CAPITAL MARKET DEVELOPMENT IN TRANSITION ECONOMIES

Country Experiences and Policies for the Future

ORGANISATION FOR ECONOMIC CO-OPERATION AND DEVELOPMENT

ORGANISATION FOR ECONOMIC CO-OPERATION AND DEVELOPMENT

Pursuant to Article 1 of the Convention signed in Paris on 14th December 1960, and which came into force on 30th September 1961, the Organisation for Economic Co-operation and Development (OECD) shall promote policies designed:

- to achieve the highest sustainable economic growth and employment and a rising standard of living in Member countries, while maintaining financial stability, and thus to contribute to the development of the world economy;
- to contribute to sound economic expansion in Member as well as non-member countries in the process of economic development; and
- to contribute to the expansion of world trade on a multilateral, non-discriminatory basis in accordance with international obligations.

The original Member countries of the OECD are Austria, Belgium, Canada, Denmark, France, Germany, Greece, Iceland, Ireland, Italy, Luxembourg, the Netherlands, Norway, Portugal, Spain, Sweden, Switzerland, Turkey, the United Kingdom and the United States. The following countries became Members subsequently through accession at the dates indicated hereafter: Japan (28th April 1964), Finland (28th January 1969), Australia (7th June 1971), New Zealand (29th May 1973), Mexico (18th May 1994), the Czech Republic (21st December 1995), Hungary (7th May 1996), Poland (22nd November 1996) and Korea (12th December 1996). The Commission of the European Communities takes part in the work of the OECD (Article 13 of the OECD Convention).

OECD CENTRE FOR CO-OPERATION WITH NON-MEMBERS

The OECD Centre for Co-operation with Non-Members (CCNM) was established in January 1998 when the OECD's Centre for Co-operation with the Economies in Transition (CCET) was merged with the Liaison and Co-ordination Unit (LCU). The CCNM, in combining the functions of these two entities, serves as the focal point for the development and pursuit of co-operation between the OECD and non-member economies.

The CCNM manages thematic and country programmes. The thematic programmes, which are multi-country in focus, are linked to the core generic work areas of the Organisation (such as trade and investment, taxation, labour market and social policies, environment). The Emerging Market Economy Forum (EMEF) and the Transition Economy Programme (TEP) provide the framework for activities under the thematic programmes. The EMEF is a flexible forum in which non-members are invited to participate depending on the theme under discussion. The TEP is focused exclusively on transition economies. Country programmes, providing more focused dialogue and assistance, are now in place for Bulgaria, China, Romania, Russia, the Slovak Republic (a candidate for accession to the OECD), and Slovenia.

FOREWORD

Capital markets in transition economies have been developing since the beginning of the transition process, including several which were created or re-established in the 1990s. It is now timely to examine these countries' experiences, to analyse the differences in the degrees of market development and to identify the main challenges to further capital market development. Highlighting the varying circumstances and policy approaches chosen by these countries can shed further light on the options available to promote the development of efficient and transparent capital markets. Meanwhile, the financial crisis affecting an increasing number of emerging market economies since mid-1997 heightens the need for such an assessment of policy choices and adds urgency to the task of eliminating weaknesses in capital market infrastructure.

For these reasons, the OECD organised a "Conference on the Development of Securities Markets in Central and Eastern Europe and Russia" in Paris on 20-21 October 1997, as part of the programme of its Centre for Co-operation with Non-Members (CCNM). This conference brought together officials from ministries of finance, central banks and securities commissions from Central and Eastern Europe and the Russian Federation, along with capital markets experts from major OECD centres and international financial institutions. They focused on four major topics:

The role of government securities markets in developing infrastructure and trading techniques, including standards, skills and practices for the benefit of the wider securities markets.

The threat posed to transparency and standards of disclosure in equity markets, in general, and minority shareholder rights, in particular, by the emergence of insider systems and "closed shop" practices.

The development of institutional and retail sectors in securities markets in transition economies and the introduction of new financial instruments.

*Market fragmentation versus centralised trading: should market participants be allowed to use the trading system they prefer in the interest of promoting spontaneous development and competition, or are there genuine cases for restricting trading to an officially designated exchange?*This publication is based on contributions from the experts and presents experiences from each country. Ms. Eva Thiel Blommestein, of the OECD's Directorate for Financial, Fiscal and Enterprise Affairs, selected and edited the conference papers and wrote the overview chapter, which summarises the transition country experiences and brings into focus the very crucial links between choice of privatisation method and equity market development.

It is also complementary to the 1997 publication in the OECD Proceedings series: "The New Banking Landscape in Central and Eastern Europe," which deals with policy issues and country experience in the development of sound banking institutions.The views expressed by the authors in the publication do not necessarily reflect those of the OECD, its Member countries or the institutions or countries they represent. It is published on the responsibility of the Secretary-General.

André Barsony
Acting Director for Co-ordination
Centre for Co-operation with Non-Members

TABLE OF CONTENTS

Section II

TRANSPARENCY AND STANDARDS OF DISCLOSURE

Section III

INSTITUTIONAL AND RETAIL SECTORS AND THE DEVELOPMENT OF NEW INSTRUMENTS

EDITOR'S NOTE

The experts' papers included in this volume were written before the true extent of the financial crisis originating in South East Asia had become clear, and they may therefore strike a more optimistic tone regarding fund flows to emerging markets than seems justified at the time of publication (although some of the papers have in fact been updated to take into account the contagion effect on financial markets in transition countries). In the case of the article on the Russian corporate securities market, no updating has been attempted, as the bouts of severe market turbulence in that country are still coming in rapid succession. The only conclusion that could be ventured at the moment is that the strong market upswing described in this article happened *in spite of* the structural shortcomings in the Russian securities market environment, particularly with respect to corporate governance and protection of minority shareholders' rights. Thus, the subsequent internally generated aggravation of the contagion effect coming from outside is due largely to the continued existence of these structural deficiencies.

Overview

THE DEVELOPMENT OF SECURITIES MARKETS IN TRANSITION ECONOMIES - POLICY ISSUES AND COUNTRY EXPERIENCE

by
Eva Thiel Blommestein
Economist and Principal Administrator, OECD Financial Affairs Division

1. Introduction

This article is primarily intended as a review of the experience to date with the creation and functioning of securities markets in the more advanced transition economies in Central and Eastern Europe as well as Russia. In several of these countries, notably in the Czech Republic, Hungary, Poland, the Slovak Republic, Slovenia and Russia, equity markets were created or re-established already in the beginning of the 1990s, government securities markets have been actively developed and, in some cases, corporate bond markets have begun to flourish. Yet, many problems remain in achieving desired levels of market efficiency and transparency and the policy choices to promote these objectives as well as further integration of the fledgling markets into the international capital markets are not always straight-forward and free of controversy.

It is frequently stated that securities markets activities in the region remain less developed than banking activities, even though most of the countries in question established the basic legal and regulatory framework required for securities issuance and trading several years ago. In particular, it is noted that these markets do not yet perform the key functions of providing an alternative to bank funds for debt and equity finance to the private sector and of offering a secondary market in ownership. Both these functions are of course critical for the transition process as a means of encouraging enterprise restructuring. In order to gauge the relative success in developing securities market activities we normally look at capitalisation and liquidity ratios in equity markets. Where these remain low in the face of significant advances in macroeconomic stability, *e.g.* in Slovenia and the Slovak Republic, to cite only two countries fairly well advanced in other aspects of the transition process, lack of development of effective regulation and institutions, inadequate financial disclosure and insufficient transparency of trading are usually cited as the key reasons. Here, the intention is to go a little further in depth, first by discussing the main problems and policy challenges in advancing securities market development and secondly, by shedding some more light on the possibilities and options available to promote the development of efficient and transparent markets through a discussion of the different policy approaches chosen by individual countries in the region.

Based on the experience of the countries under review, three major problem areas have been identified, which merit further study and exchange of views among experts and policymakers. These are: *a)* The threat posed to transparency and standards of disclosure in equity markets, in general, and minority shareholder rights, in particular, by the emergence of insider systems and "closed shop" practices; *b)* The need for further growth of institutional and retail sectors in securities markets in transition economies and its implications for market development; and *c)* The conflict between trends towards spontaneous market fragmentation and ambitions to centralise trading in the interest of promoting transparency.

Several of these problems and challenges are in many respects the same for emerging markets as for longer-established OECD markets, but here we are also concerned with the special angle brought by the transition stage. Furthermore, a discussion of developments in the securities markets of Central and Eastern Europe as well as Russia will of course, today, be seen against the backdrop of the recent events in South East Asian markets, where bursting of asset price bubbles combined with additional structural problems have had serious contagion effects on other emerging markets. Whatever the timeframe required for this acute crisis to subside, it is nevertheless clear that emerging market investment will continue to grow despite the recent turmoil. As developed country populations age, technology is diffused around the world and trade and investment barriers continue to fall, investors in the more advanced markets in the world have few options but to continue to diversify into emerging markets.

Before moving on, first to compare the development to date in terms of a number of quantitative, concrete criteria and secondly, to discuss recent experience in terms of the three major areas singled out above, it is important to highlight the interlinkages between the privatisation process and equity market development, as well as the stimulus to the wider securities markets deriving from the development of active secondary markets in government securities.

2. The impact of privatisation methods on securities market development

While it is fairly clear that the design and implementation of privatisation methods in the transition countries was not significantly influenced by objectives regarding the development of equity markets, it is an accepted fact that equity market development has been significantly affected by the choice of privatisation method. In some countries, notably the Czech Republic and Russia, mass privatisation via voucher schemes took place early in the transition, well ahead of the emergence of well-functioning secondary markets within a tried and tested system of regulation and oversight. Market infrastructure and regulation was thus developed *ex post* in response to demands from market participants for improvements in services and supervision. In other countries, such as Poland and, somewhat later, Romania, the creation of capital markets infrastructure and gradual privatisation through initial public offerings was seen as an integrated process. The regulation of the public offerings and trading on the secondary market was drawn up according to the highest standards of major OECD markets. In this government-led *ex ante* approach, with its emphasis on very ambitious disclosure and fiduciary standards, combined with the slow pace of privatisation, capitalisation and turnover has grown more slowly, with market activity initially dominated by short-term speculation. Other countries -- the Baltic Republics constitute an example -- following more "mixed" privatisation paths, have achieved progress with institution-building and regulation more in parallel with the development of capitalisation and trading activities. The table and chart below are offered as illustrations of this broadly sketched pattern.

Table 1 shows the choice of principal privatisation method, where the countries italicised, (Czech Republic, Estonia, Hungary, Russia, the Slovak Republic and Slovenia) have all achieved privatisation of near or above 50 per cent of previously state-owned assets via different combinations of methods. Chart 1 overleaf sets out two key indicators of stock market development (total market capitalisation as a percentage of GDP -- size -- and total market turnover relative to capitalisation -- liquidity). By way of illustration, the chart includes 1996 values for five large OECD economies, merely to give an approximate idea of how far the transition economies here discussed have advanced towards developed OECD market characteristics of capitalisation and liquidity.

Table 1. **Methods of privatisation of medium-sized and large enterprises**[1]

	Voucher privatisation				
	Equal access	With significant concessions to insiders	Sale to outside owners	Management Employee Buy-outs	Other[2]
Albania	-	-	**Primary**	-	-
Bulgaria	Secondary	-	**Primary**	-	-
Croatia	-	-	-	**Primary**	-
Czech Republic	**Primary**	-	Secondary	-	-
FYR Macedonia	-	-	-	**Primary**	-
Hungary	-	-	**Primary**	-	Secondary
Poland	Secondary	-	Tertiary	**Primary**	-
Romania	-	-	Secondary	**Primary**	-
Slovak Republic	Secondary	-	-	**Primary**	-
Slovenia	-	-	Secondary	**Primary**	-
Estonia	-	-	**Primary**	Secondary	-
Latvia	**Primary**	-	Secondary	-	-
Lithuania	**Primary**	-	-	Secondary	-
Russian Federation	-	**Primary**	Secondary	Tertiary	-
Ukraine	Secondary	-	-	**Primary**	-

1. Primary, secondary and tertiary denote the first, second and third most important privatisation methods in a particular country, according to their contribution to privatisation of state-owned enterprise assets.
2. Includes asset sales through insolvency proceedings and a mass privatisation programme based on preferential credits.
Source: EBRD.

Chart 1. **Indicators of stock market development**

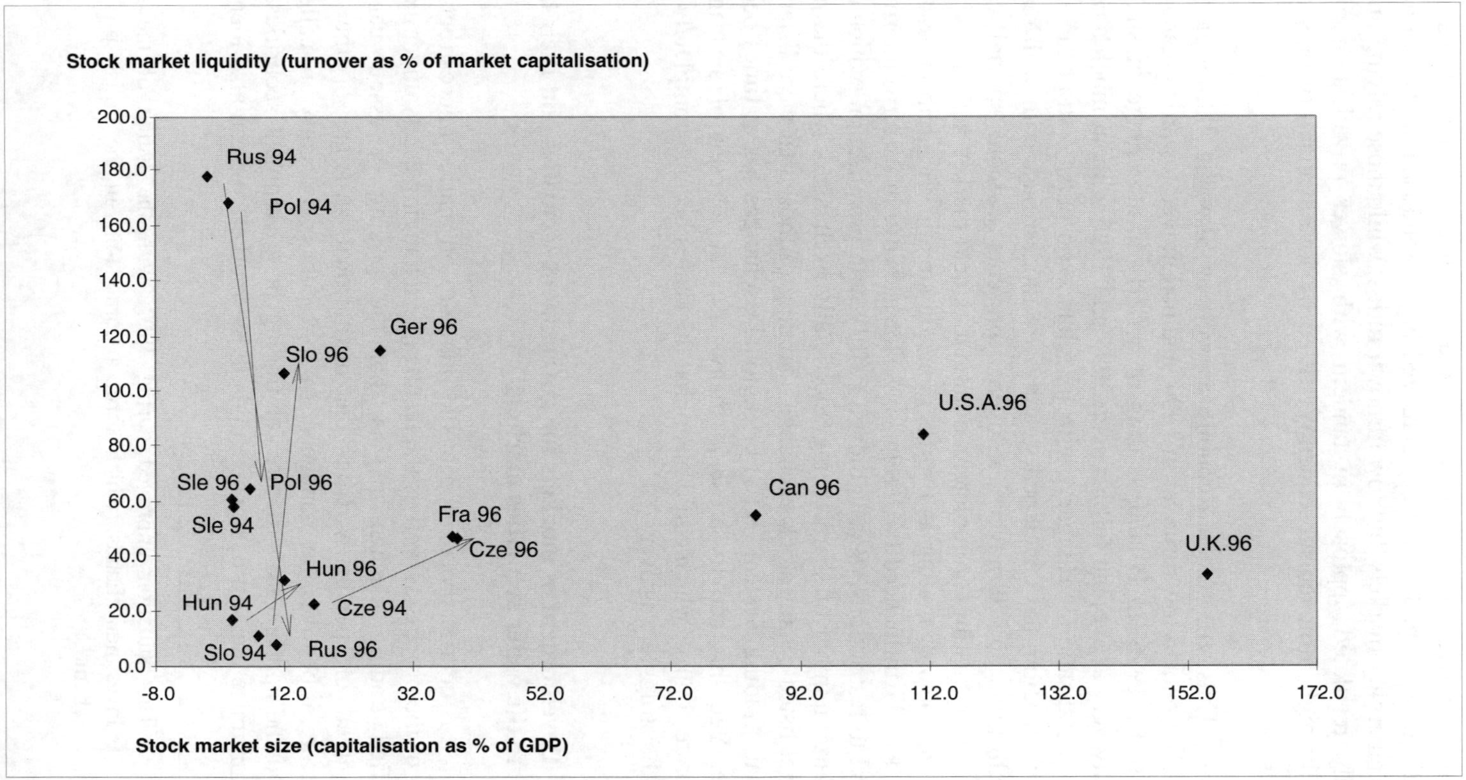

Several things can be read from this chart. First, in line with the reasoning above, it is shown that the countries relying on early mass privatisation methods generally achieved high capitalisation levels relative to other emerging markets, but low turnover ratios, while those relying on a more heavily regulated approach in tandem with slower privatisation exhibited initially high turnover subsequently stifled by low availability of shares for trading.

Thus, the Czech Republic as well as Slovakia exhibit fairly high capitalisation and low turnover in 1994, and had moved towards greater trading activity by 1996. In Poland, trading of a fairly limited range of shares was initially very active, but fell between 1994 and 1996 without much advance in total capitalisation.[1] Hungary, with its reliance on outside strategic investors for privatisation, has developed steadily at a modest pace both with respect to capitalisation and turnover. Slovenia presents a more special case, as privatisation listings completely dominate stock market activity with very sporadic bouts of trading as listings come on stream. In addition, trading has been heavily influenced by foreign investor activity, in its turn, intermittently subject to restrictions. Russia moved swiftly with privatisation, which resulted in a large number of shares being unofficially exchanged, where the majority was not listed on any stock exchange. Trading of those that were listed on the Russian Trading System (RTS) or regional exchanges has at times been very active. Yet, this activity arose in many cases as a result of a struggle for corporate control, which could mean that the shares became completely illiquid once the struggle was over.

3. Development of markets for government securities and their benefits to the wider securities markets

A central proposition in the literature on market microstructure (the study of the process as well as the results of exchanging assets under explicitly specified trading mechanisms) is that the pricing of assets cannot be determined independently from the institutional structure of the market. Therefore, it behoves the managers of public debt in a country are called upon to find the appropriate structure for trading of government securities, which will minimise the cost of raising funds in the market. We can also identify the

---

1. This situation improved during 1997, with the listing of the National Investment Funds, which form a cornerstone in the Polish privatisation scheme.

authorities' interests as regulator, provider of infrastructure and agent of financial broadening and deepening in the economy to promote the establishment of efficient securities markets in general. It is often emphasised that the development of an efficient market structure (*i.e.* beyond setting up the basic regulatory and supervisory framework) cannot be left solely to the private sector. First, vested interests of intermediaries may support less than efficient market structures. Second, the cost of certain elements of market infrastructure, such as electronic trading networks, clearing and settlement systems as well as information systems may prove too costly for market participants to develop spontaneously. Thus, the task of the government authorities may comprise all or several of the following components: *i)* defining market structure, *ii)* defining the type of intermediaries and their role and obligations vis-à-vis the market and the public, *iii)* selecting the intermediaries, *iv)* designing, managing and providing the trading system, *v)* providing the physical location of the market. Further, in the context of encouraging transition from nascent to well-developed markets the authorities can establish transitional supporting arrangements aimed at promoting market development and the efficient functioning of markets as well as smooth transition as development progresses to further stages. The debt manager could take direct roles such as establishing or sponsoring dealer firms, possibly as a direct shareholder; act as market-maker through a separate window to promote secondary market liquidity; act as an inter-dealer broker through brokering transactions of market participants and displaying price information. Price stabilisation measures are also an option as are indirect support arrangements, *e.g.* through credit lines. Over the longer term, achieving a balanced maturity structure for the government debt portfolio would be an important contribution to better market conditions, providing benchmarks across the yield spectrum.

The government securities markets of the countries discussed in this article provide an example of the variety of choice available amongst the various support options for market development. Among the more important benefits deriving from a well-developed government securities market in evidence are the setting of benchmark yields for corporate bond markets, enhancing market infrastructure and skills and setting regulatory and supervisory standards. In addition, for some of the countries, the establishment of primary dealer systems has provided benefits for the financial markets generally by *e.g.*, resulting in better capitalised market participants. As concerns the experience in Russia, it is quite clear that the creation of a high-tech trading system for government securities is gradually bearing fruit in terms of introduction of non-government corporation bonds and that the system is quite adequate for the organisation of primary placement and trading in corporate securities. It is also notable that since the introduction of the primary dealer system in October 1996, the banks and securities firms in question are beginning to be guided in their activities by concerns for maintaining market stability as opposed to quick-fix profits, which is of benefit in fostering a more securities-oriented culture. In Hungary, where the government securities market started to expand quite rapidly in 1992, this sector has played a very significant role in restoring to the Hungarian capital market some of the depth and efficiency which characterised it before the last World War. The same is true to a lesser extent for Poland, while the Czech, Slovak and Slovenian government securities markets have, in line with the lesser reliance on deficit financing, been slower to realise this type of benefits. However, looking at the experience in other emerging markets where governments have similarly low borrowing requirements, measures can still be taken to help getting corporate bond markets off the ground. Thus, both the Hong Kong and the Singapore governments have stepped in to auction governments bonds in order to provide a benchmark risk-free rate. Several other Asian governments have sponsored the establishment of rating agencies for corporate bonds and strengthened the legal infrastructure for such issues.

4. The current state of securities market development in a selected number of transition economies

According to the transition indicators developed by the EBRD, above average progress with securities markets development has been achieved by the Czech Republic, Estonia, Hungary, Poland, the Russian Federation, and Slovenia. This means that these countries have reached the point where there is substantial issuance of securities by private enterprise, where adequate clearing and settlement procedures exist and independent share registries have been established; where there exists some minimum protection of minority shareholders; where non-bank financial institutions such as investment funds, private insurance companies and pension funds have begun to emerge with the associated regulatory framework for such institutions. The highest EBRD rating awarded within this group of countries goes to Hungary and Poland, where securities laws and regulations are deemed to be approaching IOSCO standards. The table below attempts to elaborate somewhat on this description, by giving specific information on market size, liquidity, trading structure, regulation and oversight.

As can be seen from this table, all the countries here discussed have opted for allowing their banking institutions to become fully involved in capital market activities, acting as brokers, dealers, fund-managers, custodians and depositories. This so-called universal banking model was also recently adopted by Hungary, which initially had created barriers for banks' involvement in securities market activities. To some extent, this choice reflects continental European tradition but it is also a consequence of the fact that the type of arms-length finance exercised in the Anglo-Saxon type of market-based model requires a higher degree of information disclosure and dissemination as well as legal protection than currently available in the transition economies. Control-oriented finance also puts fewer demands on market infrastructure in the form of specialised providers of financial analysis, audits and similar functions. It is notable that one reason for the significant involvement by Russian banks in the equity market is the need to protect their lending engagements to different firms by taking sizeable blocks of their equity, in the absence of standard loan contract enforcement.

For regulation and oversight, most of the countries in question now have separate agencies or commissions that act independently of ministries and central banks, with an exclusive mandate for market supervision and enforcement. The Slovak Republic is a notable exception, and the exclusivity in this area of the Securities Commission in Russia is contested by the Central Bank of Russia when it comes to the securities market activities of banking institutions. In the Czech Republic, parliament has recently adopted a new Securities Law, which allows for the setting up of a Securities Commission as well as significant strengthening of capital markets regulation, specifically to address some of the problems discussed in the next section of this paper.

The main characteristics of the Polish capital market are strong supervision, high disclosure requirements, equal access to information and dematerialised and electronic trade, with strong centralisation of trade. Certain problems with respect to market infrastructure still remain, however. *E.g.*, the settlement system functions adequately for small investors, but has been criticised as inefficient for large trades by foreign investors. A specific feature of the Czech market often referred to as a major shortcoming is the absence of a single clearing and settlement centre. The Securities Centre, established for the voucher privatisation, maintains millions of accounts, but functions only as registrar with no cash services. Thus, most OTC trades are settled on the public market.

In several countries, the dominance of non-organised OTC trading is typical with perhaps the most extreme example provided by Czech Republic, where only 3 per cent of actual trade is executed on the Prague Stock

Exchange. The existence of multiple trading systems can mean that the same stock can be traded in four different places simultaneously, with different disclosure requirements and at different prices. This situation results partially from the fact that the privatisation-linked RMS trading system was already in full operation when the stock exchange was reopened in 1993.

As for Russia, equity trading principally occurs within the framework of RTS -- the first screen-based trading system licensed by the Securities Commission or direct inter-dealer trading with large blocks of shares with no reporting in any information system. However, there has recently been some renewal of exchange-based trading, both on the MICEX and on the newly established Moscow Stock Exchange. Significant improvements in market infrastructure took place during 1997 (by mid-1997 there were 200 licensed registrars and 6 licensed depositories in operation) and preparations for the establishment of a central depository are well underway. The legal and normative basis for the securities markets is already in place and the remaining work is more a case of perfection and concretisation of this basis as well as, importantly, achieving effective co-ordination between the legislature and policies implemented by different authorities.

5. The threat posed to transparency and standards of disclosure in equity markets, in general, and minority shareholder rights, in particular, by the emergence of insider systems and "closed shop" practices

The development of equity markets in transition countries has been fraught with problems, including lack of transparent dealmaking and investor protection once trading activity began to develop and markets for corporate control came into existence. Despite a slow take-off in some cases, equity markets have by now become a significant social and political factor for most of the countries concerned. It is therefore of utmost importance that confidence in the standards of fairness, accountability and protection of rights given by law is upheld in the process of exchange of contracts giving ownership title to productive assets. In addition, the disclosure and reliability of information regarding the operations of major market participants, including potential conflicts of interest, is important for attracting funds from domestic and foreign investors alike.

It has been surmised that the emergence of what we here call "closed shop practices" or "clubism" could, in some instances, be related to the type of privatisation process implemented, in particular its speed and completeness. It is further argued that certain methods of privatisation, in particular management-employee buy-outs, are more conducive to the emergence of non-transparent practices. Comprehensive mass privatisation followed by rapid transfer of ownership from a multitude of voucher-holders into the holding of a number of core investment funds is advocated by some experts as preferable in transition situations where information is unreliable and disclosure limited. Against this line of reasoning can be argued, however, that the concentration of ownership in an environment with weaknesses in the system of legal and fiduciary controls can engender conflicts of interest situations which are very detrimental to general investor confidence. In the case of the Czech Republic, the core investment funds, established by banks, have in turn evolved into holding companies with large majority stakes in a select number of firms. The banks, as owners of these holding companies, would seem to end up with classic conflict of interest situations as both indirect owners of and lenders to major firms. As the government had, until recently, adopted a "hands-off" approach to regulation, with only minimal disclosure requirements, minority shareholders already involved as well as prospective outside investors naturally harboured some doubt that standards of fairness and transparency would be safeguarded. In Poland, on the other hand, the authorities designed what was to be an integrated process of capital market infrastructure development and gradual privatisation -- with the intent to instil the high standards of the West in terms of transparency and prudent behaviour form the outset. Ample criticism has been levied against the Polish method as well, to the effect that equity market trading activity has been held back by over-ambition in terms of disclosure and fiduciary standards. Russia, in turn, presents a mix of its own as mass privatisation strongly favoured workers and managers and largely resulted in insider ownership, with "outside" ownership, including via state holding companies, estimated at between 15 and 20 per cent. Infringements on minority shareholders rights are legion, with investor protection further weakened by problems with registration and enforceability of property rights. An additional complication in the Russian context stems from the lack of universal high-level legitimacy of regulation, with power ambiguously distributed or contested.

Table 2. **Comparative market develoment data**
Stock market size and liquidity

	Capitalisation[1]		Volume of Trading[1]			
	US$bn	% GDP	US$bn	% of capitalisation	# of Listed Shares[1]	# of Securities Dealers
Czech Republic	18.1	39	8.4	47	>1000 as a result of mass privatisation - liquid issues <50	460 traders licensed (only 20% members of Prague Stock Exchange)
Hungary	5.3	12	1.6	31	50 in two categories (listed 'A' and listed 'B')	77 brokerage firms with general license (55 of which members of BSE) 21 dealer firms with limited license (no proprietary trading)
Poland	8.4	7	5.4	64	129 (including NIFs) (mid-97)	50 (including 16 banks)
Russian Federation	68 (mid-97) 37.2	11	3.0	8	150 (RTS and regional stock exchanges)	
Romania	0.9 (end 97)	2	0.5	55	60+ (in two tiers)	100+ (members of stock exchange association and/or RASDAQ)
Slovenia	2. 5 (end 97)	15.9	0.7	33	73 (Aug 97)	42
Slovakia	2.2	12	2.3	106	19 (market dominated by a few large companies)	

Note: 1) End 1996 values unless otherwise indicated.

Table 2. **Comparative market develoment data** (continued)

Securities market structure

	Universal	Organisation of Trading		Clearing and Settlement		
	Banking	**Bonds**	**Equities**	**Bonds**	**Equities**	**Derivative Trading**
Czech Republic	Yes	Stock Exchange Central market handles only 3% of all trade. The bulk is handled by the unofficial OTC market (90%), the remainder by the RM system (now mainly retail) Bonds are listed on Prague Stock Exchange central market		UNIVYC (100% owned by stock exchange) settles most trades on OTC mkt and all trades on central stock exchange; TKD System run by Czech National Bank provides DVP for T-Bills. The Securities Centre is a central depository /registry for all securities including T-Bills.		Options and futures contracts traded on OTC market
Hungary	Initially no, but banks have been allowed to engage in securities market activities since 1997.	25% of total govt. securities trade on Budeapest Stock Exchange. Bulk of OTC trade electronic (Reuters)	86% of trade in listed shares takes place on Budapest Stock Exchange	KELER Ltd. performs all clearing & settlement for BSE trades, and only government securities failed on OTC market		Well developed both on Budapest Stock Exchange and Budapest Commodity Exchange. In both cases, settlement via KELER.
Poland	Yes	Bonds and equities trade on the Warsaw Stock Exchange. Since 1997, equities also trade on the official OTC market		National Depository for Securities performs all depository and clearing functions		Index futures traded on Warsaw Stock Exchange

Securities market structure (continued)

Russian Federation	Yes	Govt securities (GKOs, OFZs) traded on MICEX* plus 8 regional exchanges	Russian Trading System (RTS); Moscow Stock Exchange since May 97; and regional exchanges	Preparation for central depository under way. Settlement and clearing services provided by several separate institutions	Currency futures (25%) GKO and OFZ futures (80%) unregulated clearing and settlement
Romania	No, but proposal for allowing banks to engage in securities market activities pending in Parliament.	Bucharest Stock Exchange; mkt RASDAQ for privatisation shares (3700 companies listed). No bonds traded yet.		Central SRO National Company for Clearing and Settlement.	None except Commodity Exchange.
Slovenia	Yes	Lubljana Stock Exchange (A&B for listed securities and C for unlisted securities)		Central clearing corporation (KDD)	Forex and equity futures previously traded on the Lubljana Commodity Exchange. (Not under jurisdiction of Securities Agency).Exchange closed dut to insolvency end 1997
Slovakia	Yes, with some restrictions on banks'proprietary trading of securities	Secondary bond mkt provided via Bratislava Stock Exchange and the RM-System Slovakia. State bonds traded mainly on BSE.	All equities trading on BSE-listed, registered and free markets.	SCP provides registry and clearing (securities centre) services for all securities including T-bonds. Cash settlement via Banking Clearing Centre for Slovak Republic	Official mkt in preparation by Stock Exchange.

Table 2. **Comparative market develoment data**

Market regulation and supervision

	Independent Securities Commission	**Insider Laws and Enforcement**	**Investor Protection**	**Disclosure and Compliance Regulation and Enforcement**
Czech Republic	In process of creation, to function from beginning 1998	Contained in New Securities Law recently approved by Parliament.		Enhancement of standards and strengthening of enforcement capabilities needed
Hungary	Capital market and banking supervision integrated into one independent institution under Government supervision	Legal provisions and regulation converging towards IOSCO standards		Standards well developed
Poland	Yes, since 1991	Legal provisions and regulation converging towards IOSCO standards		Standards well developed
Russian Federation	Yes, since 1993	Yes, since entry into force of new securities law in April 1996 but no enforcement procedures established	Yes, since April 1996	Being developed by joint CBR/Securities Commission Working Group; no effective system of control in place.
Romania	Yes, National Securities Commission on reports directly to parliament.	Certain provisions exist in 1994 Securities Law, but enhancement being undertaken in line with market development.		Regulations developed by National Securities Commission and SRO's but enforcement procedures not in place.
Slovenia	Securities Market Agency fully independent from Ministry of Finance	Provisions exist in 1994 Law on Securities Market. New law in drafting stage will bring harmonisation with EU legislation.		Standards developed and enforcement capabilities being strengthened.
Slovakia	No, Control Office within Ministry of Finance exercises supervision	New securities law containing such provisions presented to Parliament for approval during first quarter 1998. Enforcement procedures not yet established.		

An issue of interest to regulators of emerging markets is the scope for and role of self-regulatory organisations, particularly the extent to which authorities can rely on these organisations to impose rules of good conduct on market participants. Regulatory systems for financial markets in OECD countries generally have three components: Government sponsored statutory and regulatory provisions, self-regulation by legal bodies encompassing specific industry segments or activities and corporate governance by individual financial institutions. The mix and degree of reliance on these three pillars underpinning financial market activities varies from country to country, although the scope for self-regulation seems to broaden with the increasing complexity and diversity of financial market activity. In cases where there has been heavy reliance on self-regulatory organisations, such as in the United Kingdom, the rationale has usually been that only the industry itself can resolve many of the conflict-of-interest problems without having to resort to legal action as would be required for a government-appointed body. In addition, in most countries where insider trading is a criminal offence it is proving difficult to provide sufficient proof to obtain convictions in court for transgressions. Self-regulatory organisations can more easily impose fines or other sanctions on member firms or individual employees of these firms. In order to be effective, however, self-regulation requires a substantial body of experienced market practitioners with vested interest in the reputation and good-will residing in their market image. It also requires a generally accepted set of business ethics applied by member firms. Such more or less intangible capital assets take time to build up and are extremely vulnerable to erosion during the build-up stage.

6. The need for further growth of institutional and retail sectors in securities markets in transition economies and its implications for market development.

Institutional investors have become an increasingly important factor in financial markets over the past decades. Total assets under management by OECD institutional investors rose from 38 per cent of GDP in 1981 to 106.5 per cent in 1995, with still higher levels estimated for 1996. Their increasing relative importance is naturally mirrored in the growing impact of institutional investors on the functioning of financial markets as well as their own reliance on and need for market depth, liquidity and efficient infrastructure. In most OECD countries, institutional savings institutions -- in particular pension funds -- now play a key role in domestic financial systems.

While the importance of institutional investors (domestic as well as foreign) has increased in emerging markets as well, it is still less significant, for two main reasons. First, many of these countries are still in the process of putting the basic elements in place within their domestic economies, such as pension system reform and insurance market regulation, which will promote the emergence of large institutional investors. Second, in something of a chicken-and-egg relationship, the securities markets of these countries do not yet exhibit all the criteria for well-functioning required by international institutional investors.

Nevertheless, foreign institutional investors have played an important role in the development of emerging securities markets, notably stock markets. There has been a dramatic increase in portfolio flows from institutional investors to emerging markets, with professionally managed investment funds taking the lead. The rise in the number of regional and global emerging market funds in the past decade is well documented, and for transition countries in Central and Eastern Europe and the former Soviet Union this has been an important source of foreign capital inflows in the 1990s. Emerging market exposure of OECD-based pension funds remains fairly modest, however, partly because of home bias partially linked to portfolio restrictions.

To date, the lack of progress in developing the insurance industry, pension funds and the mutual funds industry in transition countries gives an indication of the tremendous scope for further development of the domestic institutional investor sector. This becomes even clearer as demographic factors and the need for pension system reform have been an extremely important determinant in the growth of the institutional sector in OECD economies, and the demographic structure in Central and Eastern Europe is in many respects similar to that of major OECD countries. Yet, in these transition economies, as well as in the former Soviet Union, funded pension systems hardly exist. Only three CEECs have adopted legislation for regulating the activities of private pension funds. Other countries have prepared drafts of new laws or simply have laws allowing the existence of private pension funds but *not* their regulation.

Looking at the obstacles to the development of domestic institutional investors in transition economies, one could probably argue that policies to deal with such obstacles also serve to promote further development of securities markets. Deregulation and modernisation of the financial sector, including the formation of integrated financial groups and the development of products to meet the growing demand by private households for retirement benefits, are prime examples of such two-pronged policies. In particular, continued progress in the restructuring and modernisation of the banking sector in the transition economies will contribute significantly to the development of the institutional investor sector, as banks can be expected to develop such activities, including money management services.

When the mass privatisation schemes were put into effect, it was expected that the privatisation investment funds established as part of these schemes would over time come to play important roles as domestic institutional investors in these markets. What is the experience in this respect so far? It is at the moment only possible to make a meaningful assessment of the port-privatisation situation of the investment funds in Russia and the Czech Republic, as the programmes in other countries are of later date, while the elaborate Polish scheme was delayed for several years by political wrangling over the selection of management companies for the National Investment Funds (NIF). The Russian and Czech privatisation investment funds are thus alone in having had to face the test of surviving in a post-privatisation environment with the portfolios acquired during the programmes. In both countries, the number of funds have decreased drastically.

In Russia, only half of the more than 600 investment funds existing by end 1993 remained active at the close of 1996, and still more have ceased operations or merged during 1997. It is estimated that less than 30 privatisation investment funds have played any significant role in the capital market, maintaining active portfolios with long-term prospects for survival. A major reason that these few have fared better than the rest is -- apart from fortunate initial portfolio choices -- the opportunity to link up with strong financial-industrial groups, which could provide bridging finance to safeguard the maintenance of attractive long-run investment portfolios. The authorities have, on the other hand, done very little to facilitate the transformation of the privatisation investment funds into the new type of unit funds now actively encouraged, which enjoy some regulatory and tax advantages compared to the former.

In the Czech Republic, the first wave of privatisation resulted in the establishment of more than 400 investment funds, while the second wave saw another 221 funds set up. These funds enjoyed better general market conditions and more lenient conditions than their Russian counterparts. Thus, a much greater proportion of the Czech funds survived as active investors, to some extent even exercising the kind of corporate governance of their investment objects hoped for by the designers of the mass privatisation schemes. However, as discussed at greater length in Section 5, the close interrelationships between investment funds and banks and the consolidation of many of the former into regular holding companies have brought serious problems of collusion and insider dealings, to such a degree that many investors have become wary of this type of intermediary.

Thus, a tentative conclusion based on the experience of these two countries is that the early stage of capital market development at the time the funds were created made it difficult for them to evolve into viable financial intermediaries of the kind originally envisaged. Generally illiquid markets did not allow them to maintain short-term cash flow required for survival, while raising funds from the general public ceased to be an alternative due to various unscrupulous activities engaged in by some funds. Their very visible exploitation of opportunities for wealth creation by collusion and arbitrage in the absence of comprehensive information disclosure rules, as well as overall regulation and oversight quickly eroded public confidence in the institutions as such. In the Polish model, with its carefully regulated approach, it is more likely that the NIF will develop further and retain a role as viable intermediaries in the securities markets.

7. The conflict between trends towards spontaneous market fragmentation and ambitions to centralise trading in the interest of promoting transparency.

Market fragmentation can occur for two basic reasons. First, an alternative market may become more attractive to investors as a technologically superior, "stand-alone" system. An example would be the introduction of an electronic trading system, enticing order-flow away from the floor of an exchange. Second, order-flow can fragment if satellite markets offer faster execution and lower commissions, while free-riding on the price discovery and other functions provided by a major market place. While experts generally seem to be in agreement that competition by means of market architecture is desirable, the second type of fragmentation is usually seen as less beneficial when there is no contribution to price discovery and no additionality for participants who have posted quotes on the main market.

Developments in the structure of securities markets in OECD countries in the past two decades have been affected by advancing technology, deregulation, international competition and the increasing impact of institutional investor behaviour. Fully automated trading processes have been introduced in a number of OECD markets, while thriving floor-based systems continue to exist in some major market places. As technological change has made it possible to establish new regulated exchanges, in competition with established exchanges, regulation based on the assumption that trading should be concentrated in one physical place to assure market integrity has gradually been undermined. Regulators, both in OECD and emerging markets, are thus faced with the basic decision whether to uphold the principle of centralised trading in the interest of investor protection.

Many examples of new, authorised competing exchanges can be found in North American and European markets. Recently there has been considerable interest in launching stock markets targeted at small and medium-sized enterprises, both nationally and on a trans-European basis. The increasingly competitive environment for equity trading has also sharpened the controversy over strengths and weaknesses of quote-driven as opposed to order-driven systems.

In addition to competition amongst themselves, exchanges are also confronted with competition from proprietary trading systems (PTS), which are generally understood to be screen-based systems operated by non-self-regulatory organisations (*i.e.* run as independent businesses). Although hitherto mainly restricted to institutional investors and other market professionals, such systems are increasingly being adapted to attract retail investors (*e.g.* via Internet).

As competition in equity trading is becoming increasingly internationalised, regulators are being forced to re-examine regulation which is basically national in character. As long as there are possibilities for outside investors to access clearing and settlement facilities freely, then the actual trading could potentially take place anywhere -- on SEAC international, on Instinet or via remote facilities for cross-border access to national screen-based exchanges. Efforts to restrict the domestic trading system in various ways against the wishes of market participants may thus result in a non-desired loss of trading activity.

8. Conclusions

Key policy issues concerning the development of securities markets have been raised in the preceding pages, together with various details on the current status of capital market development in a number of transition countries. This overview paper is not the proper place for specific recommendations addressing the evolving situation in any particular country, but a few remarks concerning the essential choices open to policymakers can be offered as conclusion.

- A sound banking system is an important pre-requisite for the development of modern, efficient securities markets.

- Privatisation and capital market development are intimately linked. First, there is the need for achieving balance between institution building and trading activities. Second, the institutional framework for privatisation has important consequences for the formation of public confidence and trust in the fairness and transparency of capital market trading practices. Although the countries discussed above have already made the fundamental choices with respect to privatisation, there are still many remaining individual privatisation cases where these aspects should be carefully considered.

- The development of a modern government securities sector has a positive impact on the development of the wider securities market structure.

- Failure to safeguard transparency and disclosure aspects in market activity leading to inadequate protection for minority and larger (foreign) shareholders through the emergence of "crony capitalism" can have extremely negative consequences for overall market development, so that, ultimately the market cannot fulfil its essential intended functions as smaller investors vote with their feet.

- Governments in transition economies must actively facilitate the development of the institutional investor sector: pension funds (as part of the reform of the public pension system), insurance companies and investment funds. This should also include, where appropriate, facilitating the conversion of privatisation investment funds to unit funds or similar type of collective investment institution. Above all, an effective regulatory and supervisory framework for all these types of institutions should be put in place.

- The choice between allowing spontaneous fragmentation of trading or centralising trading to one regulated exchange is not a real one, as developments in communication and information technology have brought a new, increasingly competitive and internationalised trading environment. The issue for the authorities is rather to enforce transparency and disclosure rules for trading, wherever it takes place, paying close attention to the respective degree of sophistication and thus required need for protection of participants in any the particular trading situation.

Section I

DEVELOPMENT OF GOVERNMENT SECURITIES MARKETS

Chapter 1

THE ROLE OF THE GOVERNMENT IN THE DEVELOPMENT OF THE SECURITIES MARKETS

by
Lars Kalderén
Former Director General of the Swedish National Debt Office
and Chairman, Devfin Advisers

Introduction

In this paper I will discuss some aspects of the relationship between government debt management and the securities market as a whole, as well as the interplay between the sub-markets which exist in OECD countries and will develop over time also in the economies in transition -- notably those for paper issued by the central government, municipalities, housing finance institutions, infrastructure project financiers and the corporate (mainly industrial) sector. Their indirect counterparts are the investors: institutions such as banks, pension funds and insurance companies as well as large corporations with financial surpluses, who will operate in the wholesale market; and small firms, co-operatives and private individuals active in the financial retail market. Between them are the intermediaries: banks as underwriters and advisers, dealers, brokers, stock exchanges, etc. but also other "market builders" such as rating agencies.

These are the players: issuers, investors and intermediaries (the three "Is"); while the regulating authorities operating under the law of the land are the organisers of the playing field and the umpire. In a fully developed market -- if such a thing can be imagined, since dynamic change is the hallmark of finance -- there is rivalry and competition within each category of player, and also little harmony between the categories as each tries to cut costs and get more value for his money. But there are times -- and I believe there is one in Europe today, as we approach the EMU -- when certain considerations should be common to all players, and when transition economies should watch closely to learn from the problems of developed OECD markets.

The market for government securities

After considerable work by international organisations such as the OECD, the International Monetary Fund and the World Bank, there is now general agreement about the desirability of a step-by-step development of a government securities market, particularly in transition economies[1]. The primary objective for creating and maintaining such a market should always be to cover the government's borrowing needs (as well as ensuring the government's continued access to the market), but a secondary motive will be, already in the early stage of financial market reform, to facilitate the conduct of stabilisation policies by the central bank. Thus, at that stage government debt instruments and primary market issuance are often used for monetary purposes. As the stock of securities expands and becomes more diversified, commercial banks and non-bank financial institutions will strengthen their balance sheets through the acquisition of low-risk, near-liquid assets. This interactive process will provide incentives for institutional development, *e.g.* creation of capacity to handle asset-liability management by the banks or the establishment of new institutions to support secondary market trading in securities. Moreover, while the increased depth and efficiency in money and government securities markets will open up additional opportunities for effective implementation of monetary and public debt policy, the growth in government securities markets will also serve as a catalyst for the development of markets in other, more risky securities, such as corporate bonds and equities. A further objective to be served by a government securities market could be the promotion of household financial savings as a source of funding the public deficit.

The design of an appropriate program of government debt instruments and their sales needs to take into account a number of considerations , *i.a.*, that it should avoid creating distortions in credit and capital markets by adhering to selling arrangements which are market-based, with flexible and competitive interest-rate determination -- rather than instituting captive market segments where statutory reserve and liquid asset requirements, and/or interest restrictions, force financial institutions to be involuntary holders of government debt instruments. Moreover, while initially mainly concerned with the creation of money and treasury bill markets, the program should early on consider the development of a medium-and-long term bond market so as to provide more stable funding of the public sector debt, as well as opening up opportunities for financial investments by the private sector.

The government's structural debt management policies will influence the flow of funds to different financial markets, and the level and term structure of interest rates. In a situation where the authorities wish to limit the demands of the government on the banking system they will need to target potential non-bank markets such as institutional investors and households. However, the government should avoid creating a segmentation of markets by type of holders; this will lead to small volumes of instruments and restricted secondary markets, thus making the securities less liquid and therefore more expensive to the government. In particular, the tax treatment should be more or less uniform for various types of securities.

For a number of reasons the authorities should strive to encourage medium-term securities and achieve a balanced maturity profile. In higher-inflation countries this will require basing such securities on adjustable rates or on the indexation of principal (index-linked bonds) which will reduce the inflation premium that investors would otherwise require. However, one should bear in mind that adjustable rate instruments will complicate treasury and budget management and may constrain interest rate policy.

Secondary market development

Secondary markets in government securities provide liquidity for investors (the ability to move from securities to cash, and vice versa, with little delay and at reasonable cost). They also enable investors continuously to observe interest variations (price discovery) as a basis for their decisions. Moreover, secondary markets support interest rate liberalisation, as the government can rely on competitive money and interbank markets to set interest rates in line with supply and demand conditions. Realistic pricing will then attract new investors who will eventually widen their portfolios to include non-government securities as well.

Secondary markets may need the direct support of the government to come into being. This may involve introducing appropriate legislation and regulations facilitating the emergence of institutions such as dealers, brokers, clearing systems and custodial arrangements; instruments such as rediscount and repurchase facilities; and information systems that provide price transparency to market participants and allow the authorities to monitor and supervise the markets. Regulation and supervision of the markets can be achieved by establishing a securities commission (by various names) as the final authority to rule on *e.g.* capital adequacy, and generally to encourage an efficient trading system and healthy competition among market participants. Central to the success of such efforts will be an efficient and secure clearing and settlement system for transactions in government securities, which can also be expanded to cater for other kinds of securities such as private sector bonds and stocks. There are many examples of such Clearing and Settlement (C&S) systems around the world, and the component parts are well known; when working smoothly, the system ensures "delivery of securities against payment" which is the very basis of a functioning secondary market.

The role of market-maker in government securities is widely acknowledged as a condition for success of secondary market development; in most OECD countries (although there are significant exceptions such as Denmark) both primary and secondary markets are run by a group of authorised primary dealers. Another indispensable ingredient is a stock exchange that may have been established initially to conduct trades in equity but can also set up facilities for trading in bonds as well.

Debt management operations require a range of supporting arrangements of a legal and organisational nature, such as procedures for planning the regular sales of securities based on projections of the cash flow needs of the Treasury and the absorptive capacity of the market; mechanisms for regular consultations with investors and financial intermediaries about their preferences with regard to debt instruments and market arrangements; schemes for publicising the types of available instruments, the issue calendar and the size of issuance as well as regular reporting to provide market-makers, investors, market analysts and credit rating agencies with up-to-date and accurate information on the fiscal situation and the debt program.

New thinking on debt management policy in Sweden

At the request of the government, a study has recently been concluded in Sweden of the debt management policies to be followed by the State, how responsibility for its execution should be distributed and how the performance of the National Debt office should be measured.[2]

In discussing the goals of debt management the economist in charge of the study, Professor Peter Englund of Uppsala University, takes as his starting point that running budget deficits amounts to postponing taxation. Since high future levels of taxation are detrimental to growth -- *i.a.* by creating disincentives to labour supply -- and variance in tax rates over time also matters, debt policy should aim at having a tax-smoothing effect through low variance in real interest cost and a debt structure which makes interest payments low when GDP is unusually low or public expenditures unusually high -- in other words, in a recession.

Debt policy should also be designed with a view to enhancing the credibility of the government's anti-inflationary policies, by reducing the proportion of the debt which is issued in domestic nominal bonds. The idea behind this credibility goal is that the government should have as little incentive as possible to "inflate out of debt"; it does not matter if the government professes its adherence to a low target-figure for inflation, because the very existence of such an easy way out of domestic debt will cause investors to demand a risk premium in the form of higher coupon rates.

A third goal of State debt policy should be to contribute to market efficiency, including the development of new markets. A more efficient market structure will benefit the State's debt through the reduced risk and liquidity *premia* that have to be paid to the investors but also have wider positive effects on the economy at large (*i.a.* through better resource allocation and lower transaction costs).

Other effects of state debt policy are more arguable, according to Mr. Englund, and goal-setting therefore more difficult and less straight forward: thus, it is not clear if the composition of the debt portfolio -- although large in relation to GDP -- can have any (lasting) effect on domestic interest rates and exchange rates; what its results might be, under various assumptions, on the distribution of income and wealth in the economy; or how one should look at risk sharing across generations.

The study pays special attention to the question of how government debt policy could be used to improve the efficiency of financial markets. As the largest issuer of bonds in the market the State could increase liquidity by concentrating on a limited number of benchmark loans. Pre-announced issue calendars will smooth price formation at auctions and remove any suspicion in the market that an unexpected issue signals negative developments in the monetary or fiscal situation. The study recommends some experimentation with uniform instead of Dutch auctions although the gains -- if any -- are likely to be small. Mr. Englund is also in favour of indexed bonds, as a useful financial innovation which should be further exploited, and suggests the introduction of bonds with a real rate on interest tied to GDP growth. A Swedish interest future, based on State bonds, would fit well with the structure of other major European market places for securities trading.

The practical implications of the reasoning summarised above would lead to long-term indexed bonds constituting a major part of government debt. Variance in future interest burdens should be minimised through a diversified portfolio which contains bonds positively indexed to GDP; but nominal bonds could also provide insurance against adverse shocks to GDP -- because low growth is often associated with high inflation, which drives down bond prices. However, a reduction in the share of nominal bonds would improve credibility and should therefore have priority, at least so long as Sweden stays out of the EMU. A fraction of the portfolio -- but smaller than today -- should consist of foreign currency debt.

The study recommends that the general goals of the State's debt policy should continue to be determined by Parliament, acting on the advice of the Cabinet (in practice the Minister of Finance), that the Cabinet annually decides, as part of a five-year strategy, on the general composition of the debt portfolio specifying within wide margins the portfolio shares and desired duration of domestic nominal bonds, indexed bonds and foreign currency borrowing. The Debt Office would then be delegated to implement the decisions as the government's portfolio manager, including setting more precise benchmarks and creating a system for evaluation of its performance (there should be a benchmark for foreign currency borrowing, whereas domestic borrowing does not really lend itself to benchmark comparisons). Debt Office actions with regard to market efficiency should be evaluated once a year by outside experts, and its Director General as well as the Finance Minister should appear annually in Parliament for hearings on how its debt policy decisions have been implemented.

After receiving comments from a handful of interested agencies -- including the Debt Office and the Riksbank (central bank) -- the government has now proposed to Parliament certain changes in the law governing State borrowing, in partial response to the recommendations by Mr. Englund (some of those recommendations concerned the relationship between the Cabinet and the Debt Office and thus do not have to be submitted to Parliament).

According to the proposals, the name of the law should be "The Act on State Borrowing and Debt Management". Only one goal of State debt policy should be incorporated in the Act, viz. that of *cost minimisation over the longer term*. However, the government is interested in avoiding large increases in debt servicing costs as a result of excessive risk-taking in debt management -- thus the Debt Office should operate in such a way that interest costs are predictable and do not vary too much over time; this should contribute to lower over-all interest levels and therefore lower costs of debt management over time. Another restriction in the Act concerns the relation between the Debt Office and the Riksbank: thus, State debt policy and management must be conducted so as not to obstruct or contravene monetary policy. Other possible goals of State debt policy, such as those suggested by Mr. Englund, are considered either already incorporated in the cost minimisation target (tax smoothing, improving the financial markets), or better served by other aspects of economic policy (the credibility goal). Should the Debt Office wish to undertake some action designed to improve the efficiency of the market, which would run contrary to the cost minimisation goal, it should request special funds for this purpose and the request would then be judged on its merits compared to other government expenditures.

The proposals to Parliament are quite detailed with regard to the machinery for annual decision-making by Parliament, the Cabinet (Ministry of Finance) and the two agencies concerned, *i.e.* the Debt Office and the Riksbank, including dates for the submission to Parliament of *guidelines for State debt policy in the coming fiscal year* as well as the role of the Debt Office in preparing such guidelines and that of the Riksbank in commenting on them; but they are silent on the scope and substance of the guidelines. Finally, the government suggests that the Parliament should annually receive a special *evaluation report* on the results of government debt management during the past five years in relation to the goals determined by Parliament. The report would be based on material delivered by the Debt Office but also on the judgement of experts outside the government. Such reports could then be supplemented by public hearings of Debt Office and MoF staff arranged by the parliamentary Finance Committee, should this be judged desirable.

The government as a participant in the securities market

The relationship between the government debt manager and other market participants received special attention in Gunther Broker´s book *Government Securities and Debt Management in the 1990s* (OECD 1993). Broker makes the following points:

1. In a free and competitive financial market, the government would not wish to maintain practices and regulations that other market participants could regard as providing privileged access to sources

of finance, such as mandatory requirements for investment in government paper, or the issue of debt instruments offering special tax advantages. Instead, the government debt manager should step up his marketing efforts to be on a par with other issuers, and should devote more attention to the development of efficient secondary markets for government paper. Above all, achieving and retaining the confidence of investors should receive the highest attention of the debt manager.

2. In countries where the government debt is large in relation to the market and the debt manager is keen to foster a wider securities market, minimising the market impact of government debt operations becomes an important objective. This means that erratic movements in prices and yields on government securities should be avoided, both when new issues are made and when other large scale operations like redemptions are conducted. The immediate goal is to secure a steady flow of funds to the new issue market for government debt; but "maintaining orderly market conditions" is valuable also for other market segments, particularly as securities there tend to be priced off government debt. This becomes especially important when interest rate futures and options markets are based on government securities, or when corporate bonds and swaps are priced on government bonds as benchmarks. The goal of "orderly market conditions" can be secured by informing market participants on government borrowing needs, publishing an issuing calendar, choosing the right selling technique for each occasion and perhaps also intervening in the secondary market to prepare for new issues or major redemption operations. Over the longer term, achieving a balanced maturity structure for the government debt portfolio would be an important contribution to better market conditions: lengthening the average life and smoothing the time profile of the outstanding debt, constructing the issuing calendar so as to match government cash flows, etc.

To Broker´s observations can be added what Stiglitz and Uy have pointed out:[3]

"One obstacle to the emergence of bond markets in (five high-performing East Asian economies) is the absence of a market for government securities -- because the governments do not run deficits, they do not need to borrow. With no market for government securities, there is no benchmark risk-free rate, and so markets must determine both the risk-free rate and the risk premium associated with a specific corporate bond. Hong Kong´s government has responded to this limitation by auctioning government bonds -- even though it does not need the financing -- to provide a benchmark risk-free rate and eventually help create a market for corporate bonds. Malaysia and Singapore are considering doing the same." Other initiatives with the same purpose have been the establishment of a rating agency for bond issues (Malaysia), strengthening the legal infrastructure for securities (Hong Kong, Taiwan and Thailand) and providing government guarantees for private sector issuers (Korea).

Stiglitz and Uy thus corroborate the study conducted for the OECD in 1993 by S. Ghon Rhee[4] which enumerates a number of obstacles to the growth of secondary markets in countries like Korea and Malaysia, where primary markets are fairly large, *viz.*:

1. a controlled or administered structure of interest rates through which the effective yields on government bonds are kept below the levels of the credit market;

2. protection by the commercial banks of their privileged position as lenders to the private sector;

3. legal restriction on the issuance of corporate debt by enterprises;

4. high minimum denominations of new issues, which bar individual investors from participating;

5. the lack of a securities infrastructure in the form of a competitive auction system, rating agencies, and clearing and settlement systems.

The study makes the general observation that corporate bond trading receives a stimulus from an active government bond market -- and vice versa.

Clearly then, the government debt manager cannot limit himself to pursuing the immediate goal of borrowing cheaply on behalf of the taxpayer -- he must observe a much more enlightened self-interest and understand that he is involved in a symbiotic relationship with other issuers who are both competitors and supporters. The authorities above him who are responsible for the development of the financial sector in general and the securities market in particular should of course be even more broad-minded. Theirs is the responsibility to create the conditions for the healthy growth of the segments of the money and capital market serving other clients than the state, such as the housing sector, the municipalities, industrial and trading corporations, and major infra-structural projects which secure their funding in the market place. They are also responsible for the health of the securities industry which -- at least in some OECD countries -- has become a key element in the process of financial intermediation as well as a major employer. From the point of view of the authorities, neither excessive demand for funds, nor complete lack of demand in any of these segments over a period of time is attractive as it implies a loss of institutional capacity and professional competence -- quite apart from the fact that it signals imbalances in the real economy which can have far-reaching effects on investment and growth. The same effect on the securities industry can be observed as a result of wide swings in the borrowing requirements of the government -- although in that case a fall in demand for funds is usually welcomed as a sign of an improving budget balance. In any event, the reduction in the state's net borrowing needs to zero or even turning into a surplus is seldom a cause for worry since the stocks are normally so large that redemptions and refinancings normally constitute the bulk of the government's debt operations.

However, in the current situation when savings are high and in some OECD countries still rising, and when budget deficits and state borrowing needs are shrinking in preparation for the EMU, there should be scope for increased long-term funds from the non-government sectors of the securities market. To facilitate the access of other borrowers than the state to that market should then be in the interest of the authorities -- including the government debt manager who should be keen to see the market continue to receive the normal flow of funds and operating at high professional levels even in periods when there is little demand for deficit financing. He can regard the success of his colleagues (and erstwhile competitors) with equanimity, as he can be confident that if and when he wishes to return to the market he will again be accorded priority by the investors (particularly so if other borrowers have then lost some of their appetite, which is likely to be the case if the government resumes borrowing in a recession). In other words, we may now have a better opportunity than in a long time to develop securities markets that are able to serve the productive sectors as well as the government -- something which should be as important to the economies in transition as to the developed OECD countries.

The Swedish case

The mechanisms at work can be studied in Sweden today: during the first half of the 1990s trade in interest-bearing securities expanded rapidly as a result of large and growing budget deficits. Interest rates were high as inflationary expectations were slow to die and the krona regarded as a devaluation-prone currency following its depreciation in late 1992. But in a few years there has been a dramatic turn-around in the economic health of the country: exports have expanded while imports were held down by recession and low growth, the krona has strengthened significantly, inflation is near zero and shows no signs of an early resumption. The budget deficit is turning into a small surplus (if it is not going to be spent on new expenditures or tax relief in advance of next year's elections). Government will thus be less active in the primary issue market and the securities industry will have to rely more on the secondary market -- where, however, low and stable interest rates do not make for a very exciting life of the traders. Most likely competition will increase, spreads will shrink and so will profitability, forcing some firms out of the market and others to merge. The willingness to take risk may increase and the capital base of intermediaries come under pressure. Without compensating demand from other segments of the securities markets we may see attempts to broaden the Swedish market by creating stronger Nordic links, and to bring down transaction costs through more computer-based trading and a reduction in staff. Naturally, traders are looking for new products and increased volumes of issues from other sectors of the economy than the government.

So what are the chances that such increases in demand will be forthcoming, and what are the obstacles? While each country is unique, the Swedish case may nevertheless carry some lessons for other countries as well. At the present time, the signals are not very encouraging: major institutional investors are still concentrating their attention on government paper and refuse to take an active interest in other securities. And there are other reasons why the non-government segments of the market do not evidence any significant increase in their demand for funds.

The housing sector

During the building boom of the late 1980s, when the government's demand for new funds was low, the institutes financing housing and other construction were the largest issuers in the Swedish securities market. However, the boom turned to bust and the building industry has been in the doldrums for several years now, with uncertain prospects for the rest of the decade. The net demand for housing and construction finance is likely to remain low. Likewise, while some big infrastructure projects are under implementation -- such as the bridge over the straits of Öresund -- no major increase in funding requirements is expected. A recent proposal by a government expert, Mr. Anders Sahlén, is designed to better align Swedish legislation with current directives by the EU to the insurance industry, by introducing housing bonds with a "gilt edge", *i.e.* issued against mortgages below 75 per cent of market value (60 per cent for office and farm buildings). This would be in line with legislation already in force in Denmark and Germany and would make housing bonds a better substitute for government securities. The total EU market for long housing bonds is in the order of nearly US$1 000 billion.[5]

The municipalities

The Swedish municipalities are a significant category of borrowers in the domestic and the international markets, carrying a total debt equivalent to some US$13 billion. They benefit from an indirect guarantee from the state and their securities should thus be no more risky than those of the Kingdom -- nonetheless they carry a slightly higher coupon. Ten municipalities have today their own S&P rating indicating good creditworthiness, and they can borrow in the markets on better terms than the banks would offer them for loans. Smaller municipalities have come together in a co-operative institute (called Kommuninvest) which borrows on their behalf, evening out discrepancies in risk and in the demand for funds. Over the longer term the municipalities are likely to increase their market borrowing, particularly if and when the Euro will offer a risk-free currency in which to raise long-term funds. They would then provide a better substitute than today to government bonds in the investment portfolios of insurance companies and pension funds.

Corporate bonds

The corporate sector was a major borrower in the regulated Swedish market up to the mid- 1970s. The queues were long and strictly controlled by the central bank which normally did not permit borrowing abroad. The commercial banks, not the companies themselves, were responsible for the issues, and conditions were highly standardised. Two decades later there is a complete change: industrial companies are highly liquid, short term funds can be raised at home or abroad at very low cost and little exchange risk (banks are also flush with funds to lend), and savings are flowing into the equity markets as never before. Besides, getting a rating for the company is expensive and somewhat risky -- if the result is worse than expected this may cause a setback in the race with your competitors in the industry…

However, there is consensus that if the rating facilities for Swedish corporates were improved, even "junk bonds" could enter investors' portfolios, particularly if they were issued in Euros which would give better liquidity because the currency risk had been eliminated. Then credit risk would become more important and the rating institutes would have to apply greater sophistication in their work.

From a structural point of view, it could be argued that industry should strive to raise long-term capital in order to be able to conduct product and system development without demands for profitability in the short term, particularly in the case of environmentally friendly products. But many factors in modern society seem to conspire against business firms taking a long term view: the IT society which demands instant information; management systems which require accountability to shareholders every quarter; the short product cycles and the growth of short-term financial markets, etc. In many Swedish companies the cost of raising external capital has not been a problem in recent years and the advantages of issuing corporate bonds versus raising equity has seldom been fully explored. But the government can encourage greater use of the rating process, and the stock exchange can promote the trading of corporate bonds.

NOTES

1. The following paragraphs are based on the book published by the IMF in 1997 entitled "Co-ordinating Public Debt and Monetary Management: Institutional and Operational Arrangements ", edited by V. Sundararajan, Peter Dattels and Hans J. Blommestein.

2. Government Study (SOU) 1997:66, Government Bill 1997/98:154

3. In "Financial Markets, Public Policy, and the East Asian Miracle", The World Bank Research Observer, vol. 11, no. 2 (August 1996)

4. "Emerging Bond Markets in the Dynamic Asian Economies", OECD Publications, Paris 1993

5. "Säkrare obligationer", SOU 1997:110

Chapter 2

THE RUSSIAN GOVERNMENT SECURITIES MARKET

Submission by
The Russian Central Bank

Trade organisation principles

It is known that most countries whose economies may be classified as transitional sooner or later are confronted with a significant federal budget deficit and the need to finance it on a qualitatively new, market-oriented basis. Growing inflation, which is initially caused primarily by deferred demand, requires from the central bank the implementation of a restrictive monetary policy, that is restricting the fiduciary issue of money. In this situation direct government borrowings from the central bank become inadmissible and the need arises to switch to the new means of financing the budget deficit, based on the issue of government securities with market yields.

Russia began to create a government securities market in the middle of 1992 when the work on the principles of organising this market and its regulatory rules started. At that time the Russian financial market was still in the making and there was simply no system that could become an adequate alternative to exchange floor trading.

For many reasons it was decided to concentrate all trading in government bonds on one Moscow floor, the Moscow Interbank Currency Exchange (MICEX). Firstly, the government short-term bonds, or GKOs, were originally intended for a large number of big investors scattered all over Russia and that factor alone dictated the need for arranging centralised exchange trade. Secondly, the bonds were to be issued electronically in accordance with advanced international standards and that made the concentration of trading at MICEX very convenient from the viewpoint of settlements, accounting and custody of the bonds. That also increased many times the speed and reliability of settlements.

Another advantage of trading in GKOs and later in the federal loan bonds, of OFZs, at MICEX was that it made it easier to supervise market participants. This, in turn, would make the market more transparent and enable the Central Bank to pursue an effective monetary policy.

Exchange trade also encouraged competition in the government securities market. As the market expanded and trade volumes increased, the number of market players grew and that practically eliminated the possibility of price manipulation and unfair competition. At the same time, the development and expansion of the government securities market confronted the Bank of Russia with new tasks, which required some changes in the rules of trading.

Initially, all market players were divided into two groups: the professional market participants (dealers), who conducted operations on their own behalf and for their own account and also on their own behalf for investors' account and on the latters' instructions, and the investors. Both had equal bidding rights in the trading system from the viewpoint of price formation. Nevertheless, the expansion of the market and the growth in the number of market participants required the introduction in October of 1996 of "super-professional" market participants, the so-called primary dealers, who had more rights and duties than any other market participants. Specifically, the primary dealers now have the exclusive right to make out quotations on the Trading System. At the same time, one of their duties is to maintain bilateral quotations on the market, ensuring acceptable terms of trade for other market players.

Recently, exchange trade opportunities expanded for all GKO-OFZ market participants. All dealers were given the opportunity to register deals with their clients outside the trading system partly during the trading session and right after its closing. It should be noted that during the trading session over-the-counter deals on each bond issue are made at prices within the current market spread, while after the close of the trading session they are made at average weighted prices. This gives both the dealers and their clients new possibilities for striking mutually beneficial deals.

The development and evolution of the role of the government securities market

The government securities market is the most technologically advanced sector of the Russian financial market. It matches the world's best standards. Government securities worth more than 310 billion new roubles are traded in the Russian market today. The average daily turnover is around 5 billion roubles ($1 billion), almost three times the corporate stock market turnover, and it is the world's third largest market in terms of daily trade sessions.

In 1992 when Russia was just beginning to create a government securities market there was no organised stock market in the country. Almost the entire real sector of the economy was state-owned, large-scale privatisation was only beginning and there were no conditions for the creation of a corporate securities market. However, high inflation rates, which were largely caused by the direct crediting of the budget deficit by the Central Bank, dictated the need to create new instruments that would make it possible to finance the budget deficit by non-inflationary means.

The work carried out by the Bank of Russia and the Finance Ministry to establish the market principles of financing the federal budget deficit enabled the Finance Ministry first to substantially reduce and eventually abandon all direct borrowing from the Central Bank (the abolition of this practice was formalised in the Law on the Central Bank) and create a market for government short-term bonds, which by early 1995 had become one of the most powerful segments of the Russian financial market, contributing to the development of the stock market as a whole.

During the four years of its existence the GKO market has passed several stages of development. The following main changes had a significant impact on the development of the present market infrastructure:

1. Ever since its inception, the GKO market was oriented to the world's advanced technologies. Initially, all trading was conducted on the MICEX trading floor, but in early 1994 the increase in the number of traders led to the connection of remote terminals. The first to be connected were the Bank of Russia terminals. At present practically all trading in government securities is done from remote terminals. The regional expansion of the market in 1995-1996 was the logical consequence of that process. At present eight

regional exchanges trade in GKOs and OFZs in the same regime as MICEX.

2. A new instrument, the variable-coupon federal loan bond, was introduced in the market in June 1995. It allowed investors to invest for longer terms while receiving coupon income. Late in February 1997 the government securities market began to trade in the fixed-income federal loan bonds. It should be noted that recently the OFZs have become one of the most attractive and important kinds of government debt instruments as a result of a decline in yields on government securities, enhanced stability and liquidity of the federal loan bonds and market players' increasing orientation towards longer-term investments.

3. The expansion and qualitative growth of the GKO-OFZ market in 1996 required a significant restructuring. Foreign investors were granted access to the government securities market in February 1996. Initially, non-residents' participation was limited to auctions, but in August non-residents received the right to participate in trading in the secondary market, investing funds and repatriating returns through the special C-type accounts. The inflow of foreign capital to the Russian government securities market contributed not only to the development of the national banking sector, but also to the improvement in Russia's rating as a borrower in international financial markets.

   Non-residents' participation in the domestic Russian government securities market had a favourable effect on the infrastructure of the Russian financial market as a whole, especially the foreign-currency market: turnover on the spot market grew and its liquidity improved. The over-the-counter currency futures market also received a strong impetus: its turnover grew and the share of longer-term contracts increased. Overall, this has had a favourable effect on the stabilisation of foreign exchange trade.

4. In 1996 the institution of primary dealership became finally established in Russia under the impact of a rapid market growth and an increase in the number of market players (this subject was discussed in detail above).

5. For the first time in Russia two new instruments of managing bank liquidity -- Lombard credits and direct REPO operations -- were

developed and introduced in 1996 on the basis of the government securities market. Lombard credits are simply credits extended against collateral of government securities. Initially, the Central Bank extended Lombard credits at auctions and for a term of 7 and 14 days, but subsequently the range of Lombard credit operations was extended through credit term diversification from 3 days to 29 days and credits began to be granted at a fixed rate tied to the Central Bank's refinancing rate.

Direct REPO operations, which are designed not only to manage bank liquidity, but also to maintain primary dealers' activity in the GKO-OFZ market, were introduced at the same time as the primary dealership. REPO operations are transactions involving the sale of government securities with a pledge of their subsequent repurchase. In 1996 the Central Bank conducted only two-day direct REPO operations, tied to the short cash position on the results of trading or auction. This means that given a short cash position, a primary dealer had to sell securities to the Central Bank and repurchase them later. In 1997 the range of REPO operations was broadened considerably by including reverse REPO operations and REPO operations untied with the short position and the terms of operations were diversified.

Thus, the present government securities market has a high-tech and diversified infrastructure. The qualifications and expertise of most market players enable them to use effectively the existing financial instruments and create new ones on their basis, while the transparency, speed and reliability of transactions constantly attract new resources and participants to the exchanges.

A trading system capable of handling an ever growing volume of government securities as well as corporate bonds has been created. Since March 1997, the MICEX Trading System has successfully traded in the bonds of the non-governmental corporation High-Speed Railways, and trading in equities will be introduced later in the year. One of the fundamental elements of the progress made is the use of the existing infrastructure of the government securities market.

Since the GKO-OFZ market first appeared, the strategies of its participants have undergone substantial change. Previously many market players sought to make profit from speculative investments in GKOs and OFZs, whereas now their interest has shifted to medium-term investments. Primary dealers, who are now assigned the functions of market-makers, are beginning to be guided in their actions not only by a quest for quick-fix profits, but also by the need to maintain market stability, something that in the final analysis serves their long-term interests.

Thus, there is ample reason to regard the present infrastructure of the government securities market and qualifications of its participants as quite adequate for organising primary placement of and trade in corporate securities. The task now is to create conditions that would enable the enterprises capable of manufacturing competitive products to increase their working capital by issuing short-term bonds that would be placed in the same system as the GKOs.

Chapter 3

THE CONTRIBUTION OF THE GOVERNMENT SECURITIES MARKET TO THE DEVELOPMENT OF WIDER SECURITIES MARKETS IN HUNGARY

by
Attila Csajbók and Judit Neményi*

Introduction

The establishment and development of government securities markets can be considered as one of the major achievements in the Hungarian financial sector reforms.

This paper addresses the role of government securities markets in relation to the development of other capital market segments in a historical approach. In order to see how government securities markets could influence other segments of the market, the main regulatory changes and institutional developments will be listed and the different aspects/channels through which events on government securities markets affected the other securities markets will be presented.

The following characteristics influencing capital market development in Hungary should be emphasised:

– By the time the government securities market was to take off, Hungarian investors (at least those who dared to invest in new, unknown instruments) had already had some unpleasant

* National Bank of Hungary, Economics and Research Department (1850 Hungary, T: 361-3122469, F: 361-2690753. email: nemenyi@mnbpost2.mnblan.mnb.hu). The views expressed here do not necessarily reflect the official position of the National Bank of Hungary.

experiences with the emerging corporate bond market due to the surge in inflation at the end of the 1980s.

- In the early phase of transition (early 1990s) the development of government securities markets could not be backed by stable economic prospects for the Hungarian economy as a whole. In 1990-1991, Hungary managed to cope with a serious foreign exchange liquidity crisis, but still ranked among highly indebted countries (forex debt/GDP was over 60 per cent).The introduction of the new market-based budget financing system in 1992 coincided with the start of a period of growing internal and external imbalances.

- The 1995 March adjustment measures created the basis for sounder macroeconomic development (sustainable growth) which may have increased investors′ confidence. The economic trends prevailing since the adjustment programme was launched (decreasing inflation, significant cuts in the twin deficits (the current account deficit and the government borrowing requirement), growth recovery) have provided and are expected to continue to provide favourable conditions for further development of government securities (Treasuries) markets aiming at a more secure maturity profile, cost-efficient financing and improved market liquidity.

- Hungary had chosen to establish a network of brokerage firms specialised to deal in the securities business rather than opt for the universal banking approach. However, the "Chinese Wall" between commercial banking and brokerage activity was destroyed in 1996, when the prohibition for commercial banks to trade with government securities was abolished. Although the previous regulatory situation already had resulted in almost all of the commercial banks establishing their "own" securities trading subsidiary, the new regulation may give further impetus to capital market development in Hungary.

Main features of the development of securities markets

Capital markets in Hungary started to develop in the second half of the 1980s with corporate bond issues. Later the first Treasury bill issues took place and in 1990 the Budapest Stock Exchange was re-opened.

Table 1. **Development of the Budapest Stock Exchange**

	1990 21 June.	1990 31 Dec.	1991 31 Dec.	1992 31 Dec.	1993 31 Dec.	1994 31 Dec.	1995 31 Dec.	1996 31 Dec.	1997 30 Dec.
Number of stock exchange members,	42	42	48	48	47	51	56	57	63
of which:									
Brokerage houses	23	21	31	41	46	50	55	56	62
Banks	19	21	17	7	1	1	1	1	1
Registered securities,	1	6	22	40	62	120	166	167	149
of which:									
Shares	1	6	20	23	28	40	42	45	49
Government bonds			1	4	16	25	34	36	28
Corporate bonds			1	1	1	3	3	2	7
Treasury bills				10	10	31	50	50	44
Investments units				1	6	20	36	33	20
Compensation coupons				1	1	1	1	1	1

The track record of the development of government securities markets within the capital market is presented in Table 2.

Starting with a negligible stock of Treasury bills in 1990, the size of the government securities market has become more than significant by the second half of the 1990s, while the range of instruments and the maturity composition has been well diversified. As a result, the share of Treasuries in domestic financial savings and in the portfolios of different investors has been increasing, enhancing their role not only as saving instruments but also as a tool of liquidity management. This was promoted by the deepening of secondary markets.

The issuance of government securities in the early nineties was motivated by both fiscal and monetary policy considerations. The government's deteriorating fiscal position made it necessary to increase the supply of Treasuries, while monetary policy, following basically an anti-inflationary target, was directed to avoiding the monetisation of the growing government borrowing requirement, and hence supported the increase of the share of market-based financing. Policymakers agreed that the efficiency of economic policies can be increased if the privileged access of the government to cheap central bank finance was reduced (and later, abolished) although the appropriate speed of this process had been the subject of serious debates. Financing the budget at market prices (by issuing government securities) was considered as a condition of crucial importance to the transition which could help both fiscal adjustment in the budget and the development of money and capital markets. Government securities markets provide useful information to various economic agents (policymakers, bankers, investors and entrepreneurs) not only in their everyday operation but also when designing policy stances and making business plans for the longer run.

Table 2. **Government securities in the Hungarian financial system** (percent)

	1991	1992	1993	1994	1995	1996	1997
Total stock of government securities*/GDP	4.7	15.9	28.4	30.9	30.6	36.2	31.6
Treasury bonds,	2.3	10.5	22.1	23.7	22	26.1	20.9
of which:							
Marketable	1.1	5.1	9.1	10.7	8.5	10.7	12.2
Recapitalisation	0	0	8.1	7.6	6.1	5.2	3.1
Other special issues	1.2	5.4	4.9	5.4	7.4	10.2	5.6
T-bills	2.4	5.4	6.3	7.2	8.6	10.1	10.7
of which:							
Discount T-bills	1	2.2	5.1	5.4	7.2	8.3	7.8
Special T-notes*	1.4	3.2	1.2	1.8	1.4	1.8	2.9
Share of government securities in household savings	..	..	2.38	6.83	8.55	9.9	11.65
Share of government securities in the total turnover at the BSE***	2.97	81.44	85.29	63.96	62.51	54.52	56.10

* Consolidation and other special (recapiatlisation) bonds were issued mainly via private placement and not admitted to the stock exchange.

** Non-marketable savings instruments (interest bearing T-bills, savings bills, etc.)

*** BSE - Budapest Stock Exchange.

Table 3. **Capitalisation at the Budapest Stock Exchange**
(in per cent of GDP)

	1990	1991	1992	1993	1994	1995	1996	1997
Capitalisation	0.78	2.15	6.86	12.88	20.25	21.96	36.12	60.88
Shares	0.78	1.53	1.60	2.30	4.16	5.89	12.88	36.41
Government securities	0.00	0.61	2.80	8.90	14.49	14.93	21.16	22.14
of which:								
Government bonds		0.61	2.80	6.81	9.00	8.16	10.63	11.33
Treasury bills				2.09	5.49	6.77	10.53	10.81
Corporate bonds				0.01	0.04	0.03	0.02	0.44
Investment units				0.16	0.44	0.78	0.63	0.39
Compensation coupons				1.52	1.12	0.34	1.44	1.50

The development of government securities markets

Although the development of money and capital markets in Hungary started in the eighties[1], they were further widened and strengthened in the 1990s. In 1990 the overwhelming part of household savings were invested in commercial bank deposits. The share of government securities in total household savings has since increased rapidly and has exceeded 10 per cent by the end of 1996. However, the development has been burdened by adverse micro- and macroeconomic conditions and the secondary market was held back by the lack of serious institutional investors. The regulatory institutional framework of the government securities markets could only be established gradually, taking into account the features and results of the transition, while trends on the international scene also had to be considered.

- Transformational recession and unclear economic prospects made domestic savings quite volatile. While there was a sharp decline in economic activity (bottoming in 1993), the restructuring of production and the re-orientation of trade patterns, as well as the transformation of the ownership structure had begun and progressed at a steady pace. As a result, the profitability and creditworthiness of enterprises had increased to a great extent by 1996.
- This transformation coupled with the significant fiscal adjustment introduced in 1995 (the so-called "severity package"), resulted in

the consolidation of household savings at a level which by that time was in balance with the demand for funds from both the government and the corporate sector.

– General trends in the international financial markets can be characterised by: *i)* the expansion of capital markets (a relative retreat of banking activity in collecting funds), *ii)* liberalisation and globalisation leading to the increase of international capital flows and *iii)* an upsurge in financial innovation. All this affected the transition countries and, in a way, forced them to adjust their market regulation according to the above-mentioned general directions in a very early phase of market development. Trying to be always on the safe side, Hungary as well has experienced a relatively rapid liberalisation and market development during the nineties. The major part of foreign exchange current and capital transactions (except short-term operations) were liberalised by 1997. The change of the investor base as well as financial innovation could be considered quite substantial.

The development of securities markets is determined by several factors:

– *legal and regulatory framework* - in Hungary it was established quite early in the transition process, while the development of different market segments was followed and encouraged by regular amendments of the basic laws.
– *macroeconomic developments and outlook* - the less certain and favourable they are the less confidence may be expected from investors to invest for the long run (constraining demand) and the higher the risk premium issuers have to pay (constraining supply).
– *microeconomic development* - the weak performance (profitability) and adjustment capability of the enterprises before restructuring and privatisation constrained the development of equity and corporate bond markets.
– *the culture of investing in securities* - due to lack of markets and instruments in the CPE it has been emerging only slowly. This is probably a longer-term education process promoted, however, by such new developments like the pension reform, or the establishment of mutual funds (subject to tax allowance).

- *secondary market liquidity and transparency* - the deepening of the secondary markets has been essential in making securities investments more and more attractive and enhancing the interdependence of different sub-markets.
- *issuing and trading techniques, settlement and clearing system* - development in these fields is a precondition for secondary markets.
- *liberalisation of foreign exchange capital transactions* - participation of non-residents in the securities business may contribute to the deepening of markets.[2].

The first decade of capital markets development in Hungary can be characterised by a permanent change in legislation, markets (products and participants) and behaviour. The main events of legislation and institutional development, having a direct or indirect effect on the government securities markets, are given below. Three main blocks of laws can be distinguished. The first one consists of laws regulating institutions (exchanges, clearing houses and depositories and institutional investors), trading and settlement of transactions. The second block of laws is related to the government securities markets (borrowing requirement and financing the budget, the role of the central bank). The third block concerns the foreign exchange regulation and more particularly the participation of foreigners in the domestic securities markets.

Legislation[3]

Act on Business Organisations (1988)

Act on the Public Issuing of and Trade in Certain Securities and the Stock Exchange (1990)

Act on Financial Institutions and Banking (1991).

Act on the Commodity Exchange and the Central Depository (1994)

Act on Mutual Funds (1991)

Act on the Central Bank (December 1991) and the amendments to this Act (in 1993 and 1996).

The Code on Foreign Exchange (1996)

Act on the General Government

Institutional changes

Budapest Stock Exchange reopened in 1990.

Establishment of the Banking Supervisory Agency and the Securities Supervisory Agency (1991). The two institutions were merged (in 1996) into Banking and Capital Market Supervision.

Establishment of brokerage houses (1990-)

Government Debt Issues Organising Office (1993)

State Debt Management Agency (SDMA, 1995)

Treasury (January 1995), System of Primary Dealers (1996)

Mutual funds, Pension funds (1995-)

Regarding the government securities markets development the Act on the Central Bank (ACB) undoubtedly stands out as being of crucial importance among all these changes in legislation[4]. According to the ACB:

- since 1992 the budget has been financed by government securities issuance[5] (Treasury bills and bonds);

- financing the budget by the central bank was limited in 1993, 1994 and 1995 (5. 4 and 3 per cent of budget revenues was set as an upper limit to the increase in the government's liabilities to the central bank, respectively). Preferential direct credit lines ceased to exist but direct purchase of government securities by the National Bank of Hungary (NBH) was not prohibited. Since 1997 the NBH is not allowed to provide direct finance to the budget.

- at the beginning the NBH played a market maker role in the government securities markets and its retail selling activity was also quite significant. As the SDMA and the Treasury were set up and the primary dealer system began to operate (in 1996) the central bank could retire cease such activities.

- the amendment to the ACB in 1993 was enacted to swap the non-interest bearing debt of the budget[6] into marketable government bonds. The size of the debt swap was determined according to the decline in the net foreign exchange liabilities of the NBH. The 10-30 year maturity government bonds issued in exchange for the debt exceeded HUF 500 Billion (8 per cent of GDP) at the end of 1996.

The measures introduced by the ACB are of great importance from the point of view of the development and interdependence of securities markets and together with the other laws listed above determined the framework for the contribution of government securities to capital markets development.

Public debt management and securities markets development

The public debt management has affected the development of securities markets in general through different "channels". The objectives of public debt management promoted the development of other markets directly or indirectly by:

- educating investors;
- increasing the choice of capital market instruments;
- promoting domestic savings;
- developing techniques, infrastructure and network of primary issues;
- ensuring an efficient functioning of the secondary markets.

Following 1992 government securities markets started to expand quite rapidly, being nearly the only alternative of bank deposits for domestic investors. At the beginning, the presence of government securities did not mean more than they *contributed to the "education" of inexperienced investors.* As the supply of marketable instruments got larger, the portfolio approach became more and more relevant when analysing investor behaviour and propensity to save. In addition, by increasing competition for funds with the banking sector, government securities issues have probably accelerated the development of infrastructure and business operation in commercial banks[7].

A fundamental characteristic of government securities, beneficial for the development of wider securities markets, is that they represent risk-free assets or, rather, they are assets of a relatively low risk in any circumstances. This characteristic is even more important in emerging market conditions, since the presence of a low-risk asset in the securities markets may provide:

- the other markets and market participant with a *benchmark yield curve*;
- the commercial banks and other financial institutions with instruments for *strengthening their balance sheets* in a period of increasing market risk (such like the restructuring and portfolio cleaning period from 1992-1995 in Hungary);
- the enterprises with reliable *instruments for liquidity management*;
- and investors with low-risk instruments for *portfolio diversification*.

In the following we describe the government securities markets' performance with respect to the above functions.

The benchmark yield curve

The government securities yield curve has only gradually become a benchmark for different markets and market participants. As long as the borrowing requirement of the budget remained high (outside the sustainable range) and the recurrent devaluation expectations made Hungarian forint investments less attractive even if the risk premium had been increasing (during 1992-1995 Q1), the yield on government securities could not be treated as reflecting a low-risk scenario for investors.

However, as the first results of the 1995 March measures appeared, the improving conditions contributed to a reduction in the excess premium on government debt instruments and since 1996 the yield curve began to exhibit a negative slope which can be regarded as a sign of increasing credibility of government disinflation targets for the future. The increased credibility of the anti-inflationary policy made it possible to issue longer-term (5-year) fixed-interest T-bonds, in February 1997, the Hungarian yield curve lengthening significantly.

Figure 1. **Enterprises credit and deposit rates, TB-yield and inflation** (per annum)

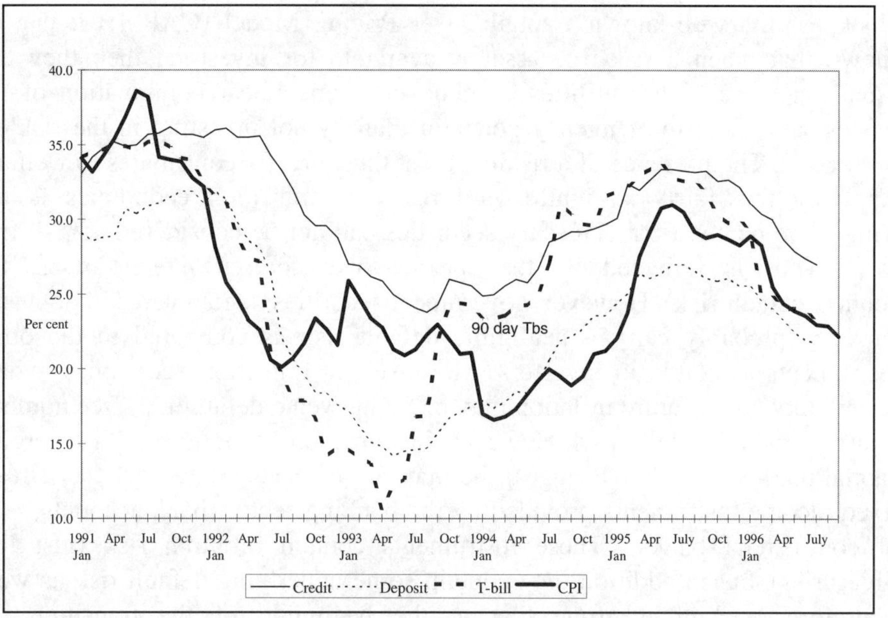

Figure 2. **Zero-coupon yield curves**

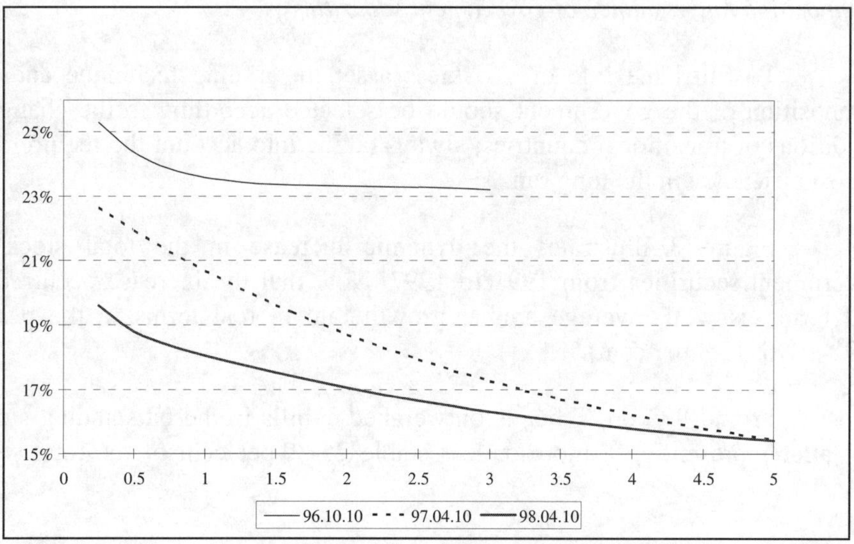

* Calculated from primary dealers' daily price quotes for 35-37 Treasury securities

Portfolio diversification

According to theoretical considerations (which also serve as building-blocks of the well-known Capital Asset Pricing Model (CAPM)) it can be shown that when a risk-free asset is available for investors, then they can usually achieve higher utilities by choosing some linear combination of the riskless asset and the tangency portfolio than by not investing in the riskless asset at all. The presence of a riskless asset thus directly contributes to welfare. Applying this fairly straightforward result to transition economies is not without problems. First, Treasury securities can not be considered as risk-free assets (this is reflected by the spreads over foreign interest rates, the country/default risk). However, government securities denominated in domestic currency probably carry a negligible default risk as compared to the other instruments available to investors. Moreover, in transition economies, where uncertainty about future inflation may be high, even a default risk-free nominal return is risky in real terms. However, in transition economies with emerging capital markets (stock exchanges) the majority of the available risky assets are fixed income instruments provided by the banking sector (bank accounts, CDs of commercial banks). These instruments contain inflation risk (just like Treasuries), but in addition they contain some underlying default risk as well. Therefore one might argue that at the beginning of the transition the introduction of government securities helped investors to reduce the risk of their portfolios and thus directly contributed to welfare.

Composition and issuance of government securities

To fulfil the role of a riskless asset the issuing technique and the composition of the government should be selected according to the changing conditions of transitional countries, always taking into account the requirement of cost efficiency in the long run.

Figure 3 illustrates the dynamic increase in the total stock of government securities from 1991 to 1997. Note that the increase occurred in real terms as well (average annual growth rate in real terms in the period 1992-1996: 13.8 per cent).

From 1992 on, T-bonds outweighed T-bills in the outstanding stock, the latter representing a more or less stable 25-30 per cent of the total stock (Fig. 4.).

Figure 3. **Total outstanding stock of Treasury securities**
(T-bonds and T-bills, private placement and public issue)

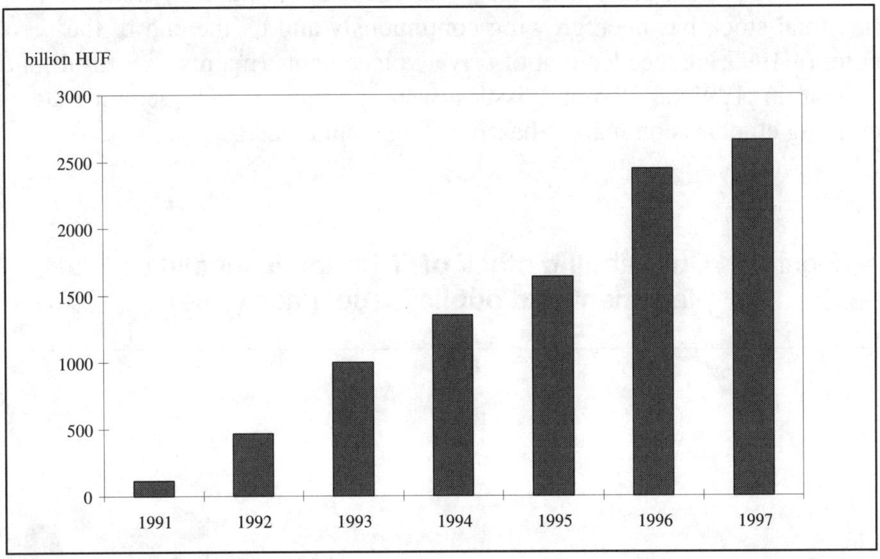

Figure 4. **Total outstanding stock of T-bonds and T-(face value) bills**

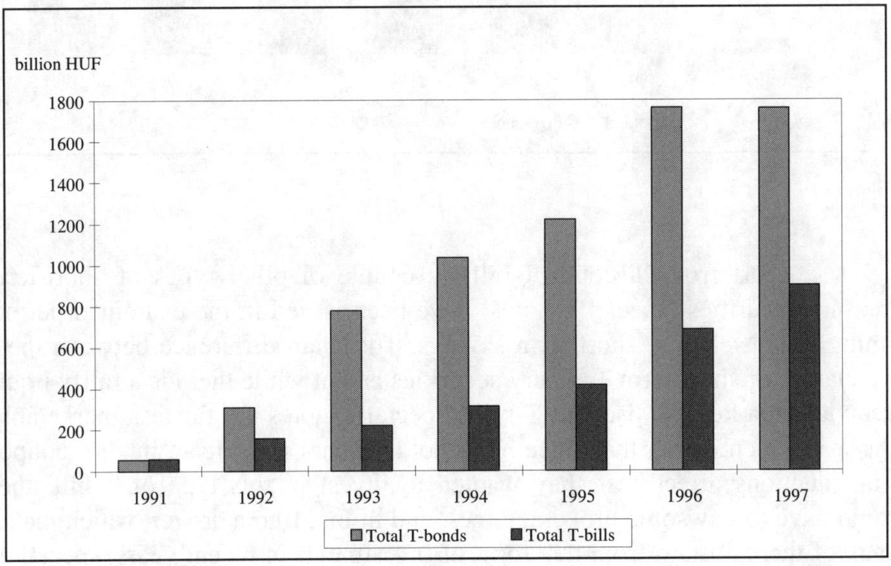

T-bill issues have been predominantly open in the past six years, while Fig. 5 shows that the major part of the outstanding stock of T-bonds have been sold via private placement. However, the share of publicly issued T-bonds in the total stock has been growing continuously and by the end of the second quarter of 1997 it exceeded that of private placements (mainly as a result of the fact that in 1997 all T-bond issues were public), which demonstrates an increasing emphasis on market-based selling techniques.

Figure 5. **Outstanding stock of T-bonds issued via private placement and public issue** (face value)

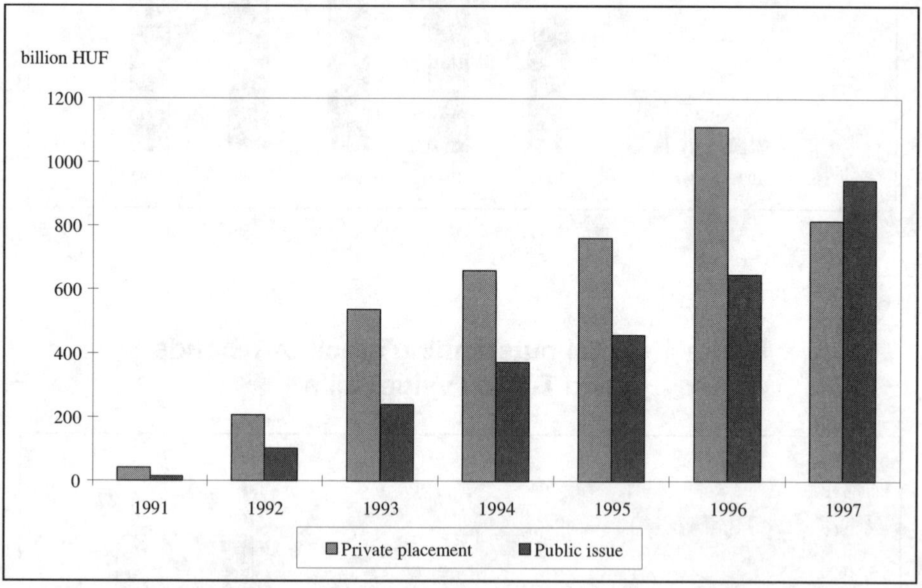

Apart from discount T-bills, a couple of other types of short-term Treasury securities (special T-notes) have been issued in the examined period, aiming at households' short-term savings. The main difference between these two classes of short-term Treasury securities is that while there is a fairly liquid secondary market for discount T-bills, special T-notes are far less marketable. It is worth mentioning that since households cannot participate in zero coupon T-bill auctions directly, if they wanted to invest in this type of T-bill, they would have to pay some brokerage fees, and in fact find a broker, which makes many of them abstain from this form of investment. In recent years, special T-notes have been heavily advertised and are now available in the outlets of major commercial banks -- of course with all the well-known principal-agent type of problems that usually emerge in this situation. The proportions of discount T-bills and special T-notes are shown in Fig. 6. Discount T-bills dominate the segment of short-term government securities, showing that investors in general are aware of the advantages of this relatively liquid instrument.

Figure 6. **Outstanding stock of discount T-bills vs. special T-notes**

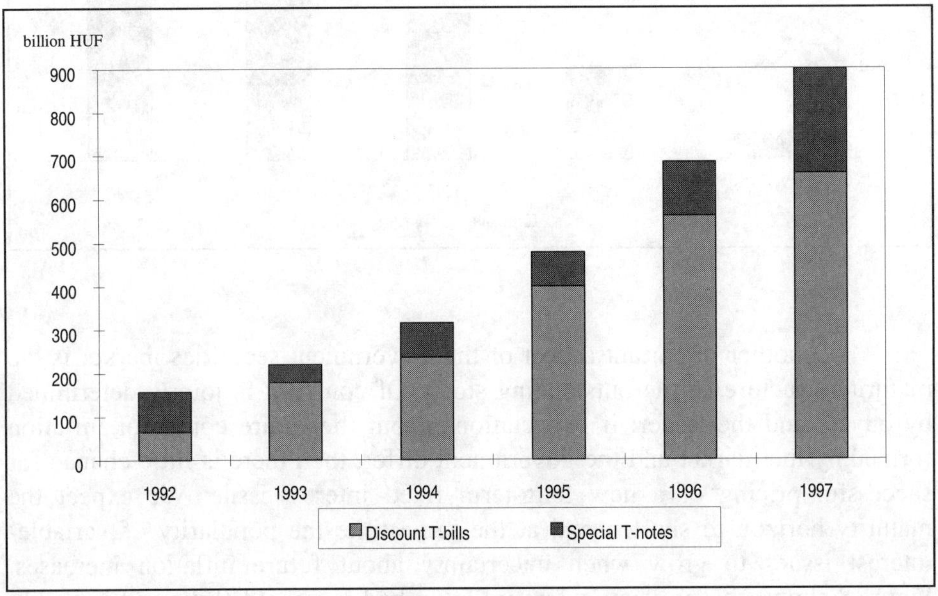

While households have no direct access to discount T-bill auctions, they can participate in fixed-price issues of T-bonds, and recently they can do so in the outlets of some commercial banks as well. Fig. 7 illustrates that although household investments in T-bonds have been increasing until 1996, shorter-term T-bills generally dominated the part of household savings allocated towards Government securities.

Figure 7. **Gross nominal household savings in Treasury securities**
(end-of-year stocks)

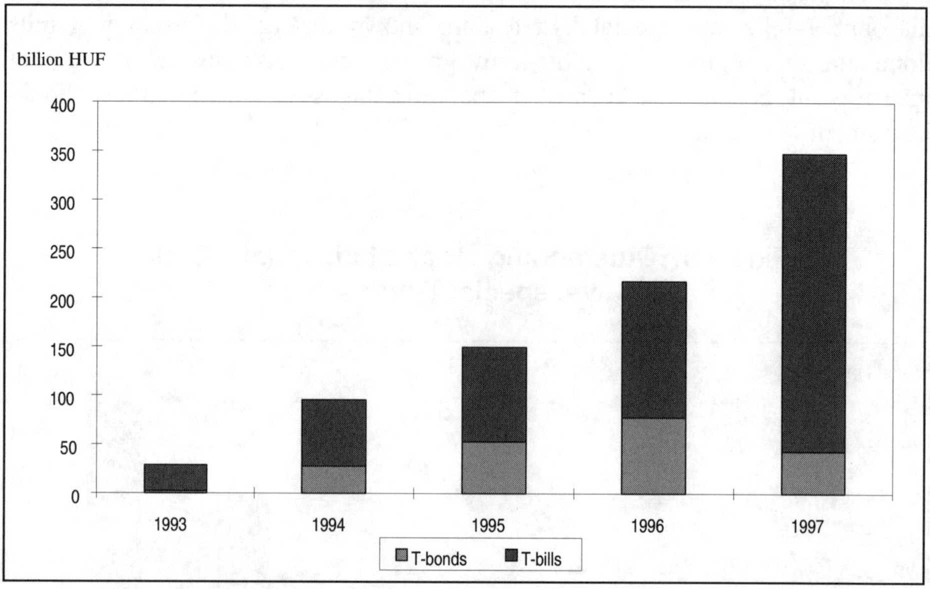

Another important aspect of the Government securities market is the maturity structure of the outstanding stock. Of course it is jointly determined by buyers and the issuer: if expectations about the future course of inflation formed by the market and the government differ, then there is little chance for successful pricing of a new long-term fixed interest issue. We expect the maturity horizon to shorten and at the same time the popularity of variable-interest issues to grow when uncertainty about future inflation increases. Figure 8 shows that in years when inflation had increased (followed probably by an increase in uncertainty about future inflation) compared to the previous year (1993 and 1995) average maturity shortened.

The picture is less clear if one looks at the changes in the proportion of fixed and variable interest instruments (Figure 9), although it is still true that the share of variable interest instruments was highest in 1995, when the highest increase in inflation had occurred.

Figure 8. **Average maturity of the outstanding stock of publicly issued Treasury securities and CPI inflation**

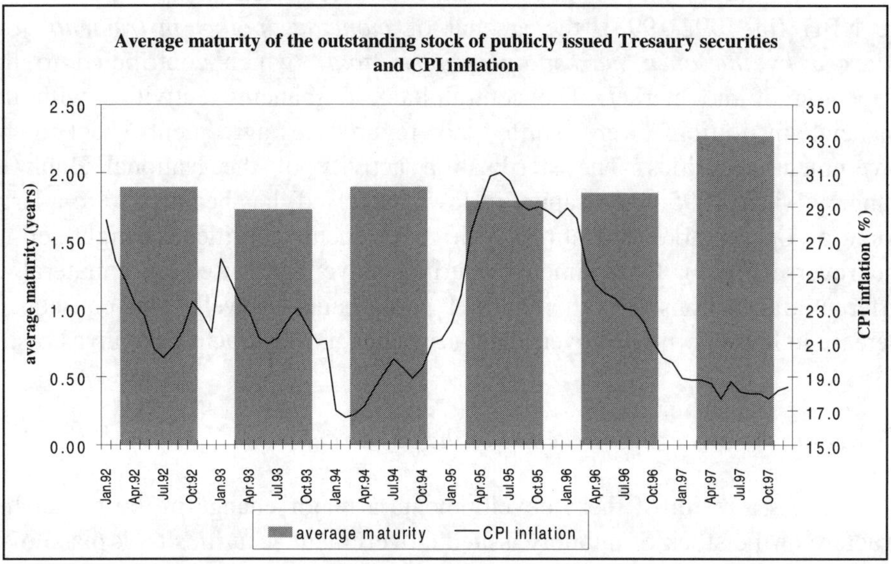

Figure 9. **Proportion of fixed and variable interest bonds in total stock of public-issue T-bonds**

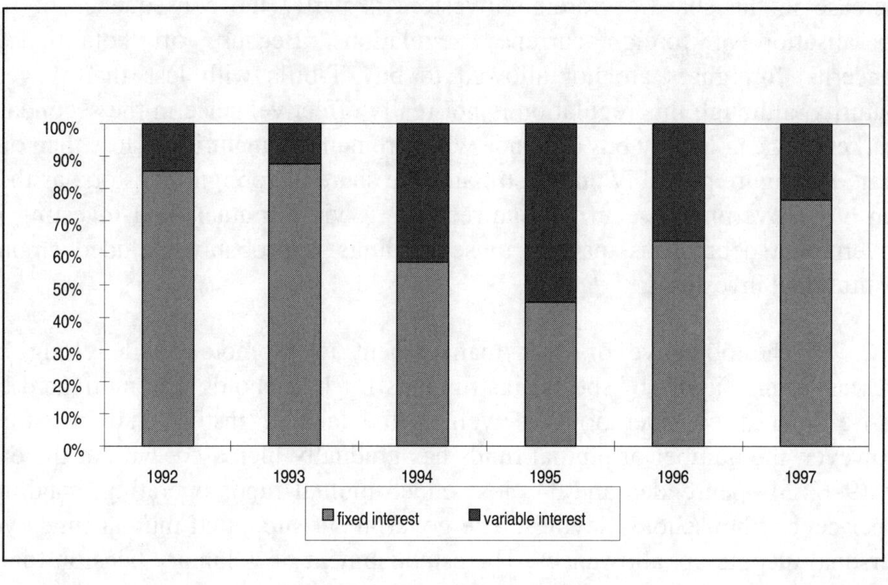

Instruments to be used as collateral

As the share of the government securities increased in the portfolio of the NBH (in 1992-1993), the arsenal of *monetary policy instruments was enlarged by the open market operations "tool"* which contributed to the deepening of the market. The central bank refinancing activities with the financial institutions were shifted to repurchase agreements backed by government securities. The sterilisation activity of the National Bank of Hungary (since 1995 when capital inflows increased) has been based to a large extent on open market operations with government securities (outright selling and reverse repos). Government securities have been used as collateral in different transactions by other market participants as well. The consequent increase in liquidity made government securities more attractive for investors.

Changes in the ownership structure of the public debt

As a result of these developments a major change in the ownership structure of the stock of publicly issued Government securities took place over the last four years (Fig. 10). The decrease of the share of the central bank was absorbed mainly by institutional investors and, to a lesser extent, by households and foreign investors.

The relative retreat of the central bank reflects an intentional policy, forcing the government to finance budget deficits from the market. The increase in the share of foreign investors is partly the consequence of the liberalisation of foreign currency regulations. Because of 'hot money' concerns, foreigners are not allowed to buy T-bills with less than 1 year maturity, although this regulation is not really effective, since in the secondary market they can legally buy T-bonds with a remaining maturity of less than one year. The figure probably underestimates the share of foreign investors, as they can buy Government securities indirectly, *e.g.* via a mutual fund investing in government debt. Thus, part of these holdings is probably included among institutional investors.

The objective of debt management to promote retail selling by increasing the supply of special instruments for households was motivated by cost-efficiency considerations as well as the lack of institutional investors. However, the number of mutual funds has gradually increased, with at the end of 1996, 24 open-ended and 34 close-ended mutual funds operating, handling 4 per cent of households savings. The government supported mutual funds via personal income tax allowances. The establishment of voluntary pension funds is allowed since 1995. Almost 300 voluntary pension funds had been established by the end of 1996, with a HUF 20 billion (US$118 million) portfolio and 500 000 members. Institutional investors still keep the majority of their assets in low-risk government securities. Recently mutual funds have started to increase their investments in domestic shares and foreign securities as well (which was made possible by further steps in the liberalisation of foreign exchange transactions).

Figure 10. **Ownership structure of the outstanding stock of publicly issued Treasury securities** (T-bonds+T-bills, end-of-year stocks)

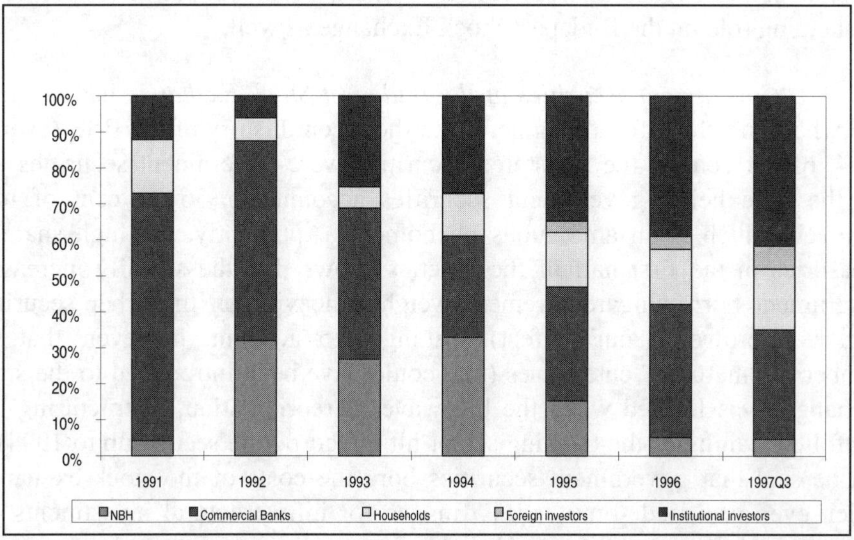

Unfortunately, data about the distribution of the institutional investors' stake in the total stock of government securities by different types of investors has only been collected very recently. What we can examine therefore is a 'snapshot' rather than a process. Nevertheless, it is interesting to see that at the end of the third quarter of 1997 mutual funds accounted for 11 per cent of the total stock, insurance companies for approx. 10 per cent, while the share of companies were quite large at about 20 per cent, second after commercial banks (30 per cent). *This fact shows that by now companies have learnt to use Treasury securities for active liquidity management.* The increase in households' share from 1994 until 1997 is also significant and demonstrates that this sector has recognised the advantages of investing in government debt as well. From 1993 households allocated an increasing share of their gross nominal financial savings towards Government securities, although this share has not yet exceeded 10 per cent of total household savings.

Increasing liquidity and deepening the secondary market

The secondary market liquidity is indispensable for fulfilment of all the above functions associated with the government securities as less risky assets in the securities market as a whole. The secondary market has two scenes in Hungary. The over the counter market (OTC) has had a significant share in the secondary trading which has been further increasing as the trading with bonds begun to expand as well. However, the government securities played an outstanding role on the Budapest Stock Exchange as well.

Government securities at the Budapest Stock Exchange had taken an overwhelming share for a long period in the recent history of the BSE (even in 1994, 65 per cent of the registered securities were government securities and for the time being government securities account for 56 per cent of total turnover) which is an ambiguous phenomena. Apparently, the high share of Treasuries in the first half of the nineties shows that the steadily increasing government borrowing requirement weighed heavily on the other securities markets ("crowding out" effect). Taking into account, however, that the number of "matured" enterprises (that could have been introduced to the stock exchange) was limited when the big wave of reorientation, restructuring and portfolio cleaning of the banking sector hit the corporate sector (up to 1994), it can be said that government securities bore the costs of the stock exchange, which even provided some excess finance for infrastructural investments. *To develop the infrastructure of trading has been one of the preconditions for the developments of wider securities markets and for attracting more and more investors (both residents and non-residents).*

The secondary market has strengthened in line with the supply of instruments and with the institutional and infrastructural developments. Security traders reported a steadily increasing turnover (Table 5). The dynamics has been exceptional especially concerning the new instruments promoted by tax benefits as well. Trading in shares has expanded as well. Although the increase in government securities turnover was lagged behind that of shares at the BSE, the structure of the total secondary market turnover (including OTC markets) remained basically unchanged. The traditionally very high share of government securities in trading can be expected to decline in the future as other markets continue to strengthen.

Table 4. **Turnover at the Budapest Stock Exchange**[8]
(in billion HUF, duplicated)

	1990	1991	1992	1993	1994	1995	1996	1997
Total (in billion HUF)	6.12	10.11	33.67	185.69	211.23	253.18	1145.4	6736.3
Total turnover	100	100.0	100.0	100.0	100.0	100.0	100.0	100.0
Equity	100	97.0	17.8	9.8	27.0	34.5	42.8	42.6
Government securities	0	3.0	81.4	85.3	64.0	62.5	54.5	56.1
of which:								
Government bonds	0	3.0	36.7	39.5	25.5	30.5	36.5	29.1
Treasury Bills	0	0.0	44.7	45.8	38.5	32.0	18.0	27.0
Corporate bonds	0	0.0	0.0	0.0	0.0	0.0	0.0	0.6
Investment units	0	0.0	0.1	0.1	0.1	1.4	0.8	0.0
Compensation coupons	0	0.0	0.6	4.8	8.9	1.6	1.8	0.7
Number of transactions	4 962	14 509	8 565	23 749	73 784	71 240	172 840	504 879
Average daily transaction	27	58	34	94	293	286	689	2 044
Average daily trading (million HUF)	33.8	40.1	133.6	736.9	838.2	1 016.8	4 618.7	27 272
Turnover per contract (million HUF)	1.2	0.7	3.9	7.8	2.9	3.6	6.63	13.3
Number of trading days	181	252	252	252	252	249	248	247

Table 5. **Turnover in the OTC market**
(in billion HUF, duplicated)

	1993	1994	1995	1996
Shares	10.7	51.0	45.7	118.9
Government Securities	146.4	731.8	1377.9	3 506.8
of which:				
Government Bonds	37.1	145.3	464.4	1 636.8
Treasury Bills	109.3	586.5	913.5	1 870.0
Corporate Bonds and Others	91.9	52.1	94.3	82.0
Investment Unitst	0.9	0.3	10.6	16.4
Compensation Coupons	23.3	30.5	18.4	15.6
Total	273.3	865.6	1 557.6	3 739.7

Infrastructural developments have been highly motivated by public debt management. Transactions in government securities are settled by the Central Clearing House and Depository Ltd. (KELER) where besides the securities accounts the stock exchange accounts of the members of the BSE are kept as well. By now the infrastructure of trading and settlement has approached the international standard. In the case of government securities the settlement could be shortened to T+2 and the KELER has opened securities account with CEDEL, which made the international trade of securities more rapid and more reliable. Hungarian brokers are, however, free to choose either KELER or they can deal directly using their counterparties′ accounts abroad.

Conclusions

The development of government securities markets has had an outstanding role in the "restoration" of the Hungarian capital market, which operated quite efficiently before the 2nd World War. The apparently adverse feature, namely that the government borrowing requirement amounted to an unbearable level, had a relatively favourable consequence on the capital market development: during the period when the Hungarian economy suffered the most painful transition shocks the public debt could contribute to the revival of securities markets by providing instruments for the investors (which can be considered as a part of a longer term education process) and profits for traders and stock exchange (allowing them to finance the infrastructural investments necessary to make capital markets more attractive for investors).

Government securities markets affected investors and markets through different channels.

Households only gradually learned the investment opportunities provided by capital markets. As a first step, to quit the products offered by commercial banks in a monopol position (often at below-market interest rates), they have been offered investment alternatives in the form of the government securities sold for retail investors (1 and later on, 2-year maturity Treasury Notes issued by subscription). Investors′ confidence could not be gained when PSBR was steadily increasing, which resulted in short term and floating rate instruments having an overwhelming share in deficit financing.

Institutional investors (mutual and pension funds, insurance companies) appeared gradually, which first held back but later on helped the development of the secondary market. They have made increasingly significant investments in government securities and they gradually started to expand

-- according to the improving conditions and appealing offers -- toward other parts of the securities markets as well. Government securities, being relatively low-risk continue to play an important role in reducing the risk of institutional investors' portfolios. Hypothetic portfolios with different maturities constructed from short-term and long-term government securities also serve as the most important benchmarks in assessing the performance of bond portfolios managed by various mutual funds.

The profits from government securities trading were an important source of funds for the infrastructural investments of market participants in the early stages of the capital market's development.

Last but not least, government securities are the most straightforward candidate for collateral in different transactions (*e.g.* in settlement, futures transactions, etc.), thus the fact that they were readily available and were backed by a relatively large and liquid secondary market has probably contributed to the evolution of various types of new financial products and activities.

NOTES

1. The two tier banking system was established in 1987. The treasury bill issues started in 1989 but up to 1992 they were considered as "supplementary" instrument of budget finance, the central bank direct credit line at preferential interest rate being the main source of funding.

2. Although this is not risk-free. Therefore in Hungary the liberalisation has been gradual and designed to take into account both macro- and micro-economic aspects.

3. Over the last decade the Hungarian financial system strengthened. According to the pace of development, the laws of crucial importance (listed below) have been amended several times.

4. The amendments of the Act on the General Government were closely related in certain respect with the change in legislation on the central bank.

5. In the previous regime the budget was financed by central bank loans at preferential interest rates. The NBH borrowed abroad in its own name.

6. The outstanding amount of the non-interest bearing debt of the budget was fully swapped into foreign exchange denominated loans on January 1. The history of non-interest bearing government debt to the central bank is not without lessons, but does not belong thoroughly to our topic.

7. Which of course was not free of danger of crowding out of the private sector. It should be mentioned that the high yields on government securities made them attractive for commercial bank as less risky investment than the corporate sector being restructured.

8. In this paper we deal only with the spot markets as a separate paper covers the derivative markets developments.

Chapter 4

THE PRESENT SITUATION AND CURRENT PROBLEMS IN THE STATE SECURITIES MARKET IN THE SLOVAK REPUBLIC

by
Juraj Jánosík
National Bank of Slovakia

Introduction

The state securities market in Slovakia underwent a series of significant changes over the past years. During a relatively brief period, not only fundamental prerequisites for the existence of this market were created, but also the market was accepted by the domestic financial community. In spite of several unresolved problems, state securities are considered an interesting asset primarily by banks, and interest in investing in state securities is growing among non-banking entities. Subsequently, this basically allows financing of a major part of the state budget deficit of the Slovak Republic in a manner generally accepted in market economies.

Development in the state securities market in 1996 and 1997

Primary market

State securities in 1996 were issued with regard to the issuer's need, but there was no timetable for issuing state securities then. However, during the year, it became an established rule that auctions of state bonds were held on Tuesdays, treasury bills were auctioned on Wednesday, and the issuing day was Thursday.

The aggregate sum of treasury bills issued in 1996 (Annex 1) was significantly higher compared with the previous year, as a result of the state budget deficit, which was three-times higher than in 1995.

As to the time structure of accomplished issues of treasury bills, most had maturity ranging from 3 to 28 days. While in the first three quarters, shorter maturity (approximately 1-month) prevailed, nine-month bills were auctioned in the last two months of the year.

Primary sale of treasury bills was carried out in the form of so-called American auctions, where neither the issue volume nor the maximum interest rate are announced in advance. However, in the last issue of the year, the issuer set a maximum interest rate in an effort to prevent further growth of the average yield. The rapid growth of interest rates on the primary market, particularly in November and December, resulted not only from the general development of interest rates on the interbank market, but primarily from the urgent necessity of the Finance Ministry to refinance the deficit, which reflected in higher issuing activity and willingness to accept most of the auction binds.

Unlike treasury bills, the aggregate volume of state bonds issued in 1996 (Annex 2) was lower than the year before. This decrease may be attributed to the low state budget deficit in 1995 that needed to the refinanced by state bond issues in 1996. Four auctions of state bonds took place, whereby three issues have been issued (in March, August, and October).

All state bond issues in 1996 were auctioned in American-style auctions. Their common feature was short maturity (12 and 18 months), which did not correspond with the overall situation on the primary market; particularly in March, the issuer did not use a chance to acquire long-term resources at favourable conditions. This was confirmed by developments on the primary market starting with the second half of the year that was negatively influenced by growth of interest rates on the money market. Issuing state bonds with a short maturity, along with the small number of issues in 1997, eliminated efforts from previous years to create a yield trend curve of state securities on the primary market.

In 1997, the Finance Ministry together with the NBS decided to issue a timetable of issuing state securities. This timetable is issued regularly for each quarter, and auctions are held regularly each week as scheduled. In the first quarter, auctions of treasury bills were held on Wednesdays in the first three weeks of each month, and on Thursday of the last week of a month, an auction of state bonds took place.

In the first six months of 1997 (Annex 3), more than half of state treasury bill auctions failed, when the issuer (the Finance Ministry) accepted none of the bids. The high number of unsuccessful auctions was a consequence of a complicated situation on the money market, manifested by liquidity shortage and growing interest rates. The development of rates on the interbank deposit market to a great extent also influenced rates offered by market participants at auctions of treasury bills.

The NBS bought treasury bills in an auction only once. Growing interest rates on the interbank market, that affected yield from treasury bills increased the participation of non-banking entities in auctions.

The situation on the money market characterised by liquidity shortage negatively influenced the possibility of refinancing the current deficit by treasury bills bought into the portfolio of commercial banks or non-banking entities. Subsequently, the Finance Ministry and the NBS twice used a specific form of issues directly into the portfolio of the NBS, in accordance with the NBS Act No. 566/1992, Collection of Laws. These issues were payable in seven days at most.

The situation on the primary market became even more complicated in the second half of 1997. The cause for this development was a steep growth of the state budget deficit associated with the necessity to issue a higher volume of treasury bills, along with the announced intention of the Finance Ministry to tax yields from state securities. The Finance Ministry's proposal included taxation of issues that had been issued before the effectiveness of this change, as long as their yield payment would fall in the period after the amendment came into force. These factors, along with the insufficiently developed market, were the main causes for the current situation, where untaxed yield from state securities are higher than interbank deposit rates that are taxed by a 40 per cent tax.

Auctions of treasury bills began to be held every week, whereby auctions of longer bills that would mature in the following year were held every last week of a month, in association with the system of financing the budget deficit used in the Slovak Republic.

The situation with state bonds in the first half of 1997 was similar to that of treasury bills, when half of the auctions ended without accepting any of the bids. A common feature of all issues was their short maturity (one-year), yield (10 per cent p.a.) and unlimited issuing price. From March, periodicity of yield payment changed from once a year to twice a year. Primary sale of individual issues was carried out in the form of American auctions and their participants could be banks, insurance companies, and securities brokers.

Unlike the short-term securities market where treasury bills and NBS bills are traded, foreign investors do have access to the capital market. Our legal system contains no provisions that would restrict their entry on the domestic market. However, foreign investors may only participate on state bonds primary market through participants of this market. The only condition for their participation in trading on the secondary market is opening an account at the Securities Centre, which serves as securities register for the capital market.

Compared with the situation in 1996, demanded yield of auction participants sharply increased as a consequence of growing interest rates on the money market. The effect of the money market on the state bonds primary market was higher also because of their short maturity. In comparison with previous years, however, increased interest of insurance companies and securities brokers who to a greater extent began participating in auctions may be evaluated positively.

With regard to the large volume of state bonds that needed to be issued to cover the 1996 state budget deficit, two-week intervals were introduced for auctions of state bonds, and in October state bond issues were held every week.

Significant growth of interest rates along with improved liquidity of banks contributed to rising demand for state bonds, hence on October 9, the last issue of state bonds to cover the 1996 state budget deficit took place. However, accepted yields from state bonds on the primary market reached their highest level since the start of their issuing.

Secondary market

Treasury bills have been a dominating instrument on the secondary market of short-term securities since its establishment. The NBS used these securities to implement its monetary policy through open market operations on the free market. Transactions between the NBS and commercial banks constituted about 90 percent of all transactions on the short-term securities market, the remaining 10 percent were transactions between commercial banks.

At the beginning of 1996, the situation on the money market was characterised by a notable liquidity surplus, and the NBS reacted by draining liquidity through open market operations. For this reason, NBS bills were used to implement the central bank's monetary policy during this period instead of treasury bills. This was done by a combination of regular issues of NBS bills and short-term REPO transactions with NBS bills from the NBS own portfolio.

Transactions with treasury bills played an important role specifically in refinancing transactions of the NBS in April (resulting from lowered liquidity by issues of NBS bills), in August (a unification of required minimum reserves from all primary deposits to 9 percent) and in the last two months of the year (draining liquidity by auctions of long-term treasury bills).

The secondary bond market is provided through two public market organisers -- Bratislava Stock Exchange (BCPB) and the RM-System Slovakia (RM-S). In accordance with the law, all securities transactions on the capital market were carried out through these organisers. State bonds are only traded at the BCPB, where they are accepted for trading on the basis of a notification, without a prospectus or an evaluation of the BCPB Trading Council.

The capital market in the Slovak Republic witnessed a marked revival in 1996. This was associated with growing demand of investors for bonds, whereby the aggregate volume of transactions more than doubled over the previous year.

Paradoxically, the development on the secondary market with state bonds (Annex 4) did not correspond with this development, when the aggregate trading volume dropped below the value of the year before. In spite of that, state bonds still ranked among the most traded instruments, and state bond transactions made up one-third of the total sum of all bond transactions.

In 1996, the NBS actively entered the secondary market through REPO transactions with state bonds. The NBS carried out these transactions on the BCPB floor throughout almost the whole year using seven-day maturity and a REPO rate set by the NBS. The reason was, that some refinancing operations could not be done using treasury bills, because not all banks had them in their portfolio.

The situation with open market operations in 1997 was influenced by a change of approach by the NBS. The NBS cancelled individual REPO rates and began using REPO tenders to implement its monetary policy. Treasury bills were used for refinancing REPO tenders, and NBS bills were using for draining liquidity.

Problems with providing liquidity for the banking sector through open market operations continued as a consequence of lower demand for treasury bills. Uneven distribution of treasury bills between individual entities surfaced.

At the beginning of the year, only directly agreed-upon transactions were carried out on the secondary market with state bonds (Annex 5), and not a anonymous transactions was concluded on the stock exchange floor, and only deals agreed-upon outside the stock exchange were settled. The reason was increased orientation of investors on the money market and high yield requirements on the demand side. Trading with state bonds only restarted in April, when prices dropped below par value and yield exceeded those of corporate bonds.

New issues of state bonds caused a revival of trading on the secondary market with a certain delay, with regard to excessively long period of assigning state bonds purchased on the primary market to property accounts of investors, and the associated length of the period from the date of issue until the start of trading at the BCPB.

Although the volume of state bonds trading still constitutes a large proportion of the secondary bond market, we can maintain that with regard to their short maturity they are losing their position of a benchmark on the bond market, because other bonds are issued with substantially longer maturity, five years on average.

Evaluation of the current situation and development potential of the domestic state securities market

We consider a sufficient range of products and offered price level as the priorities of the domestic capital market. It is necessary to achieve a suitable time structure, primarily of state bonds, where only one and very short maturity of one year now exists. We believe that resulting from the state budget deficit as well as needs of its refinancing, there will be enough of these securities on the market. From the investor's perspective, the development of yields may be evaluated positively, when particularly in 1997 the growth trend was surprising.

We consider effective functioning of transmission mechanisms of the domestic money and capital markets one of the fundamental conditions for successful and continuous financing of the state budget. The market itself, *i.e.* its ability and willingness to invest available resources in state securities is becoming a specific element of timely and sufficient coverage of financial needs of the state. For this reason, liquid and stable market has an irreplaceable role.

An important factor for creating a quality market for state securities is a standard legal environment. A majority of domestic entities consider inappropriate the most recent amendment to the Income Tax Act, according to which yields from still not repaid state bonds issued before the amendment came into force, should be taxed. We do not want to overestimate this problem, but in a phase of forming a quality market, it does not contribute to its stabilisation.

The presence of foreign investors on the state securities market is very important in the phase of creating a quality domestic capital market. Through the entry of foreign investors into the domestic market, we anticipate an improvement of its liquidity and international financial credibility, with an effect on interest of foreign business entities in doing business in Slovakia.

We anticipate an improvement in smooth financing of the state's needs from providing technical access to the state bonds market to domestic private entities. With regard to minimum risks and interesting yields, we assume higher demand for these securities in the future.

We may conclude that despite some problems, the existing system of state bonds sale and trading is technically acceptable and able to meet the requirements of the issuer, as well as to fulfil the role of the NBS as an agent. A very important factor is the economically attractive and technically simple, but at the same time reliable system. It embraces the optimising system of sales, as well as transfer and financial settlement of securities.

STATISTICAL ANNEXES

Annex 1. **Survey of treasury bills issues in 1996**

Evidence number	Face value of 1 bill in SKK	Issue date	Maturity date	DTM	Demand volume in pieces	Sold volume in pieces	Min. inter. in % p.a	Max. inter. rate in % p.a	Average inter. rate in % p.a
62501101	1 000 000	2-Jan-96	25-Jan-96	23	6 450	0	-	-	-
62501102	1 000 000	11-Jan-96	25-Jan-96	14	8 509	325	6.00	6.50	6.246
*62202103	1 000 000	9-Feb-96	22-Feb-96	13	1 000	1 000	-	-	
*61502004	1 000 000	12-Feb-96	15-Feb-96	3	1 500	1 500	-	-	
62902105	1 000 000	15-Feb-96	29-Feb-96	14	6 800	2 810	6.50	6.80	6.726
60703106	1 000 000	22-Feb-96	7-Mar-96	14	6 630	2 680	6.50	6.81	6.760
62803107	1 000 000	29-Feb-96	28-Mar-96	28	3 905	1 001	6.65	6.99	6.866
62103108	1 000 000	7-Mar-96	21-Mar-96	14	4 033	3 333	6.70	7.20	7.039
61104109	1 000 000	14-Mar-96	11-Apr-96	28	7 406	801	6.65	6.83	6.805
62504110	1 000 000	21-Mar-96	25-Apr-96	35	6 852	3 402	6.70	7.05	6.875
62305111	1 000 000	25-Apr-96	23-May-96	28	5 435	1 569	5.82	6.62	6.354
63005112	1 000 000	2-May-96	30-May-96	28	3 746	0	-	-	-
60606113	1 000 000	16-May-96	6-Jun-96	21	3 361	841	6.50	6.80	6.581
62706114	1 000 000	23-May-96	27-Jun-96	35	2 640	1 120	5.92	6.74	6.591
62706115	1 000 000	6-Jun-96	27-Jun-96	21	884	884	6.80	9.67	8.504
61107116	1 000 000	13-Jun-96	11-Jul-96	28	2 300	1 400	7.49	7.49	7.490

Evidence number	Face value of 1 bill in SKK	Issue date	Maturity date	DTM	Demand volume in pieces	Sold volume in pieces	Min. inter. in % p.a	Max. inter. rate in % p.a	Average inter. rate in % p.a
61807117	1 000 000	20-Jun-96	18-Jul-96	28	2 850	550	7.40	7.45	7.417
62507118	1 000 000	4-Jul-96	25-Jul-96	21	2 125	1 501	7.79	7.89	7.849
60310319	1 000 000	11-Jul-96	3-Oct-96	84	2 082	2 862	7.99	8.69	8.453
61508120	1 000 000	18-Jul-96	15-Aug-96	28	1 050	1 500	8.30	8.30	8.300
62208121	1 000 000	25-Jul-96	22-Aug-96	28	2 297	514	8.20	8.70	8.671
62808122	1 000 000	1-Aug-96	28-Aug-96	27	1 408	0	-	-	-
62208123	1 000 000	15-Aug-96	22-Aug-96	7	990	640	8.19	8.35	8.314
62609124	1 000 000	5-Sep-96	26-Sep-96	21	323	0	-	-	-
61710125	1 000 000	24-Sep-96	17-Oct-96	23	2 600	1 650	7.95	8.15	8.039
61710126	1 000 000	19-Sep-96	17-Oct-96	28	1 700	1 700	7.89	8.40	8.185
62410127	1 000 000	26-Sep-96	24-Oct-96	28	6 536	6 236	8.09	8.50	8.396
63110128	1 000 000	3-Oct-96	31-Oct-96	28	2 746	4 046	8.40	9.00	8.774
60711129	1 000 000	10-Oct-96	7-Nov-96	28	3 060	4 000	8.90	9.00	8.981
61411130	1 000 000	17-Oct-96	14-Nov-96	28	2 198	1 998	8.80	9.20	9.088
*62410031	1 000 000	16-Oct-96	24-Oct-96	8	2 005	2 005	-	-	
62111132	1 000 000	24-Oct-96	21-Nov-96	28	6 124	7 014	8.96	9.25	9.206
63107933	1 000 000	31-Oct-96	31-Jul-97	273	5 220	3 570	9.20	9.40	9.307
60708934	1 000 000	7-Nov-96	7-Aug-97	273	2 717	2 717	9.39	10.00	9.669
62501102	1 000 000	11-Jan-96	25-Jan-96	14	1 089	325	6.00	6.50	6.246
*62111036	1 000 000	13-Nov-96	21-Nov-96	8	1 003	1 003	-	-	
*62111037	1 000 000	14-Nov-96	21-Nov-96	7	3 006	3 006	-	-	
61912138	1 000 000	21-Nov-96	19-Dec-96	28	1 334	1 234	9.50	10.49	10.041
62808939	1 000 000	21-Nov-96	28-Aug-97	280	4 270	3 970	9.90	10.99	10.118
*62811040	1 000 000	21-Nov-96	28-Nov-96	7	5 010	5 010	-	-	
*62911041	1 000 000	22-Nov-96	29-Nov-96	7	1 503	1 503	-	-	

Evidence number	Face value of 1 bill in SKK	Issue date	Maturity date	DTM	Demand volume in pieces	Sold volume in pieces	Min. inter. in % p.a	Max. inter. rate in % p.a	Average inter. rate in % p.a
60409942	1 000 000	28-Nov-96	4-Sep-97	280	1 835	1 030	10.50	11.49	11.249
61912143	1 000 000	28-Nov-96	19-Dec-96	21	1 505	1 350	10.00	10.99	10.414
*60512044	1 000 000	28-Nov-96	5-Dec-96	7	3 500	3 500	-	-	
61809945	1 000 000	5-Dec-96	18-Sep-97	287	2 570	2 520	11.40	12.50	11.942
62712146	1 000 000	5-Dec-96	27-Dec-96	22	1 095	0	-	-	-
*61212047	1 000 000	5-Dec-96	12-Dec-96	7	1 200	1 200	-	-	
60210948	1 000 000	12-Dec-96	2-Oct-97	294	5 043	2 168	11.60	13.00	12.618
*61712049	1 000 000	10-Dec-96	17-Dec-96	7	1 500	1 500	-	-	
*61812050	1 000 000	11-Dec-96	18-Dec-96	7	2 600	2 600	-	-	
62509951	1 000 000	19-Dec-96	25-Sep-97	280	4 720	4 690	12.90	14.00	13.591
*62012052	1 000 000	17-Dec-96	20-Dec-96	3	4 500	4 500	-	-	
*63012053	1 000 000	20-Dec-96	30-Dec-96	10	5 500	5 500	-	-	
60910954	1 000 000	30-Dec-96	9-Oct-97	283	8 633	8 633	13.45	13.50	13.500
*63012055	1 000 000	23-Dec-96	30-Dec-96	7	1 003	1 003	-	-	
*63012056	1 000 000	27-Dec-96	30-Dec-96	3	1 602	1 602	-	-	

* direct sale to National Bank of Slovakia

Annex 2. Issues of government bonds in Slovak Republic (14 May 1998)

Number of Issue	Date of Issue	Date of Maturity	DTM in years	Amount issued	Face Value	Coupon in % p.a.	Coupon frequency	Form of sale	Demand in SKK		Accepted yields in p.a.		
									total	accepted	minimum	average	maximum
001/A	27.03.92	27.03.97	5	2 000 000 000	10 000 000	8.00%	an.	direct		2 000 000 000			
001/B	03.07.92	03.07.97	5	1 200 000 000	10 000 000	8.00%	an.	direct		1 200 000 000			
001/C	28.09.92	28.09.97	5	1 000 000 000	10 000 000	8.00%	an.	direct		1 000 000 000			
002	01.10.92	01.10.96	4	100 000 000	10 000 000	15.00%	s. an.	auction	100 000 000	100 000 000			
	01.10.92	01.10.96	4	500 000 000	1 000 000	15.00%	s. an.	auction	500 000 000	500 000 000			
003			3	0	5 000		s. an.	subs.					
004	14.12.92	14.12.96	4	1 950 000 000	5 000	D+12 5%	s. an.	auction	1 950 000 000	1 950 000 000			
005	01.03.93	01.03.96	3	76 000 000	5 000	D+8 5%	s. an.	auction	76 000 000	76 000 000			
006	03.06.93	03.06.96	3	1 124 000 000	5 000	D+5 5%	s. an.	period.		1 124 000 000			
007	02.08.93	02.02.95	1.5	1 000 000 000	5 000	D+4%	s. an.	period.		1 000 000 000			
008	09.09.94	09.09.96	2	4 460 000 000	10 000	15.00%	s. an.	subs.	4 460 000 000	4 460 000 000	-	-	-
009	09.11.94	09.02.96	1.25	3 520 000 000	10 000	10.90%	quart.	auction	8 310 000 000	3 520 000 000	8.90	10.75	11.20
010	28.02.95	28.02.99	4	2 310 000 000	10 000	11.00%	s. an.	auction	4 630 000 000	2 310 000 000	10.84	11.26	11.49
011	16.05.95	16.05.00	5	6 040 000 000	10 000	10.90%	s. an.	auction	7 230 000 000	6 040 000 000	10.00	10.97	11.10
012	15.06.95	15.06.98	3	620 000 000	20 000	10.50%	s. an.	auction	7 460 000 000	620 000 000	10.50	10.50	10.50
013	**27.06.95**	**27.06.97**	**2**	**4 460 000 000**	**10 000**	**10.00%**	**s. an.**	**auction**	**5 560 000 000**	**4 460 000 000**	**9.99**	**10.17**	**10.28**
014	**18.07.95**	**18.07.97**	**2**	**1 670 000 000**	**10 000**	**9.50%**	**s. an.**	**auction**	**3 000 000 000**	**1 670 000 000**	**9.50**	**10.16**	**10.20**
015	31.08.95	31.08.98	3	4 860 000 000	10 000	9.50%	s. an.	auction	6 430 000 000	4 860 000 000	9.50	10.13	10.25

Number of Issue	Date of Issue	Date of Maturity	DTM in years	Amount issued	Face Value	Coupon in % p.a.	Coupon frequency	Form of sale	Demand in SKK		Accepted yields in p.a.		
									total	accepted	minimum	average	maximum
016	14.09.95	14.09.99	4	4 260 000 000	20 000	10.00%	s. an.	auction	5 760 000 000	4 260 000 000	10.00	10.18	10.20
017	28.09.95	28.09.00	5	6 640 000 000	20 000	9.80%	s. an.	auction	8 260 000 000	6 640 000 000	9.80	10.00	10.08
018	12.10.95	12.10.98	3	4 000 000 000	50 000	9.00%	s. an.	auction	6 060 000 000	4 000 000 000	8.89	9.59	10.12
019	23.10.95	23.10.99	4	3 305 500 000	50 000	9.50%	s. an.	auction	7 340 000 000	3 305 500 000	9.40	9.48	9.50
020	**12.03.96**	**12.09.97**	**1.5**	**3 000 000 000**	**100 000**	**7.80%**	**s. an.**	**auction**	**8 425 000 000**	**3 000 000 000**	**7.02**	**7.66**	**7.75**
021	**22.08.96**	**22.08.97**	**1**	**6 120 000 000**	**100 000**	**9.00%**	**s. an.**	**auction**	**6 120 000 000**	**6 120 000 000**	**8.42**	**8.94**	**9.00**
022	**26.09.96**	**26.09.97**	**1**	**0**	**100 000**	**8.50%**	**s. an.**	**auction**	**180 000 000**	**0**	**-**	**-**	**-**
023	**17.10.96**	**17.10.97**	**1**	**2 179 200 000**	**100 000**	**9.00%**	**s. an.**	**auction**	**4 580 000 000**	**2 179 200 000**	**8.68**	**9.16**	**9.20**
024	**31.01.97**	**31.01.98**	**1**	**0**	**100 000**	**10.00%**	**s. an.**	**auction**	**1 240 000 000**	**0**	**-**	**-**	**-**
025	**28.02.97**	**28.02.98**	**1**	**1 110 000 000**	**100 000**	**10.00%**	**s. an.**	**auction**	**1 310 000 000**	**1 110 000 000**	**12.50**	**14.66**	**15.50**
026	**27.03.97**	**27.03.98**	**1**	**2 040 000 000**	**100 000**	**10.00%**	**an.**	**auction**	**4 090 000 000**	**2 040 000 000**	**13.99**	**14.88**	**15.70**
027	**24.04.97**	**24.04.98**	**1**	**0**	**100 000**	**10.00%**	**an.**	**auction**	**2 350 000 000**	**0**	**-**	**-**	**-**
028	29.05.97	29.05.98	1	1 010 000 000	100 000	10.00%	an.	auction	1 130 000 000	1 010 000 000	15.10	15.87	16.99
030	10.07.97	10.07.98	1	2 480 000 000	100 000	11.00%	an.	auction	2 800 000 000	2 480 000 000	15.00	16.81	17.50
031	24.07.97	24.07.98	1	2 420 000 000	100 000	11.00%	an.	auction	3 010 000 000	2 420 000 000	14.97	17.80	18.21
032	30.07.97	30.07.99	2	1 000 000 000	100 000	9.00%	an.	auction	-	-	-	-	-
033	07.08.97	07.08.98	1	1 120 000 000	100 000	11.00%	an.	auction	1 550 000 000	1 120 000 000	18.45	19.39	20.00
034	21.08.97	21.08.98	1	2 380 000 000	100 000	11.00%	an.	auction	2 950 000 000	2 380 000 000	19.30	20.35	21.40
035	04.09.97	04.09.98	1	2 750 000 000	100 000	11.00%	an.	auction	2 930 000 000	2 750 000 000	21.00	22.15	24.00
036	18.09.97	18.09.98	1	3 370 000 000	100 000	11.00%	an.	auction	3 780 000 000	3 370 000 000	21.00	23.88	25.00
037	02.10.97	02.10.98	1	3 640 000 000	100 000	12.00%	an.	auction	4 340 000 000	3 640 000 000	24.40	25.93	26.94
038	09.10.97	09.10.98	1	5 575 000 000	100 000	12.00%	an.	auction	5 585 000 000	5 575 000 000	24.50	26.73	29.18
039	13.11.97	13.11.99	2	500 000 000	100 000	9.00%	an.	auction	500 000 000	500 000 000	9.00	9.00	9.00
040	**08.01.98**	**08.01.99**	**1**	**0**	**100 000**	**12.00%**	**an.**	**auction**	**1 060 000 000**	**0**	**-**	**-**	**-**
041	22.01.98	22.01.99	1	1 350 000 000	100 000	13.00%	an.	auction	3 020 000 000	1 350 000 000	19.50	21.60	22.00
042	**05.02.98**	**05.02.99**	**1**	**0**	**100 000**	**13.00%**	**an.**	**auction**	**880 000 000**	**0**	**-**	**-**	**-**
043	**12.02.98**	**12.02.99**	**1**	**0**	**100 000**	**19.00%**	**an.**	**auction**	**830 000 000**	**0**	**-**	**-**	**-**
044	**19.02.98**	**19.02.99**	**1**	**0**	**100 000**	**19.00%**	**an.**	**auction**	**830 000 000**	**0**	**-**	**-**	**-**

Number of Issue	Date of Issue	Date of Maturity	DTM in years	Amount issued	Face Value	Coupon in % p.a.	Coupon frequency	Form of sale	Demand in SKK		Accepted yields in p.a.		
									total	accepted	minimum	average	maximum
045	22.02.98	22.02.99	1	530 000 000	100 000	18.00%	an.	auction	530 000 000	530 000 000	18.50	22.46	25.00
046	05.03.98	05.03.99	1	1 150 000 000	100 000	18.00%	an.	auction	2 660 000 000	1 150 000 000	19.99	23.45	24.00
047	12.03.98	12.03.99	1	2 230 000 000	100 000	18.00%	an.	auction	3 824 000 000	2 230 000 000	21.00	23.33	23.50
048	19.03.98	19.03.99	1	2 230 000 000	1 000 000	18.00%	an.	auction	3 680 000 000	2 230 000 000	21.99	23.05	23.50
049	26.03.98	26.03.99	1	1 110 000 000	1 000 000	18.00%	an.	auction	2 120 000 000	1 110 000 000	22.40	23.39	23.50
050	02.04.98	02.04.99	1	1 070 000 000	1 000 000	19.00%	an.	auction	1 440 000 000	1 070 000 000	22.99	24.66	25.98
051	09.04.98	09.04.99	1	2 170 000 000	1 000 000	17.00%	an.	auction	2 420 000 000	2 170 000 000	23.44	25.22	26.00
052	16.04.98	16.04.99	1	1 030 000 000	1 000 000	17.00%	an.	auction	1 850 000 000	1 030 000 000	23.50	25.75	26.00
053	23.04.98	23.04.99	1	1 350 000 000	1 000 000	17.00%	an.	auction	1 350 000 000	1 350 000 000	24.99	26.50	27.95
054	30.04.98	30.04.00	2	3 460 000 000	1 000 000	17.00%	an.	auction	3 660 000 000	3 460 000 000	23.00	27.19	28.90
055	07.05.98	07.05.99	1	2 220 000 000	1 000 000	17.00%	an.	auction	3 190 000 000	2 220 000 000	25.99	28.13	29.50
056	14.05.98	14.05.99	1	2 460 000 000	1 000 000	17.00%	an.	auction	6 970 000 000	2 460 000 000	27.79	28.49	28.99

TOTAL **118 149 7000 000**

OUTSTANDING **80 640 500 000**

- redeemed issues
- issues listed on BSSE
- not successful issues

D - discount rate of NBS

Annex 3. **Survey of treasury bills issues in 1997**

Evidence number	Face value of 1 bill in SKK	Issue date	Maturity date	DTM	Demand volume	Sold volume in pieces	Min. inter. rate in % p.a.	Max. inter. rate in % p.a.	Average rate in % p.a.
73001101	1 000 000	2-Jan-97	30-Jan-97	28	753	1 000	12.30	12.80	12.549
70602102	1 000 000	9-Jan-97	6-Feb-97	28	959	959	13.00	14.00	13.643
*71601003	1 000 000	9-Jan-97	16-Jan-97	7	-	1 003	-	-	
71302104	1 000 000	16-Jan-97	13-Feb-97	28	1 251	0	-	-	-
72404305	1 000 000	23-Jan-97	24-Apr-97	91	1 903	800	13.00	14.00	13.964
70603106	1 000 000	6-Feb-97	6-Mar-97	28	127	0	-	-	-
71303107	1 000 000	13-Feb-97	13-Mar-97	28	37	37	13.65	14.00	13.957
72205308	1 000 000	20-Feb-97	22-May-97	91	293	0	-	-	-
70304109	1 000 000	6-Mar-97	3-Apr-97	28	800	0	-	-	-
71004110	1 000 000	13-Mar-97	10-Apr-97	28	1 402	718	12.90	13.70	13.277
71505211	1 000 000	20-Mar-97	15-May-97	56	325	0	-	-	-
*72704012	1 000 000	24-Mar-97	27-Mar-97	3	-	1 502	-	-	
72404113	1 000 000	3-Apr-97	24-Apr-97	21	1 280	0	-	-	-
71007314	1 000 000	10-Apr-97	10-Jul-97	91	648	448	13.45	15.80	14.844
71610615	1 000 000	17-Apr-97	16-Oct-97	182	1 356	0	-	-	-

Evidence number	Face value of 1 bill in SKK	Issue date	Maturity date	DTM	Demand volume	Sold volume in pieces	Min. inter. rate in % p.a.	Max. inter. rate in % p.a.	Average rate in % p.a.
*72404016	1 000 000	21-Apr-97	24-Apr-97	3	-	1 002	-	-	
*72804017	1 000 000	23-Apr-97	28-Apr-97	5	-	2 005	-	-	
72905118	1 000 000	2-May-97	29-May-97	27	1 325	0	-	-	-
*73004019	1 000 000	28-Apr-97	30-Apr-97	2	-	1 500	-	-	
70506120	1 000 000	9-May-97	5-Jun-97	27	3 393	2 203	12.80	14.95	14.214
71408321	1 000 000	15-May-97	14-Aug-97	91	861	0	-	-	-
72011622	1 000 000	22-May-97	20-Nov-97	182	73	73	14.25	14.25	14.250
*72805023	1 000 000	26-May-97	28-May-97	2	-	2 002	-	-	
70307124	1 000 000	5-Jun-97	3-Jul-97	28	150	0	-	-	-
*71206025	1 000 000	5-Jun-97	12-Jun-97	7	-	3 009	-	-	
71112626	1 000 000	12-Jun-97	11-Dec-97	182	250	0	-	-	-
*71906027	1 000 000	12-Jun-97	19-Jun-97	7	-	3 009	-	-	
*71906028	1 000 000	13-Jun-97	19-Jun-97	6	-	1 504	-	-	
71007129	1 000 000	19-Jun-97	10-Jul-97	21	680	300	14.50	15.50	15.000
72606030	1 000 000	19-Jun-97	26-Jun-97	7	-	4 714	-	-	
72407131	1 000 000	26-Jun-97	24-Jul-97	28	2 977	2 107	13.00	15.49	13.524
*70207032	1 000 000	25-Jun-97	2-Jul-97	7	-	3 511	-	-	
*70307033	1 000 000	26-Jun-97	3-Jul-97	7	-	3 000	-	-	
73107134	1 000 000	3-Jul-97	31-Jul-97	28	2 391	1 141	12.50	15.45	14.022
*70907035	1 000 000	2-Jul-97	9-Jul-97	7	-	3 510	-	-	
*71007036	1 000 000	3-Jul-97	10-Jul-97	7	-	2 507	-	-	
*71107037	1 000 000	4-Jul-97	11-Jul-97	7	-	2 321	-	-	
71408138	1 000 000	10-Jul-97	14-Aug-97	35	1 520	2 420	15.40	17.49	16.048

Evidence number	Face value of 1 bill in SKK	Issue date	Maturity date	DTM	Demand volume	Sold volume in pieces	Min. inter. rate in % p.a.	Max. inter. rate in % p.a.	Average rate in % p.a.
*71007039	1 000 000	9-Jul-97	10-Jul-97	1	-	1 000	-	-	
*71607040	1 000 000	9-Jul-97	16-Jul-97	7	-	2 507	-	-	
*71707041	1 000 000	10-Jul-97	17-Jul-97	7	-	1 004	-	-	
*71707042	1 000 000	11-Jul-97	17-Jul-97	6	-	2 307	-	-	
*71607043	1 000 000	14-Jul-97	16-Jul-97	2	-	1 502	-	-	
71610344	1 000 000	17-Jul-97	16-Oct-97	91	955	955	16.00	19.60	18.248
*72307045	1 000 000	16-Jul-97	23-Jul-97	7	-	5 016	-	-	
**72407046	1 000 000	16-Jul-97	24-Jul-97	8	-	1 300	-	-	
*72407047	1 000 000	17-Jul-97	24-Jul-97	7	-	3 312	-	-	
71408148	1 000 000	24-Jul-97	14-Aug-97	21	3 845	725	17.50	18.90	18.196
*73007049	1 000 000	23-Jul-97	30-Jul-97	7	-	5 018	-	-	
*73107050	1 000 000	24-Jul-97	31-Jul-97	7	-	3 312	-	-	
71106951	1 000 000	31-Jul-97	11-Jun-98	315	1 210	440	18.50	20.00	19.404
*70608052	1 000 000	30-Jul-97	6-Aug-97	7	-	5 018	-	-	
**72808153	1 000 000	31-Jul-97	28-Aug-97	28	-	1 010	-	-	
*70708054	1 000 000	31-Jul-97	7-Aug-97	7	-	3 313	-	-	
**72808155	1 000 000	31-Jul-97	28-Aug-97	28	-	1 200	-	-	
70409156	1 000 000	7-Aug-97	4-Sep-97	28	2 157	1 257	17.60	20.00	19.287
*71308057	1 000 000	6-Aug-97	13-Aug-97	7	-	4 200	-	-	
71408058	1 000 000	7-Aug-97	14-Aug-97	7	-	3 514	-	-	
71311359	1 000 000	14-Aug-97	13-Nov-97	91	1 915	1 615	18.00	22.50	19.926
*72008060	1 000 000	13-Aug-97	20-Aug-97	7	-	4 016	-	-	
*72108061	1 000 000	14-Aug-97	21-Aug-97	7	-	4 332	-	-	

Evidence number	Face value of 1 bill in SKK	Issue date	Maturity date	DTM	Demand volume	Sold volume in pieces	Min. inter. rate in % p.a.	Max. inter. rate in % p.a.	Average rate in % p.a.
71809162	1 000 000	21-Aug-97	18-Sep-97	28	4 550	3 250	17.90	21.50	20.264
*72708063	1 000 000	20-Aug-97	27-Aug-97	7	-	4 016	-	-	
*72808064	1 000 000	21-Aug-97	28-Aug-97	7	-	4 332	-	-	
71806965	1 000 000	28-Aug-97	18-Jun-98	294	2 345	1 475	20.00	23.00	21.963
*70309066	1 000 000	27-Aug-97	3-Sep-97	7	-	4 016	-	-	
**72509167	1 000 000	28-Aug-97	25-Sep-97	28	-	1 523	-	-	
*70409068	1 000 000	28-Aug-97	4-Sep-97	7	-	4 332	-	-	
70210169	1 000 000	4-Sep-97	2-Oct-97	28	5 596	5 596	19.00	26.50	22.094
*71009070	1 000 000	3-Sep-97	10-Sep-97	7	-	1 363	-	-	
*71109071	1 000 000	4-Sep-97	11-Sep-97	7	-	5 650	-	-	
70611272	1 000 000	11-Sep-97	6-Nov-97	56	3 083	1 230	21.50	25.00	22.070
*71709073	1 000 000	10-Sep-97	17-Sep-97	7	-	1 360	-	-	
*71709074	1 000 000	10-Sep-97	17-Sep-97	7	-	790	-	-	
*71809075	1 000 000	11-Sep-97	18-Sep-97	7	-	5 650	-	-	
71610176	1 000 000	18-Sep-97	16-Oct-97	28	4 826	3 976	22.49	26.00	24.629
*72409077	1 000 000	17-Sep-97	24-Sep-97	7	-	2 150	-	-	
*72509078	1 000 000	18-Sep-97	25-Sep-97	7	-	5 650	-	-	
72506979	1 000 000	25-Sep-97	25-Jun-98	273	4 040	1 800	23.50	26.00	25.030
*70110080	1 000 000	24-Sep-97	1-Oct-97	7	-	2 150	-	-	
*70210081	1 000 000	25-Sep-97	2-Oct-97	7	-	5 700	-	-	
72410182	1 000 000	26-Sep-97	24-Oct-97	28	5 808	4 683	23.00	27.00	25.890
*70210083	1 000 000	25-Sep-97	2-Oct-97	7	-	500	-	-	
70204684	1 000 000	2-Oct-97	2-Apr-98	182	1 608	0	common price auction		-

Evidence number	Face value of 1 bill in SKK	Issue date	Maturity date	DTM	Demand volume	Sold volume in pieces	Min. inter. rate in % p.a.	Max. inter. rate in % p.a.	Average rate in % p.a.
*70810085	1 000 000	1-Oct-97	8-Oct-97	7	-	2 150	-	-	
*70910086	1 000 000	2-Oct-97	9-Oct-97	7	-	6 200	-	-	
73110187	1 000 000	3-Oct-97	31-Oct-97	28	4 110	1 530	common price auction		26.001
**72312388	1 000 000	3-Oct-97	23-Dec-97	81	-	1 045	-	-	
71311189	1 000 000	9-Oct-97	13-Nov-97	35	6 206	4 386	22.70	28.49	26.402
**70910090	1 000 000	6-Oct-97	9-Oct-97	3	-	300	-	-	
**71410091	1 000 000	7-Oct-97	14-Oct-97	7	-	1 000	-	-	
*70910092	1 000 000	7-Oct-97	9-Oct-97	2	-	1 500	-	-	
*71510093	1 000 000	8-Oct-97	15-Oct-97	7	-	2 150	-	-	
*71610094	1 000 000	9-Oct-97	16-Oct-97	7	-	7 700	-	-	
70705795	1 000 000	16-Oct-97	7-May-98	203	5 290	4 790	26.50	32.00	29.879
**73010096	1 000 000	16-Oct-97	30-Oct-97	14	-	202	-	-	
*72210097	1 000 000	14-Oct-97	22-Oct-97	8	-	3 500	-	-	
*72210098	1 000 000	15-Oct-97	22-Oct-97	7	-	650	-	-	
72011199	1 000 000	17-Oct-97	20-Nov-97	34	5 056	4 056	28.49	33.00	30.617
*723100100	1 000 000	16-Oct-97	23-Oct-97	7	-	5 250	-	-	
*724100101	1 000 000	17-Oct-97	24-Oct-97	7	-	2 300	-	-	
**709079102	1 000 000	20-Oct-97	9-Jul-98	262	-	700	-	-	
**730122103	1 000 000	22-Oct-97	30-Dec-97	69	-	315	-	-	
714057104	1 000 000	24-Oct-97	14-May-98	202	5 656	5 436	25.00	31.00	26.579
*729100105	1 000 000	22-Oct-97	29-Oct-97	7	-	2 400	-	-	
*730100106	1 000 000	23-Oct-97	30-Oct-97	7	-	5 250	-	-	
*731100107	1 000 000	24-Oct-97	31-Oct-97	7	-	700	-	-	
704121108	1 000 000	30-Oct-97	4-Dec-97	35	3 025	1 000	26.00	26.00	26.000

Evidence number	Face value of 1 bill in SKK	Issue date	Maturity date	DTM	Demand volume	Sold volume in pieces	Min. inter. rate in % p.a.	Max. inter. rate in % p.a.	Average rate in % p.a.
*706110109	1 000 000	30-Oct-97	6-Nov-97	7	-	6 200	-	-	
718068110	1 000 000	6-Nov-97	18-Jun-98	224	4 622	2 830	25.00	26.00	25.964
*713110111	1 000 000	6-Nov-97	13-Nov-97	7	-	4 600	-	-	
*714110112	1 000 000	7-Nov-97	14-Nov-97	7	-	1 050	-	-	
716078113	1 000 000	13-Nov-97	16-Jul-98	245	8 409	6 656	23.88	26.00	25.470
*713110114	1 000 000	13-Nov-97	20-Nov-97	7	-	6 000	-	-	
*721110115	1 000 000	14-Nov-97	21-Nov-97	7	-	1 000	-	-	
723078116	1 000 000	20-Nov-97	23-Jul-98	245	6 909	5 949	24.50	26.00	25.556
724110117	1 000 000	17-Nov-97	24-Nov-97	7	-	1 500	-	-	
*727110118	1 000 000	20-Nov-97	27-Nov-97	7	-	6 030	-	-	
*701120119	1 000 000	24-Nov-97	1-Dec-97	7	-	1 500	-	-	
730078120	1 000 000	27-Nov-97	30-Jul-98	245	4 767	2 960	24.75	25.80	25.035
*704120121	1 000 000	27-Nov-97	4-Dec-97	7	-	3 015	-	-	
703099122	1 000 000	4-Dec-97	3-Sep-98	273	7 464	2 984	24.50	25.00	24.814
*711120123	1 000 000	4-Dec-97	11-Dec-97	7	-	3 517	-	-	
710099124	1 000 000	11-Dec-97	10-Sep-98	273	5 129	2 521	24.00	24.85	24.662
*717120125	1 000 000	10-Dec-97	17-Dec-97	7	-	2 000	-	-	
724099126	1 000 000	18-Dec-97	24-Sep-98	280	2 370	1 295	24.00	24.60	24.476
*723120127	1 000 000	17-Dec-97	23-Dec-97	6	-	3 500	-	-	
712033128	1 000 000	23-Dec-97	12-Mar-98	79	625	0	-	-	-
*731120129	1 000 000	23-Dec-97	31-Dec-97	8	-	3 100	-	-	
702043130	1 000 000	31-Dec-97	2-Apr-98	92	3 827	3 217	23.70	24.60	24.219

* direct sale to National Bank of Slovakia.

** direct sale to select participant of short-term securities market.

Annex 4. **Monthly positions in the secondary sale of government bonds on BCPB in 1996**

ISSUE No.	Form of sale	jan	feb	mar	apr	may	jun	jul	aug	sep	oct	nov	dec	Total
004	floor BCPB	0	0	0	26 972	0	0	79 966	0	0	0	0	THE ISSUE	106 938
	directly sale	0	0	0	0	0	0	0	0	0	0	0	WAS REDEEMED	0
005	floor BCPB	THE ISSUE WAS REDEEMED												0
	directly sale													0
006	floor BCPB	0	0	10 404	392 146	437 299	THE ISSUE WAS REDEEMED							839 849
	directly sale	61 900 228	0	0	0	0								61 900 228
007	floor BCPB	THE ISSUE WAS REDEEMED												
	directly sale													0
008	floor BCPB	18 659 200	0	0	52 364 180	52 725 000	0	318 425 100	0	THE ISSUE WAS REDEEMED				442 173 480
	directly sale	0	110290 000	0	52 295 850	0	0	0	591 206 345					753 792 195
009	floor BCPB	THE ISSUE WAS REDEEMED												0
	directly sale													0
010	floor BCPB	38 504 860	0	43 465 840	21 986 940	24 545 056	78 387 670	16 720 410	0	0	42 058 880	110 076 255	219 566	375 965 477
	directly sale	53 775 000	0	0	11 072 780	11 228 330	55 742 200	0	0	0	121 083 445	36 609 865	52 296 400	341 808 020
011	floor BCPB	0	0	56 958 420	11 514 810	13 443 618	0	141 999 786	130 966 440	239 406 420	105 347428	257 650 600	0	957 287 522
	directly sale	0	0	0	0	0	11 200 560	53 317 500	0	32 299 640	85 136 382	92 489 100	200 266 958	474 710 140

ISSUE No.	Form of sale	jan	feb	mar	apr	may	jun	jul	aug	sep	oct	nov	dec	Total
012	floor BCPB	0	0	0	0	0	0	0	0	0	10 555 835	0	0	10 555 835
	directly sale	0	0	0	0	0	0	0	50 875 000	10 268 333	51 732 925	0	0	112 876 258
013	floor BCPB	0	0	0	0	10 697 780	0	40 846 660	481 705 790	781 039 500	0	0	0	1 314 289 730
	directly sale	0	0	0	996 500 000	10 747 780	0	0	707 864 068	182 165 464	415 426 800	470 741 875	0	2 783 445 987
014	floor BCPB	0	0	0	0	0	0	20 151 660	0	51 045 850	0	0	0	71 197 510
	directly sale	0	20 100 000	0	0	0	0	20 320 000	0	10 160 970	0	0	0	50 580 970
015	floor BCPB	0	0	21 003 470	21 219 030	21 433 750	0	0	0	0	0	0	214 364	63 870 614
	directly sale	3 071 592	31 236 000	0	11 374 285	21 421 176	161 068 926	0	0	50 440 700	7 858 400	0	0	286 471 079
016	floor BCPB	0	0	0	0	10 963 890	0	0	0	51 775 000	0	0	109 822	62 848 712
	directly sale	497 000 000	0	0	96 306 001	0	54 688 900	0	0	0	0	0	109 822	648 104 723
017	floor BCPB	21 702 440	0	0	0	10 982 500	65 871 730	0	0	107 775 550	0	0	102 150 550	308 482 770
	directly sale	0	0	0	0	22 132 110	0	0	0	0	51 600 000	0	0	73 732 110
018	floor BCPB	51 863	0	0	0	0	0	0	0	0	0	4 967 250	50 464 250	55 483 363
	directly sale	0	0	0	10 904 445	0	0	40 236 000	0	0	0	0	101 750	51 242 195
019	floor BCPB	0	0	0	0	0	0	0	17 933 899	0	0	0	0	17 933 899
	directly sale	0	0	0	0	0	0	0	17 796 699	0	0	0	0	17 796 699
020	floor BCPB	-	-	-	0	0	20 451 000	20 526 000	0	0	0	0	0	40 977 000
	directly sale	-	-	-	0	253871 670	0	153 492495	0	197 323 340	70 223 831	59 827 002	0	734 738 338
021	floor BCPB	-	-	-	-	-	-	-	-	-	0	0	0	0
	directly sale	-	-	-	-	-	-	-	-	-	0	240 000 000	0	240 000 000
023	floor BCPB	-	-	-	-	-	-	-	-	-	-	-	-	0
	directly sale	-	-	-	-	-	-	-	-	-	-	-	-	0
	Total	694 665 183	161 626 000	121 438 134	1 285 957 439	464 629 959	447 410 986	826 115 577	1 998 348 241	1 713 700 767	961 023 926	1 272 361 947	405 933 482	10 353 211 641

Annex 5. **Monthly positions in the secondary sale of government bonds on BCPB in 1997**

ISSUE No.	Form of sale	jan	feb	mar	apr	may	jun	jul	aug	sep	oct	nov	dec	Total
010	floor BCPB	0	0	0	9 730 280	0	4 839 165	0	0	0				14 569 445
	directly sale	31 209 990	10 373 610	0	0	0	0	118 869 580	0	0				160 453 180
011	floor BCPB	0	0	0	9 757 190	91 303	8 224 999	0	0	0				18 073 492
	directly sale	52 925 833	0	675 207 105	0	377 102 150	17 359 838	0	23 666 725	0				1 146 261 651
012	floor BCPB	0	0	0	0	0	0	0	0	0				0
	directly sale	0	0	0	0	60 412 170	0	0	0	0				60 412 170
013	floor BCPB	0	0	0	0	51 753 900	0				0	0	0	51 753 900
	directly sale	50 217 443	780 475 245	1 327 664 713	350 998 000	2 919 217 023	1 524 382 979							6 952 955 403
014	floor BCPB	0	0	0	0	0	0	0						0
	directly sale	0	0	0	0	0	0							
	directly sale	0	0	0	0	0	0	0						0
015	floor BCPB	0	0	0	0	38 464 880	0	0	0	0				38 464 880
	directly sale	0	396 065 334	0	0	0	0	0	0	0				396 065 334
016	floor BCPB	0	0	0	0	0	0	0	0	0				0
	directly sale	0	0	0	0	0	0	0	0	0				0
017	floor BCPB	0	0	0	0	0	0	0	0	0				0
	directly sale	0	0	0	0	0	0	0	0	0				0

ISSUE No.	Form of sale	jan	feb	mar	apr	may	jun	jul	aug	sep	oct	nov	dec	Total
018	floor BCPB	0	0	0	0	18 725 000	0	2 862 000	0	0				21 587 000
	directly sale	0	0	0	97 325 000	243 225 000	252 363 693	0	0	145 125				593 058 818
019	floor BCPB	0	0	0	0	0	0	0	0	0				0
	directly sale	102346225	0	0	0	0	0	0	0	0				102 346 225
020	floor BCPB	0	0	0	98 510 000	49 450 000	0	0	0	0		redeemed		147 960 000
	directly sale	20 393 117	247 321 902	0	0	0	0	0	0	0				267 715 019
021	floor BCPB	0	0	0	216 728 000	50 250 000	0	0						266 978 000
	directly sale	0	606 177 000	0	446 450 500	1 657 035 165	0	206 650	20 845 000		redeemed			2 730 714 315
023	floor BCPB	0	0	0	50 275 000	0	0	0	102 925	0				50 377 925
	directly sale	10 000 000	0	0	0	0	0	0	102 050 000	0				112 050 000
025	floor BCPB	0	0	0	0	40 035 741	3 876 267	23 768 841	10 185 010	0				77 865 859
	directly sale	0	0	0	0	328 366 950	2 386 658	9 185 220	0	0				339 938 828
026	floor BCPB	0	0	0	0	0	0	0	0	0				0
	directly sale	0	0	0	0	0	0	248178 935	2 319 759	0				250 498 694
028	floor BCPB	0	0	0	0	0	0	0	0	0				0
	directly sale	0	0	0	0	0	0	283282 000	0	0				283 282 000
030	floor BCPB	0	0	0	0	0	0	0	0	0				0
	directly sale	0	0	0	0	0	0	0	0	0				0
031	floor BCPB	0	0	0	0	0	0	0	0	0				0
	directly sale	0	0	0	0	0	0	0	0	0				0
032	floor BCPB	0	0	0	0	0	0	0	0	0				0
	directly sale	0	0	0	0	0	0	0	0	0				0
033	floor BCPB	0	0	0	0	0	0	0	0	0				0
	directly sale	0	0	0	0	0	0	0	0	0				0
	Total	267 092 608	2040 413 091	2 002 871 818	1 279 773 970	5 834 129 282	1 813 433 599	686 353 226	159 169 419	145 125	0	0	0	14083 382 138

Chapter 5

BUILDING INFRASTRUCTURE FOR THE CAPITAL MARKET IN POLAND AND THE COMPETITION BETWEEN GOVERNMENT SECURITIES AND OTHER INSTRUMENTS IN THE MONEY MARKET

Submission by
The Polish Ministry of Finance

The paper consists of three parts. The first part discusses the development of the capital market infrastructure, including government securities. The second part comprises some conclusions based on the Polish experience concerning the interaction between the government instruments and other sector money market instruments. The third presents one of the greatest challenges faced by the public debt manager, *i.e.* a necessity to be competitive *vis -à-vis* other participants of the money and capital market, illustrated by the Polish money market example.

1. Creation of the institutional framework for the Polish capital market in transition

The program of transformation from a centrally planned to a market economy was launched at the end of 1989. During the first two years substantial systemic reforms were introduced, including price and trade liberalisation and facilitating private business. After the economic disruption observed in the late eighties, Poland became the first country among those undergoing transformation to achieve significant economic growth: in 1992 the Gross Domestic Product (GDP) increased by 2.6 per cent, in 1993 -- by 3.8 per cent, in 1994 -- by 5.2 per cent, in 1995 -- by 7.0 per cent, in 1996 -- by 6.1 per cent, while the increase in 1997 is expected to reach 5.7 per cent and in 1998 -- 5.6 per cent (according to the projections for the 1998 budget). Inflation has been showing a permanent tendency to decline, having dropped slightly below

20 per cent year on year (yoy) in 1996 and being likely to go down to 14.8 per cent in 1997 and 11 per cent in 1998 (according to the projections for the 1998 budget).

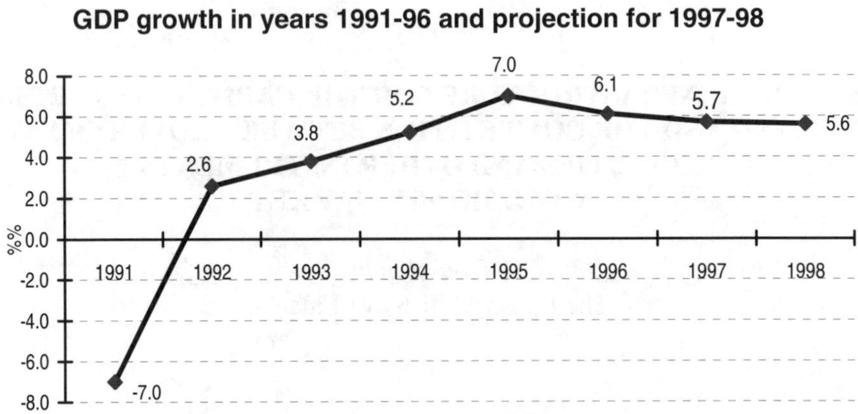

As one of the fundamentals for structural changes, the transformation programme provided for the establishment of the capital market, including the treasury securities market. The main steps in building the institutional and legal framework for the Polish capital market can be described as follows:

a) the legal basis was constituted by "The Law on the Public Trading of Securities and Mutual Funds, ratified on 22 March 1991 and currently replaced with "**The Law on Public Trading of Securities**". The first act was elaborated primarily by the Ministry of Privatisation in close co-operation with experts from the Ministry of Finance. At this stage of transformation, the capital market in Poland was in a process of creation -- the main institutions were established later. The second act was mainly prepared by the Securities Commission in co-operation with the major participants of the capital market and the Ministry of Finance. So, the Ministry of Finance and the Public Debt Department in particular played an important role in creating the legal grounds for the development of the capital market in Poland,

b) the main regulatory institution of the capital market, **The Securities Commission** (SC), was established in 1991. The SC is responsible for supervising the observance of the rules for honest trading and competition in the public trading of securities and the Minister of Finance delegates his representative to the Securities Commission,

c) the **Warsaw Stock Exchange** (WSE) was established in 1991. It is a joint stock company with more than 50 shareholders, including the largest banks and stock brokerage houses, the State Treasury being the primary shareholder and representatives of the Ministry of Finance having a significant influence on the WSE strategy, including the WSE regulations, trading techniques, the settlement system etc.,

d) the **National Depository for Securities** (NDS) was separated from the structures of the Warsaw Stock Exchange in November 1994 and became an independent depository institution, responsible for clearing transactions on the Polish capital market. NDS performs all depository and clearing functions for publicly traded securities, including Treasury Bonds issued on the domestic market.

2. Role of the public debt manager (Ministry of Finance) in the development of infrastructure and standards for the wider capital market

The Polish experience can be summarised as follows.

At the initial stage of capital market formation, the authorities responsible for government debt management, capital market development and supervision played an important role in building the legal and institutional framework for the capital market. The main institutions of Polish capital market (including: *a)* regulatory body -- the Security Commission, *b)* the main place of trade -- the Warsaw Stock Exchange, *c)* depository-clearing institution -- the National Depository for Securities) were established for the most part by the Minister of Privatisation and the Ministry of Finance. To conclude, the role of the Minister of Finance (public debt manager), at this stage, was to co-operate with other capital market participants in designing the main regulations for the capital market and in creating proper organisational infrastructure (including international standards -- the Polish National Depository for Securities follows the pattern of the French Central Depository (SICOVAM), the Warsaw Stock Exchange -- of the Company of French Stock Exchanges (*Société de Bourses Françaises*), while the Securities Commission has the responsibility and law empowerment similar to those applied in USA).

The next stage of the capital market evolution can be characterised by the increasing scale of competition on the capital market. Government securities face increasing competition from NBP Bills, corporate debt instruments (mostly commercial papers), municipal bonds (non-public and public issues), and joint-stock companies' share placements. This phenomenon is accompanied by a low supply of domestic resources to the financial market as a result of a low level of national savings and underdeveloped sector of institutional investors (including investment funds, insurance companies). All the above results in significant difficulties with the financing of the government borrowing requirements. Moreover, these needs are significant because of high social security budgetary expenditures during the transformation, implementation of the pension system reform, foreign debt redemption and the so called secondary crisis of public finances following fiscal consolidation and observed in some Economies in Transition. All this creates quite a new challenge to public debt management. The competition facing government bonds does not come from similar debt products of other sectors, but arises from the dynamic stock market and the banking deposits offered to general public. Until now, the State bonds are the only debt instruments listed on the Warsaw Stock Exchange, municipal bonds, appearing in small amounts are non-public issues and they are not marketable. The only exception is the Ostrów Wielkopolski bonds, with the redemption date 31 Dec. 1999, coupon based on 52-week T-Bills, which are traded on the regulated, non-stock exchange market -- CETO S.A. market -- "Polish NASDAQ". As compared with the medium and long-term debt instrument market, the competition on the money market is increasing rapidly (see Part 3). The Treasury instruments -- T-bills are competitive to the National Bank of Poland money bills (instruments used by the NBP as intervention tools on the monetary market). Moreover, a dynamic growth of commercial papers placement will provide a great challenge for T-Bills too.

The government securities market is also vital for the general market because:

a) government securities serve as a pattern for other issuers (as regards construction of financial instruments, interest rates etc.);

b) government securities in economies in transition are usually the only securities covering the whole time horizon and showing sufficient liquidity to be used for the construction of the reference interest yield curve. Treasury bonds are the only debt instruments traded on the Warsaw Stock Exchange and the fixed-rate T-Bonds

(2- and 5-year bonds) are the only longer-term, fixed-rate debt instruments on the Polish market.

The role of government securities market for the benefit of wider market may not be discussed disregarding the facilities accessible to the government debt manager and not to the wide market. The National Bank of Poland, fulfils the function of an issue agent for the government securities and of a depository-clearing institution for the T-bill market (The Central Register of Treasury Bills). It organises and conducts auctions and facilitates the secondary market of T-bills ensuring high liquidity. This function can exclusively be performed in relation to government securities and is inaccessible to the general securities market. This is so because of a limited direct access of non-bank institutions to the NBP settlements system. Thus, for other market segments, it is not possible to follow T-Bill settlement standards before an efficient real time settlements system has been set up to serve the capital market or over-the-counter market.

Another tool, which could be used to promote government securities sales (mainly to individuals), not generally accessible consists of applying tax relief. In Poland, income of individuals from interest on capital is not subject to taxation. Tax incentives used to be applied in Poland between 1993 and 1996, to promote Treasury Securities among individual investors. They were constructed in the following way: amounts invested in government securities (one-year and three-year bonds), up to a set limit were not subject to personal income tax. Thus such tax incentives simply increased the coupon offered to investors.

The main challenge for the government debt manager to be faced in the nearest future is to improve the settlement and trading system on the secondary market for the State Treasury bonds. The secondary market for government bond in Poland uses the Warsaw Stock Exchange system of settlements. So the secondary market of T-Bonds is much less liquid in comparison with that of T-Bills for the following two reasons:

a) a considerable time lag between the payments and delivery, caused by present settlement system applied by WSE,

b) high commission charged by the WSE (2.5 bp) and NDS (1 bp).

In the opinion shared by nearly all the market participants, there is no doubt that this system should be improved significantly. The question is whether government bond trading among big investors should be carried out in the general system or whether it would be necessary to construct a separate system, similar to that used for T-Bills. In the latter case, standards accessible to the government bond trading (in the sense of settlement and cost of transactions) would not be attainable for the wide market.

3. Development of the money market in Poland during the last three years

The establishment of nine commercial banks in 1989 (from the structure of National Bank of Poland) can be treated as a starting point for the Polish money market. The need to develop a liquidity management instrument brought about the creation of the interbank deposit market based on the presently existing two Gross Payments Settlement Systems (SYBIR -- paper-based and ELIXIR -- fully electronic). The NBP bills constitute another money market instrument. They were launched in July 1990 but between May 1991 (first Treasury Bills issue) and November 1994 the issuance was stopped because Treasury Bills were then used as a NBP intervention instrument. Afterwards NBP Bills started to be the main instrument of NBP intervention on the money market, the reason being that the NBP had sold almost all T-Bills from its portfolio. Subsequently, the role of NBP Bills on the Polish money market has become significant (see Table 1) and the T-Bills issued by the Minister of Finance have to be confronted with highly competitive instruments.

Table 1. **Outstanding value of money market instruments**
(nominal value, billion z³)

	XII'9 4	share %	XII'9 5	share %	XII'9 6	share %	V'97	share %
Interbank deposits	2.6	7.7	4.6	10.5	6.3	12.2	8.0	13.2
Reverse REPO operations	1.9	3.0	3.7	8.4	2.1	4.1	0.9	1.5
Treasury Bills	27.3	81.3	28.9	65.8	29.4	57.0	31.4	51.6
NBP Bills	2.0	6.0	5.8	13.2	12.5	24.2	18.1	29.8
Commercial Papers	0.7	2.0	0.9	2.1	1.3	2.5	2.4	3.9
Total	33.6	100.0	43.9	100.0	51.6	100.0	60.8	100.0

The first issue of commercial papers in Poland took place in June 1992 and the issue agent was the Polski Bank Rozwoju S.A. In Poland as well as in other countries commercial papers are issued by companies in a relatively good financial position and the main task of such issues is to gain financial resources at a cost lower than that of a bank credit. Typically, they are issued within the framework of long-term financing plans and their attractiveness is based on the interest rate level which should be lower than that of bank credit and higher than that of bank deposits. Other advantages for the issuer, investors and the bank -- the placement agent can be summarised as follows:

Graph 1. **Comparison of NBP Bill and T-Bill yield, 1995 - 1997**

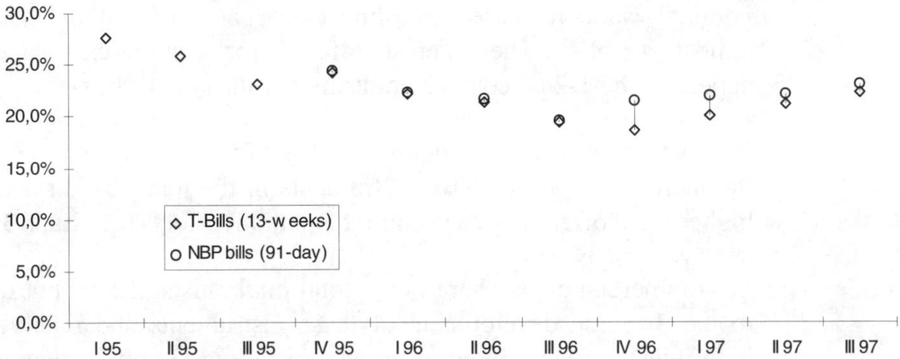

Graph 2. **Comparison between the mean market interest rates in 1997** (3-month, average)

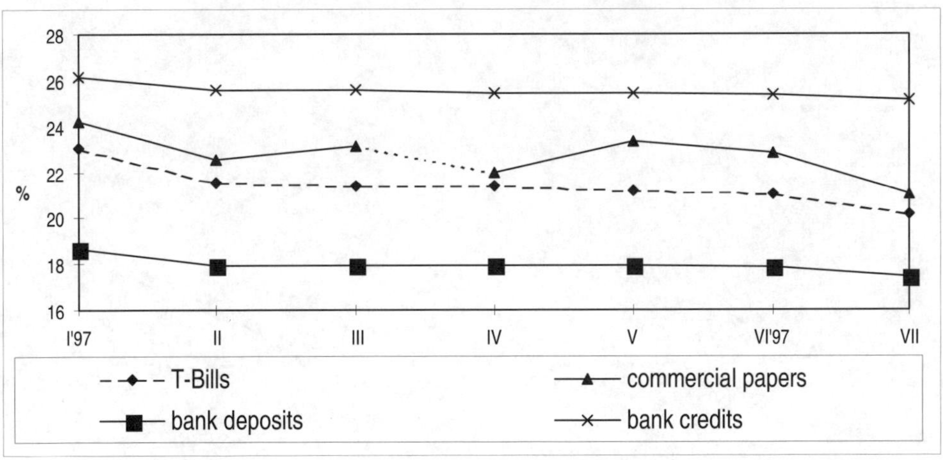

To conclude:

a) since the end of 1994, the share of T-Bills in the total outstanding value of money market instruments has dropped sharply from 81.3 per cent to 51.6 per cent,

b) in the reporting period the share of NBP bills and interbank deposits increased significantly, the share of NBP bills reached almost 30 per cent of the total market (the outstanding NBP bills increased 8 times according to the nominal value),

c) commercial papers showed a dynamic increase, the outstanding nominal value increased by almost 250 per cent and the share almost doubled. The interest offered for commercial papers appears to be 1-2 percentage points higher than on T-Bills,

d) T-Bills faced a strong competition of NBP Bills which is proved by the increased share of NBP instruments in the total market and a higher yield offered by the central bank to investors (see Graph 1),

e) the commercial paper share in the total market is still low, but due to the dynamic development of these instruments and relatively high interest rates offered to the investors (see Graph 2), they are likely to create one of the most dynamic subsectors of the money market in Poland.

Section II

TRANSPARENCY AND STANDARDS OF DISCLOSURE

Chapter 6

THE THREAT POSED TO TRANSPARENCY AND ACCOUNTABILITY OF EQUITY MARKETS

Submission by
The Czech Ministry of Finance

In 1990, 97 per cent of the GDP in the Czech Republic was created by state enterprises; in the middle of 1996, 90 per cent of the GDP was created by the private sector. About 48 per cent of the total volume of property were privatised through the voucher privatisation method, with participation by almost all the adult population of the country. Issues connected with voucher privatisation have thus become a subject of interest for a wide range of citizens, have been reflected in the attitudes and programmes of political parties and are a very frequent topic for discussion in the mass media. One of the main reasons why the capital market has become a target for criticism from the general public can be considered to be the large number of cases where individuals or groups of individuals have prospered and obtained considerable financial gains at the expense of ordinary citizens. A great number of dubious operations are taking place on the capital market, which leads to suspicious reactions on the part of the general public and also of domestic and foreign investors.

A similarly serious problem is the fact that it has not yet been possible to create ownership structures that would be an incentive for growth in labour productivity and for an increase in the overall economic prosperity of the country. Analyses concerned with the evaluation of enterprises show that companies where investment funds own a large portion of the shares usually have less favourable economic results than companies in which these funds own smaller portions of shares. However, this conclusion is often not valid for bank investment funds.

It is thus necessary to state that, as far as forming a capital market and changing the behaviour of economic entities are concerned, privatisation has fulfilled its purpose only to the extent of creating prerequisites for further changes. In fact, it could not have had other objectives. Thus, it should be our goal to define the individual steps in the process that would follow on from this initial conversion.

The influx of foreign and especially portfolio investments reacted to a considerable degree to the individual waves of voucher privatisation. Its trends are apparent from the following table.

Table 1. **Annual increments in foreign investments in CZK billions:**

Year	Direct	Portfolio	Total
1993	16.6	46.7	63.3
1994	24.8	24.6	49.4
1995	67.0	36.1	103.1
1996	37.7	19.7	57.4
I.Q. 1997	7.9	-9.5	-1.6

Source: Czech National Bank.

On the other hand, it can be argued that foreign investors are prepared to return to our capital market immediately as soon as they can see changes that have taken place to make it more attractive. However, the solutions to these problems will not be easy. The market would be made more attractive by a better dividend policy based on growth in the profits of joint stock companies. However, any profit growth for most joint stock companies in this country is dependent on the entry of a foreign investor, who would provide the means for modernising company technology. There is no way in which conditions can be changed rapidly, through some magnanimous measure or decision. We can rather expect quite a long-term process of partial and gradual changes in which it is necessary to utilise each opportunity that will have an impact on the capital market and on the economy, however small.

In order to gain a deeper understanding of the difficulties encountered in the regulation of institutional investors and thus in the search for remedies, it will be useful to describe a number of ways of "handling" the property of investment funds and unit trusts that constitute failure to comply with Law No. 248/1992 Sb., and the consequences of which lead to a decrease in property value and detriment to both shareholders and unit holders. The practices encountered include the following:

- *the interconnection of several companies*, especially investment companies, investment funds and securities dealers, pension funds, banks and other companies. These interconnections are informal, hard to identify, and utilise puppets.

- *large conventional fines* - conventional fines are agreed on in agreements on securities transfer, the amount often being a multiple of the value of the agreed deal; in case of failure to comply with the conditions of the agreement, one contracting party, as set forth in the agreement, is obliged to pay this considerable sum. Simultaneously, failure to comply with conditions is ensured by the above interconnection of persons in the contracting parties.

- *purchases of worthless shares* - persons controlling investment companies or investment funds found a normal joint-stock company, whose shares are based on worthless property (*e.g.* receivables, know-how) and then these shares are purchased into the property of the investment fund or unit trust.

- *concluding unfavourable options and futures contracts* - such agreements do not cover the risks associated with unfavourable developments in the prices of securities held by the investment fund or unit trust, but rather make these funds hold the shares irrespective of developments in their prices, in order to be able to supply the agreed securities at the time set in the agreement. The customer for these securities has a contract that includes the right of choice of whether to purchase these securities or not.

- *transfer of advances for the purchase of securities* - the investment company or investment fund transfers a considerable amount of money from the assets of the investment fund or unit trust to the account of a securities dealer; this cash is not subject to payment of interest by the dealer and thus does not yield any income for the fund holders; the dealer makes use of this money for dealing in his own name and the money is transferred without any guarantees or at least control; for example, to a securities dealer with negligible assets, a securities dealer who is a natural person, to unreliable dealers.

- *long settlement periods for securities sold* - an investment company sells securities from the assets of a unit trust or investment fund and sets a long settlement period. Cases are known where the settlement period is several years, or where settlement is made in instalments spread over a period of up to 30 years. In the meantime the company owing the money declares bankruptcy and is liquidated.

- *loans of securities* - Law No. 248/92 Sb. permits the loan of securities to other persons for a maximum period of 30 days under conditions of perfect security. In practice, neither condition is met and the securities are loaned from the assets of an investment fund or a unit trust without any guarantees and even without any payment for the loan.

- *poorly drawn-up agreements on the transfer of securities* - the agreements do not cover basic obligations, such as the date of supply of the security, date of settlement of advances for the purchase of the securities, poor designation of the contracting parties (*e.g.* an investment company acts in the name of and at the expense of a unit trust, which is not a legal entity, and which it manages, pursuant to Law No. 248/1992 Sb.; it follows from the wording of the agreement that the investment company acts in its own name and on its own account).

- *irrational movements of securities* - there are entire chains of trades in a single type of security; over a few days or weeks or even months, the respective security is owned by a whole series of companies and then returns to the fund at an entirely different price than that when it left. These practices have a great many modifications and are very difficult to uncover. In the light of the known deformations of prices on the stock exchange where negligible quantities of securities are traded so that it is very easy to manipulate their prices, the stock exchange price has no indicative value. It is difficult to demonstrate dishonest intentions and damage to shareholders or fund participants, especially when a considerable period of time has passed between the sale and purchase of the security owned by the fund. The interconnection amongst individual companies again plays a considerable role in these operations.

- *trading in securities at ridiculous prices* - such operations can be carried out especially because there is no objectively determinable price for most securities as the price-creating function of the public market fails to operate. Pursuant to section 5e of Law No. 248/1992 Sb., investment funds and unit trusts may accept loans or credit that are not secured by so-called "repo operations", *i.e.* transfer of securities as security for the loan. The fund may accept a monetary loan, *e.g.* from a bank and the bank secures repayment of the loan by the fund transferring ownership of securities from its assets to the bank. These securities remain in the banks for the entire period of loan repayment. However, Law No. 248/1992 Sb. prohibits funds from loaning money from their assets to other (*i.e.* third) parties. Funds evade this restriction by concluding an agreement on the sale of securities from their assets to some other legal entity, usually an associated one, at a very low price. A verbal agreement is then made that this associated person will sell the securities back to the fund after a certain period of time, again at a very low price. The low price is agreed so that the associated companies need not pay large sums, which they do not usually have.

  The person who purchased the securities from the fund can use them for a certain period of time, trade them, realise profit from such trading or brokerage fees and, after a certain period of time, returns the securities back to the fund. These operations are based on friendly agreements only, the partner need not comply with the verbal agreement, may run disproportionate risks, may be the object of speculation from hostile groups and the entire agreed operation need not be completed; *i.e.* the fund need not regain ownership of the securities. Written agreements do not cover these risks. The Ministry of Finance considers such trading as failure to exercise due care and failure to comply with section 5 or section 14 of Law No. 248/1992 Sb.

- *disadvantageous purchases and sales of securities* - this is only a slight modification of the above practices, *e.g.* underwriting of new issues for large sums while these shares can be purchased on the market at much lower prices. These operations once again occur between associated companies. A joint-stock company issues a certain volume of its shares and these shares are traded on the public market. This company then decides to increase its registered capital and makes a new issue. An investment fund or a unit trust, as an existing shareholder, subscribes to a part of this new issue and pays for these shares a sum decided by the general meeting. Simultaneously, shares from a previous issue with identical properties as the newly issued shares can be purchased on the public market for a much lower sum.

– *trading by management on its own account* - these practices tend to belong in the category of failure to comply with ethical standards and are also associated with the misuse of confidential information, obtained on Boards or Directors of joint-stock companies, whose shares are part of the assets of the fund; this information is supplied to the management, employees, or relatives, or the shares are sold to such persons at low prices.

Investment funds or unit trusts may own up to 20 per cent of the shares of joint stock companies. On the basis of a relatively large ownership share, the representatives of the fund or investment company demand a seat on the Board of Directors of such a joint-stock company and at Board meetings or in some other way they learn confidential information on future contracts or agreements that are being prepared that will affect the prosperity of the company and thus the price of its shares on the market. Timely purchases of these shares at a lower price on the basis of inside information ensure that persons who obtained this information then can sell the shares at a much higher price when it increases.

– *concentration of considerable amounts of cash in the accounts* of investment funds or unit trusts in banks. This method formed the basis for subsequent "tunneling" into unit trusts managed by the CS Fund, an investment company. The method was based on the fact that the investment company gradually sold securities from the assets of the unit trust and when the entire assets were transferred in the form of deposits to a bank, the deposits were withdrawn and transferred to an account abroad. The concentration of fund property in monetary form is very difficult to control, because monetary form of property is quite legal pursuant to Law No. 248/1992 Sb.

The retention of a large share of the assets of a fund in the form of deposits with a bank can have other reasons. Especially small banks, which are informally connected with the management of an investment company or an investment fund, can solve the problem of insufficient liquidity by retaining part of fund assets in an account with such a bank. In this way, the bank hides its own difficulties from bank supervision and postpones its decline: when the bank does finally fail, the assets of the fund are also affected by the measures of the Czech National Bank.

– *failure to comply with limits for restricting and spreading risks* -- section 24 of Law No. 248/1992 Sb. sets forth limits for holding securities in relation to the total volume of assets owned by an investment fund or unit trust or to the total volume of issued securities owned by an investment fund or a unit trust. Cases have been registered in which investment funds purchased the shares of banks and thus exceeded the limits for restricting and spreading risks pursuant to section 24 of Law No. 248/1992 Sb. These investment funds thus failed to comply with Law No. 248/1992 Sb. in these purchases. Simultaneously, the banks whose shares were owned by the funds encountered difficulties, were subjected to compulsory administration or entered liquidation, their shares fell to zero value and the investment funds often suffered considerable losses. Funds often behave like securities dealers and purchase control shares in joint-stock companies that often exceed the permitted limit of 20 per cent, and then sell them at a premium to other entities.

– *"tunneling" into companies is a frequent phenomenon.* Current "corporate raiders" have discovered a risk-free method of removing money from companies. This method consists of holding a general meeting of shareholders, in which the "raiders" have a voting majority; this meeting passes a decision on a transaction involving company property (*e.g.* the purchase or sale of other shares) and the Board of Directors of the company then carries out this operation, with consequent damage to the company. No (minority) shareholder can blame the Board of Directors of the company for this operation as it is bound by the decision of the general meeting where the decision was made by the "raider".

These ways of "handling" the assets of investment funds and unit trusts are combined in practice and are very difficult to demonstrate and penalise.

To a certain extent, this is also a documentation of very unfavourable effects of privatisation. It has provided considerable room for persons whose primary goal is their own gain at any cost. We have paid dear for the fact that those who organised the privatisation process were always "a few steps ahead of the lawyers", that warnings by foreign experts of the risks that redistribution of property always involves were ignored. Now we all remain behind an aggressive class of new owners who do not respect the rules that are common elsewhere in the world.

Investment funds have fulfilled their role in the voucher privatisation process. Their continued existence after the completion of privatisation has a considerable detrimental impact on the Czech capital market. Compared to closed-end unit trusts, investment funds have the advantage that investors have the right to vote at general meetings. This advantage tends to be formal only. Most fund managers have gained a predominant portion of shares in "their" investment funds, either directly or through associated entities, and thus have no reason to fear transfer of ownership of the funds or any other active counter-measures in a general meeting. Conditions are thus similar to those in closed-end unit trusts. The only advantage is perhaps the fact that the fund manager owns a certain portion of the fund managed and could thus have at least some interest in good management. However, this motivation is not effective in most cases and can, in fact, have the opposite consequences, as the fund manager was often forced to purchase his portion in the fund at a very unfavourable price at a time when he was attacked by a group that wished to take over the fund. Such a fund manager is thus interested in regaining these losses by other methods than through good management of shareholders´ equity.

Joint/stock companies in which investment funds have significant ownership shares generally show less favourable economic results than companies without such strong contact with investment funds. The only exceptions are companies owned by bank investment funds. However, this could rather be used to demonstrate the close interconnection between banks, investment companies and investment funds. Moreover, this statement provides no information on the general effectiveness of such a connection.

However, one of the serious consequences of the continued presence of investment funds on the Czech capital market is the fact that they slow down the process of searching for a final owner and the influx of funds for restructuring programmes, and thus also for renewed growth in labour productivity and economic growth in the country. Investment funds have a tendency to behave like securities dealers and these two groups often retain control over companies, in many cases through shareholding contracts. They speculate at reaching maximum prices, which foreign investors cannot accept, on the basis of a simple economic calculation. Following trading of this kind, after a majority is obtained, the remaining shares lose their value; this fact is a reason for the great instability and sudden fluctuations in the prices of shares on the Czech capital market.

We are faced with the task of defining a strategy on how to transform these investment funds, which have already fulfilled their role, as rapidly as possible into a form which is suitable and favourable for the post-privatisation period. Three method of remedying the situation are recommended in discussions -- conversion into open-ended unit trusts, conversion into "holding" companies and liquidation, *e.g.* through withdrawal of licences. This would in no way prevent prospering investment funds from continuing to exist.

Open-ended unit trusts in this country will continue to function under different conditions than classical "mutual funds". There is a lack of suitable, liquid securities, fund managers cannot adopt a pure portfolio strategy, and thus they should be allowed to protect their investors by owning large shares in the assets of joint-stock companies where they can force management to improve the quality of its work or change such management. However, it is not recommended to keep the limit of a 20 per cent ownership of shares in a single company; this share should be decreased to 10 per cent as soon as possible and then to 5 per cent in the next stage. It is also recommended that the current limits of charges for fund management be abolished. Regulations may remain valid for current investment funds. However, it is necessary to ensure that the structure of charges be made public before an investor decides to invest his funds. Competition in the levels of such charges would seem to be the best means of regulation.

The most frequent topic of discussion in relation to the Czech capital market is its (lack of) transparency. This concept is used very frequently in spite of the fact that its semantics is rather dubious. Where arguments for understanding and justifying a number of phenomena occurring in the capital market in this country, often caused by facts that that are in no way connected with the actual capital market, are insufficient, many individuals employ the expression "lack of transparency" as a justification for anything at all. Thus, an attempt will be made to separate this (lack of) transparency into three separate areas:

- trading prices
- information on issuers and
- information on ownership structures.

Discussions on the subject of increasing price transparency lead to the statement that an effective solution depends on two decisions. The first consists of regulation of state intervention, and its content would consist of limiting trading over the counter of the Securities Centre for all entities to which government or non-government institutions issue licences for providing financial services. This approach would require an amendment to the Law on Securities. The second decision would consist of the acceptance of measures by the market makers and the Securities Centre, which would lead to a decrease in the share of direct trading.

The Securities Office will have to prepare for changes in the behaviour of securities dealers who will attempt to avoid the impact of these measures.

In the interests of objectivity of this analysis, it should be stated that some opinions place requirements on price transparency in a somewhat different position.

The transparency of a market is defined in terms of the extent of information published and available on trading carried out in real time. It is necessary to realise that transparency is a concept that has appeared only recently, as it is only recent developments in technology that have permitted an increase in transparency. Although we have a tendency to understand transparency as a favourable and beneficial phenomenon, it must be realised that transparency as such has no sensible explanation of benefit. Greater market transparency is beneficial only if it improves the functioning of the market. Unfortunately, there is no indication that could make us believe in such a turn-about. In some cases, the transparency of information can be an impediment to the implementation. The statement that greater transparency can create better conditions for trading outside the central market is interesting.

As there is a considerable variety of positive and negative effects, some foreign experts recommend that it should be left to the market to find the best degree of transparency given by the conditions. Regulation and enforcement can bring greater detriment than benefits. Numerous attempts to increase transparency are motivated by efforts to copy as far as possible the practices in markets in developed economies. It can be demonstrated easily that such imitation is not suitable. Measures that can be implemented to regulate the environment in New York need not be effective in Prague. In addition, these experts point out that some practices do not even make sense in their own domestic environment.

A certain role is played in this respect by the fact that privatisation has not yet been completed. It can be pointed out that the shares in joint stock companies that the National Property Fund is gradually selling in block trades through the RM-System (or on the Stock Exchange) are greatly under-priced; the prices should also contain premiums, as these consist of significant portions. It can be observed that sales often occur when prices in the AOS BCPP (Prague Stock Exchange) drop to a minimum.

As for information on issuers, a specific characteristic in this country is the fact that only a small part of issuers provide information that is comparable with international standards. Most issuers do not publish documents on which transparency is based, but they provide reliable information on themselves in that they do not wish transparency or participation in the capital market. This would not be detrimental if they were not forced to enter that capital market and if it were easy to exit from it.

The voucher privatisation "produced" about 2 200 shares: out of these, two hundred can be considered to be "stabilised" shares and the remainder as lottery tickets. Failure to deal with this problem constitutes a serious danger for the Czech capital market. The market is losing its good reputation and, more seriously, such a volume of poor-quality share issues cannot be controlled even using known regulation methods.

The following mesures are recommended to deal with this situation:

- companies whose shares are not publicly traded should leave the market,
- regulations should be made stricter for the companies remaining on the market.

It is considered unrealistic to introduce regulation standards employed, *e.g.*, in the USA. One of the ways of protecting minorities could the requirement of a "super-majority" in making decisions on matters that could have very unfavourable consequences for such minorities, such as restructuring of the company and transactions between companies and associated companies. The management of companies should have a legal imposed liability for damage caused by neglecting their obligations and providing untrue information should be considered a criminal act.

In the transition period it is recommended that conditions be created, *e.g.* in relation to requirements connected with public tradability, so that the company itself would feel the positive consequences of its shares no longer being publicly tradable. Publicly tradable issues should only be those that comply with the condition of a minimum volume provided to the public markets. The actual transition process should be as simple as possible. A sensible approach would be the creation of a temporary "fast path" procedure permitted only to companies created in voucher privatisation and making it possible for them to privatise themselves. As the obligation of the company to offer to repurchase shares in case of a decision to abolish public tradability of shares would act counter-productively to the goal defined above, it is considered sensible to temporarily entrust some institutions (*e.g.* the Securities Commission) with deciding, *e.g.*, on the amount of compensation to be obtained by minority shareholders. A decision on compensation could be based on general guidelines and should contain information on the amount of compensation, payments should be spread over a period of time, etc.

The lack of transparency in ownership relations seems to be one of the most serious problems in the Czech capital market. For example, there is no obligation to even inform supervisory institutions of a change in the ownership of an investment company, which may often manage assets in the value of many thousands of millions of CZK in funds. A change in ownership, the election of new bodies acting entirely for the benefit of the new owner can occur within a single day and the property can be embezzled from such a fund within a single day, too. The only solution to this problem seems to be for the Law to state that such a change must be approved beforehand by the supervisory body. The current inadequate legislation leads to a high probability that tunneling of funds will rapidly be followed by intense tunneling of joint stock companies.

One of the ways of preventing these practices could be an improvement of the position of minorities, which could be achieved by utilising the concept of cumulative voting. For example, if a majority shareholder owns 80 per cent of shares and minority owners own only 20 per cent, and each share-holder votes for each member of the body separately, the minority shareholders have no way of supporting their candidate effectively. In case of cumulative voting, the majority shareholder has 80 per cent and the minority shareholder has 20 per cent of votes for all the members of the Board of Directors. Each may choose the number of votes to be awarded to each candidate; in this way it is possible to ensure that the bodies of the company contain at least proportional representation of investors in relation to the number of shares owned. If the obligation to employ cumulative voting in the election of the members of company bodies were incorporated in the Law (Commercial Code), minority shareholders would also be able to elect their representatives on the bodies of the company and would thus be able to obtain otherwise inaccessible information on happenings in the company. It is also useful to recall here the concept of a legally imposed super-majority requirement in voting on issues that are vital for the company.

Chapter 7

TRANSPARENCY AND ACCOUNTABILITY OF EQUITY MARKETS IN HUNGARY

by
Lászlo Vörös
Director General, Hungarian Banking and Capital Market Supervision

1. Building the legal framework for securities in Hungary

The year 1997 has brought major changes in the regulation of the Hungarian money and capital market. On the basis of the assumption that in market economies enterprises have two financing patterns complementing each other, the rules which were adopted in a different economic environment during the former years have been revised this year under the same economic conditions, in harmony with each other and at the same time. Thus the rules governing the securities market changed significantly on 1st January 1997 and this transformation has still not been completed.

During the formulation of the rules it was taken into account that (in my opinion) usually credit institutions have the function of financing enterprises on a short-term basis, and long-term financing takes place primarily from the securities market. Both types of financing is based on, and requires a prime condition of, a fully transparent business seeking financing. This should provide security for the investors and depositors ensuring that the funds lent by them will be recovered.

It is a basic difference that, in the case of bank financing, the full transparency of a company must be demonstrated to the bank, although financing takes place using the borrowed funds of depositors, and in the case of capital market financing the business must be transparent for investors and potential investors. In theory the specialised experts of a bank receive the same information as the private individuals, intermediaries and analysts of the market acting as participants in the capital market. While bankers are able to assess the risks of an investment (financing) from the information received, in the case of techniques applied at the developed securities markets the non "expert" investors cannot understand the received information. Therefore there was a need to create and regulate by law some institutions which had not existed in the Hungarian market or had been less regulated before. At the same time, when regulations were drafted, attention had also to be paid to the fact that, due to their large number, private investors assessed their capital market investments based on different aspects and thus a wider range of disclosure requirements had to be specified. In my opinion, this involves a significantly larger control over the issuer than that available to banking experts.

Modification in legislation was also necessary because the Securities Act of 1990, which had been established before the political conditions for the transformation into a full market economy were created, could only assume a few private enterprises participating in the market. Although when the Securities Act was adopted, the Company Act had been in force for two years allowing for the establishment of joint stock companies. However they were primarily state-owned companies and no real securities trade could be expected in relation to them and the market transparency closely related to that was not such an important issue at that time either, as it is these days.

Following the political change in 1990, privatisation of state-owned assets became the primary political and economic goal. In 1990 state-owned assets represented 95 per cent of the total assets of the country. In 1997 this ratio was only 25 per cent. We are close to the very end of the privatisation process because we plan to retain approximately 15-18 per cent of the remaining approximately 25 per cent to be owned by the State on a long-term basis.

The existing securities market has played a very important role in the privatisation process. The public issue of shares of the most important Hungarian companies took place on the basis of the provisions of the Securities Act of 1990. In many cases these Hungarian companies were sold with the involvement of foreign securities markets.

As the political and economic situation of 1990 changed fundamentally, the Securities Act also had to be amended. Naturally, modifications were also required in relation to the fact that Hungary achieved significant results in its efforts related to the Euro Atlantic accession. The signature of the Association Agreement, as the first step in the EU accession, and full OECD membership all called for harmonisation between the Hungarian regulations to be drafted and the regulations in the member countries of these organisations.

In the economic legislation package adopted at the same time at the end of last year the following Acts affected the securities market activities:

- The new Securities Act entered into force on 1st January (Act No. CXI. of 1996 on the offering of securities, investment services and the stock exchange. Compared to the previous Act in 1990, this Act defines more detailed and accurate rules for the issue of securities, operation of capital market institutions and also provides stronger rights to the Supervision in many aspects. Further references will be made to the main features of the latter one.
- A new Act was also adopted to regulate the activities of financial institutions (Act No. CXII. of 1996 on the Credit Institutions and the Financial Undertakings), replacing the Act on Financial Institutions which was passed by Parliament in 1991 and has been modified several times since then.
- Significant changes took place also in the institutional system of Government regulations concerning the money and capital market. In order to ensure uniform regulations for the capital and money market, the Hungarian Banking and Capital Market Supervision was established, which is the general legal successor of the former State Securities and Exchange Commission and the State Banking Supervision.
- Among the changes in the regulatory system we also need to mention the changes in the Act on foreign exchange which were related to the issue of Hungarian securities abroad and trading of foreign securities in Hungary. A significant change involved a reduction in the range of securities for the purchase of which a permit is required from the foreign exchange authority. Accordingly, no permission is required from the foreign exchange authority for the purchase of shares and bonds of corporations registered in OECD member countries if at least one of the five international credit rating agencies, accepted by the NBH, gives "investment grade" rating instead of the formerly required "AAA" rating or, in the case of bonds, the maturity at the time of issue is at least one year, while earlier the same requirement

counted the one year outstanding term of the bond from the time of purchase.

The experience of the regulatory and licensing, control and enforcement activities complying with the new regulations can only be analysed on the basis of sufficient experience during the first year, especially because certain regulations can only be applied following a transition period.

Therefore the presentation intends to focus on the "theory" of regulations included in the Securities Act.

The general purpose of securities market regulations is to protect the interest of investors but, in addition, they should also meet a number of other criteria which are sometimes contradictory amongst themselves, including the following:

- they should provide assistance for the development of the instruments and institutions of the Hungarian securities market, financial innovations and their successful introduction,
- the regulations should involve prudent rules promoting sound and prudent operations as much as possible,
- at the same time, they should not restrict fair competition among the financial institutions,
- bearing in mind the principle of necessary and sufficient regulations, they should decide what and at what level should be regulated, where to apply framework regulations or detailed regulations and what should be left for the institutions to regulate themselves,
- the regulations should assist gradual accommodation to the international financial and economic system and law harmonisation which is required for the EU association and future accession, *i.e.* our economic policy objective,
- the "peak" of the Hungarian economic regulations, the various laws related to the economy, including the Company Act, the Bankruptcy Act, Act on Financial Institutions, Tax and Accounting Acts and statutory regulations should at all times be harmonised and reflect relative stability.

The objectives listed above should be implemented in a way that investors should also be able to protect their own interests. In addition to control from the directing organisations, investors should be given adequate legal and institutional guarantees as a result of which they can effectively protect their own interest.

The first Act providing comprehensive regulations, Act VI. of 1990, represented a very important step in the development of the Hungarian capital market. The Act fulfilled its main functions, facilitated the establishment of investment companies, regulated issue and trading of securities as well as the foundation of the most important institution at the public market, the Stock Exchange. The previous Act created the State Securities and Exchange Commission, also providing the conditions for state control over the capital market.

The situation of the capital market has changed considerably during the past few years. A large number of investment enterprises has been established, including some with a large amount of capital, which offer a great deal of assistance in orientation at the capital market. At the moment slightly more than a hundred securities trading companies are operating on the Hungarian securities market. There is also a need for them because the public securities market includes nearly 300 corporate participants at present. At the moment 48 shares are traded on the Budapest Stock Exchange. The Hungarian securities have appeared on the securities markets of numerous countries, including primarily Luxembourg, Austria, Germany and the UK. Although it is not typical yet, foreign securities have already been issued in Hungary too, and signs can also be observed indicating the activities of international institutions in Hungary. EBRD and EIB have already issued bonds, and IFC is also interested in the Hungarian market.

Higher and higher investors' expectations have occurred in relation to the capital market institutions. Compared to the initial peculiarity, investment into securities and stock exchange products has become an everyday activity for numerous Hungarian savers.

A large number of foreign investors has also appeared in Hungary including some important institutional investors. They require a similar regulatory environment and a level of safety which they have in their own country. Hungary's intention to join the European Union also justifies the efforts of harmonising its capital market regulations with the regulations of the EU member countries concerning the principles and standards and making sure that the safety of investors is close or identical with the safety in their own countries.

It is obvious based on the above facts that the Hungarian securities market is becoming more and more developed and sophisticated and average investors think it is more and more difficult to find their way. This is why special emphasis has been laid on information provided to investors and on high standard supervisory activities.

From the point of investors purchasing securities the public issue of securities is considered safe if they have sufficient quantity and quality of information at the right time so that they can fully assess the risk of investing in that particular type of securities. In order to ensure that, Act CXI./1996 contains significant, strict provisions concerning the contents, evaluation and the approval of the prospectus for public issues.

Unlike the Polish or Slovene regulations, in the area of public issues the Act did not introduce the requirement of issuing all securities through the stock exchange but it contains a provision that, following an issue of securities in excess of HUF 200 million, in which a wider range of investors is interested, attempts should be made to list the securities on the stock exchange. This requirement will be mandatory only for the securities issued after 1st January 1998 and listing on the stock exchange should be initiated for those which are traded at the market at that time.

In order to further protect the interest of investors, the scope of the Act extends to the private placement of securities in a way that, by requiring mandatory reporting, the Supervision learns about it and controls compliance with law to check whether the issue qualifies as a private placement. This way the law intends to avoid situations in which investors obtain securities which fall within the scope of the Act but were not issued in accordance with it, thus limiting or nullifying their protection.

In the area of stock exchange regulations the Act has retained and strengthened the self-governing and self-regulating nature of the stock exchange. This has worked during the last few years and ensures that the stock exchange, *i.e.* the most important institution of the capital market, can perform its tasks free of harmful intervention.

One of the most important parts of Act CXI. of 1996. is the regulations concerning investor protection. The requirement of stronger protection for investors is reflected through the whole Act. In order to increase the safety of investors, the Act has made it compulsory for organisations involved in securities trading to establish an Investor Protection Fund, ensuring considerable reduction of losses for small investors should the investment service provider become insolvent.

Below we shall describe the instruments included in the regulatory framework of the Hungarian Securities Act, how they are used to protect investors and in what way they improve the transparency of the securities market.

2. Published market information

Since, in order to provide transparency, the Hungarian securities market regulations were formulated on the basis of a principle which leaves it to the investor to take the risk and does not guarantee investments with state liability, a special role is given to disclosure requirements. This means that investors and potential investors need to have all the necessary information required for their decision making process. Therefore the government should not classify investments or decide on their risks, but guarantee accurate information at the right time. This is why the authority supervising the securities market has created and runs a daily paper which contains all the information necessary for decisions in investment. Consequently, the resolutions of the Supervision, resolutions of the exchanges, KELER decisions, data of exchange deals, net asset values of investment funds as well as rules of SROs operating on the exchanges are all published. At the moment the Supervision is working on how to make this daily paper available on the Internet in an electronic format too.

3. Benefits of dematerialisation

The former regulations made it compulsory to generate publicly issued securities in a printed format.

The new Act introduced the concept of securities dematerialisation in Hungary. On the basis of the issuer's decision, as an alternative to the printed production, securities can now be generated in a computerised format (dematerialised securities). In such cases the issuer must deposit in the central safe a document which contains all the compulsory elements of the securities, the contents of which are defined by the document. In the future trade is based on this document.

Dematerialised securities issued in Hungary can only be transferred as a result of a debit and credit entries in securities accounts. Therefore the securities function as registered securities, trade is safe and can be monitored and the rights of the owner of securities can be enforced and protected more easily.

The Central Clearing House and Depository Ltd. (KELER) is responsible for making sure that the aggregate total of central securities accounts should be identical on a continuous basis with the issued quantity of the type of securities. Hopefully, although the new Act does not make dematerialisation compulsory, more and more issuers will choose this form when they issue new securities and will also convert their old bearer securities into a dematerialised format. Thus the majority of Hungarian securities can be entered into the records of the Central Clearing House and Depository Ltd and the transparency and safety of the total Hungarian securities issue and trade will be improved.

However, full dematerialisation could not begin yet, because the Government Decree containing the detailed regulations for it is expected to be issued in the next few days.

4. Disclosure functions

From the point of investors, one of the most important, if not the most important function is disclosure. The new Hungarian Securities Act has increased significantly the regular and extraordinary reporting obligations for public companies. Missing these obligations involves strict sanctions and penalties.

a) Regular reporting obligations of securities issuers

With the exception of government securities, issuers must inform the public regularly on the major data of their assets, income and operations. The regular reports should be provided in the form of annual flash reports and the annual reports.

The annual flash report is a new element in the regulation and is aimed to ensure that investors and the other participants in the market should obtain information on the previous year's activities of the business as soon as possible. This is essential in order to avoid potential insider trading.

Issuers must publish their flash reports by 15th February following the reporting year, at the latest. These reports should also be sent to the Supervision.

Issuers must allow investors to inspect the annual reports by 30th April following the reporting year, at the latest. In contrast with the former regulations and also considering international practice, the Act moved the time of publication of annual reports forward by one month. The issuers must also publish the place and time of inspection of their annual reports. Annual Reports must be made available for public inspection seven days after their publication, at the latest. The annual reports must be sent to the Supervision by 30th April following the reporting year, at the latest and, simultaneously with that, a statement should also be made concerning the daily paper in which and the time when the announcement will be published.

The Supervision may oblige, and set a deadline for, the issuers to prepare or modify annual reports if their annual reports do not meet the provisions of this Act.

The annual report must include a declaration from the issuer concerning their liability that the report contains true and fair data and statements, does not conceal facts which are material for the purpose of assessing the position of the issuer.

Issuers who publish a prospectus between 1st January and 30th April following the reporting year, are not obliged to prepare an annual report on the reporting year, proving that the prospectus contains the data of the annual report. The prospectus and public offering must contain a statement that, following the publication of the prospectus, the issuer shall not publish an annual report.

The new regulations also allow for continuous issue of bonds.

In the case of a continuos/tap issue the issuer and his investment services firm must also prepare a simplified prospectus in accordance with the economic, financial and legal position by 30th June of the current year and publish it by 30th September. The annual reports published during the term of the issue must be completed with the up-to-date data and information of the continuous issue.

b) Extraordinary reporting obligations of securities issuers

Issuers must send to the Supervision within two days, and publish all information directly or indirectly related to the value or yield of the securities.

The Act contains a long list of this information with examples. Thus, for example, in addition to the natural information (date of the Shareholders' meeting, changes in managers, etc.) issuers must also publish the following information which is material for economic considerations:

- report on the private placement securities issues by the issuer,
- any contract between the owners of the issuer which have an impact on the issuer or the other owners of the securities,
- any decision made by the Board of Directors which significantly affects the operation or market position of the company,
- loans exceeding 25 per cent of the equity,
- law suits by or against the issuer if the value involved in the law suit exceeds 10 per cent of the equity,
- changes in securities of the issuer held by managers, etc.

If securities of the issuer have been issued abroad, the issuer must publish also in Hungary the same data and information which need to be published in accordance with the law of the country of issue, simultaneously with the securities offering abroad.

5. Stock exchange listing requirement

It is a provision in the new Securities Act that following the public issue of securities in excess of HUF 200 million (US$1 million), the issuer must make an attempt to list the securities on the stock exchange.

The objective of the Act was to include more and more securities in the regulated, transparent and adequately supervised market. This investor protecting rule also serves the purpose of providing sufficient liquidity for the issued securities, *i.e.* investors should be able to sell the purchased securities too and be able to buy new ones. This does not mean that the trade outside the stock exchange should disappear completely, because there will be securities which, for various reasons, will not be traded at the Stock Exchange but, according to the plans, the majority of the Hungarian securities will become instruments available at the Hungarian Stock Exchange and their trade will be directly supervised by the stock exchange, which is a self-regulating organisation with adequate competence.

6. Insider information and insider persons

Among the abuses on the securities markets insider trading is the most important activity representing the biggest hazard for the market. The Act clearly bans insider trading

The Act specifies the range of insider information, which have not been published yet, but their publication might significantly influence the value and price of the particular securities. Naturally, such information corresponds with the data and information included in the issuer's obligation to provide regular and extraordinary information.

In order to retain a fair securities market in Hungary and prevent price manipulations, the following incompatibility rules and specific rules concerning insider persons and insider trading apply to the issuers of securities.

Managers of the issuer and other insider persons who were involved in the preparation of the annual accounts of the issuer, may not conclude deals for the securities issued by the issuer between the balance sheet date and the date when the annual accounts are approved.

It is banned to use insider information to conclude a deal, or order such deals for securities or Stock Exchange products affected by the insider information.

Insider information according to the Hungarian Securities Act is the following:

- information concerning the economic or legal position or expected changes in that of the issuer, investment service provider, guarantor or surety provider, especially information related to the issue of securities, major deals, organisational restructuring, bankruptcy, initiation of liquidation;
- information related to persons or enterprises holding 25 per cent or a higher share or similar voting rights in the issuer;

- information concerning enterprises in which the issuer holds 25 per cent or a higher share or similar voting rights;
- information on the securities market, especially intentions to acquire a business, a concluded commissioning agreement, preliminary decisions on purchase or sale, changes in HUF foreign exchange rates, syndicate agreement between the owners, voting agreements, and
- information related to preparations for the public issue of securities which were issued privately before,
- information which has not been disclosed to the public yet but if disclosed, is likely to have a significant influence on the value or price of the securities.

In accordance with the Act, the following persons are insider persons:

a) relevant officers, leading official and members of the Supervisory Board of the issuer and legal entity or a business without legal entity in which the issuer holds a 25 per cent or higher share or similar voting rights,

b) relevant officers, leading official and members of the Supervisory Board of the issuer and legal entity or a business without legal entity which holds a 25 per cent or higher share or similar voting rights in the issuer,

c) persons employed by or having other legal relations with the issuer within six months prior to the date when the information is used, if they might have had access to insider information in relation to the work,

d) relevant officers, leading officer of any organisations involved in the organisation of the issue and trade, and other employees of these organisations and the issuer participating in the issue and trade;

e) private individuals holding ten percent or more in the shareholders' equity (equity capital) of the issuer,

f) leading officials, members of the Supervisory Board and relevant officers of the account keeping credit institution,

as well as close relations of the private individuals listed above.

Reporting liability of insider persons:

Insider persons must report to the Supervision within two days if they have concluded a deal for securities issued by an organisation which included among the organisations listed in a)-f). The report must include the title, quantity, price of the securities involved in the deal, the date of the deal and the tittle of the investment service provider implementing the deal. The Supervision must publish the report in the official paper.

7. Investor protection fund (SRO)

An important element in the Act includes the rules related to the establishment and operation of the Investor Protection Fund. This fund must be established by all business organisations which, at the time of entry into force of the Act, were actively involved in the trading of securities.

The task of the Fund is to provide partial compensation to the customers of the members should debts be frozen at the member organisations. The insurance offered by the Fund relates only to contracts concluded after 1st July 1997.

The financial resources of the Fund can only be used if the liability of a member of the Fund is frozen, in other words the member organisation is unable to pay its customer his due funds within five days from the due date. The compensation provided to one customer is only partial and the compensation amount paid to one customer may not exceed HUF 1 million. Compensation may take place involving money or, based on the customer's agreement, government securities.

The Act also specifies the deadlines related to the payments to be made by the Fund, the announcements about payments and the payment methods.

Any organisation applying for securities trading licences after the entry into force of the Act must declare to the Board of Directors of the Fund that it would join the Fund before the licence application is submitted. Members of the Fund must pay a joining fee when they join the Fund and later on they pay an annual fee.

Taking into account the special position and tasks of the Fund, its account is kept by the National Bank of Hungary and it can only keep its money in cash or Government securities. The Fund may not conduct business activities.

Joining the Fund and being a permanent member is mandatory for organisations involved in securities trading. Therefore, they may leave the Fund only when they have terminated all the activities which were insured by the Fund and have certified that all the liabilities to customers have been met. The Board of Directors of the Fund is entitled to take measures against the Fund members if they fail to meet their obligations in time, provide wrong information in their announcements about the deals insured by the Fund, or their records do not allow for the monitoring of the deals insured by the Fund. In the case of repeated or serious violation of obligations the Board of Directors of the Fund may initiate a sanction against the Fund member at the Supervision, and may also decide to exclude the member from the Fund.

8. Protection of minority rights, acquisitions

At present Parliament is discussing the amendments and supplements in the Company Act and, parallel with that, the Securities Act.

Among others, the amendments in the Company Act strengthen protection for minority rights and define the rules for acquisitions in companies. The new chapter of the Securities Act contains detailed rules about the acquisition of joint stock companies.

a) Concern right

In accordance with the draft Company Act any domestic or foreign legal subjects, *i.e.* private individuals, legal entities and business organisations without legal entity, could be in the position of a voting member. However, only joint stock companies and limited liability companies may be in positions of control.

Not all acquisitions result in influence, only relatively significant ones. Thus the Hungarian Company Act distinguishes between significant (over 25 per cent), majority (over 50 per cent) and controlling shares (over 75 per cent). Usually the concern law regulations govern only direct acquisition and, apart from one exception, regulations do not cover indirect acquisitions The extent of ownership control of the shares is determined on the basis of voting rights.

The purpose of the Act is to give an opportunity to the minority to prevent undesirable majority or, in the case of already acquired majority shares, to prevent violation of the interests of minorities. In the case of foundation of new companies the concern rules cannot be applied. They are only applicable in later acquisitions. If the majority ratio established at the time of foundation remains the same or falls later, the concern regulations cannot be applied either. In other words, the concern law works only from the bottom to the top and not from the top to bottom.

One of the instruments in legislation is the disclosure of acquisitions. It is the obligation of the acquiring party to report to the Court of Registration, and publish in the Company Gazette, his acquired share. If that does not take place, the acquiring party cannot exercise his voting rights.

The draft Act intends to eliminate the mutually significant influence, "cross-participation". A company which acquires a significant share in the other one later, must sell its share in excess of 25 per cent of the votes and until it meets this obligation, it cannot vote with its shares offered for sale. Another rule, also aimed at the elimination of "cross-participation" is that following the establishment of a majority share, the controlled company may not acquire a share in the controlling member and must sell its full existing share within a specified time.

The rules of incompatibility, according to which the same person may not be a leading official or a member of the Supervisory Board in the controlling entity and the controlled company, are still in force.

Another provision is aimed to protect the minority. According to this, within 60 days from the publication of the majority share, any shareholder may request the controlling member to purchase his shares unless the majority was established on the basis of a public purchase offering.

In a controlled company shareholders possessing 5 per cent of the shares may, at any time, call a Shareholders' Meeting, indicating the reason for, and purpose of, the meeting. If the management of the company fails to meet the request, the Shareholders' Meeting is called by the Court of Registration. A significant legal consequence of a majority share is if the controlled company is liquidated and outstanding claims remain, upon the suit initiated by the creditor, the Court may establish full and unlimited liability of the controlling member for the debts.

b) ***Rules related to the acquisition of joint stock companies***

The Securities Act has been extended with a new chapter which contains detailed rules for the acquisition of joint stock companies.

The main instrument of the regulation is the definition of a public purchase proposal, its announcement and counter-proposals.

A public purchase proposal must be submitted for the acquisition of shares with a voting right in a public company if they will exceed 33 per cent. The public purchase proposals must be aimed at the acquisition of shares exceeding 33 per cent and a voting ratio of at least 50 per cent. If the joint stock company has also issued convertible bonds, the public purchase proposal must also extend to those. The public purchase proposal must be made for all shareholders and convertible bond holders of the joint stock company who have an equal chance to accept or refuse the proposal.

The bidder must disclose to the public his business policy ideas concerning the future operation of the company.

The price offered for the shares may not be less than

a) the weighted stock exchange average price of 90 days prior to the public purchase proposal in the case of shares listed on the stock exchange,

b) the weighted OTC average price of 180 days prior to the public purchase proposal in the case of shares not listed on the stock exchange

The period available for the approval of the public purchase proposal may be at least sixty and maximum ninety days.

Within the period available for the approval of the public purchase proposal, the Board of Directors of the joint stock company may not make a decision which disturbs the procedure, *e.g.* may not decide to increase the equity capital or acquire the own shares of the company, etc.

Within the period available for the approval -- by the deadline -- other persons, legal entities, are also entitled to make a public purchase proposal (counter proposal) if that is more favourable for the shareholders (higher purchase price, better payment conditions, etc.). If the counter purchase proposal complies with the rules and is accepted by the Supervision, the original public purchase proposal will lose its force.

If, on the basis of the accepting statements of the shareholders entitled to approve the public purchase proposal it may be established that the approval does not reach the number of shares specified in the public purchase proposal,

a) the bidder is entitled to withdraw from his proposal, in accordance with the terms and conditions specified in advance in the proposal,

b) with the lack of exclusion of the right of the bidder to withdraw or conditions for withdrawal, the shares will be transferred in accordance with the purchase proposal and the approving statements.

If according to the approving statements the number of approved shares exceeds the public purchase proposal, the approval will take place under the conditions included in the public purchase proposal or, if that is missing, in accordance with the ratio of face values of the shares of shareholders who made the approving statements.

The above take-over rules having only been drafted and proposed, legislation has not been passed yet regarding their introduction.

Chapter 8

TRANSPARENCY, COMPLIANCE AND DISCLOSURE ISSUES IN RUSSIA

Submission by
The Central Bank of The Russian Federation

One of the main problems of the stock market in any country, especially the Russian stock market with its high systemic, credit, interest-rate, liquidity, currency, political, legislative and other risks involved in securities transactions, is that of investor confidence. Investment in stock market instruments normally only happens when an investor is convinced that his rights are protected by law. This applies equally to domestic as well as foreign investors.

It is very important therefore to make an in-depth analysis of the ways of increasing reliability and stability of the operations conducted by financial market players. This involves protecting investors as well as other market players and their customers and partners, when they conduct operations in the financial markets, by enforcing compliance with the securities legislation, preventing any infringement of the rights of investors in the financial markets and settling conflicts of interests with maximum consideration for the investors' interests.

The enactment regulating the relations arising from the issue and circulation of securities and guiding the activities of the securities market players in Russia is the Federal Law on Securities, which came into effect in April 1996. With the aim of protecting the rights of investors in the securities market and ensuring stable and crisis-free development of the securities market, that law:

- established requirements for the financial market participants engaged in any professional activity in the securities market (specifically, it also regulates the activities of advertisers who participate in the securities market in a professional capacity) and also for the securities issuers;

- imposed restrictions on market players combining different activities in the securities market;
- established requirements for securities market players and issuers with respect to information disclosure;
- banned the use and transfer of inside information and defined the range of persons with access to inside information;
- imposed a ban on price manipulation in the securities market.

Specifically, to prevent conflicts of interests and unethical situations, in which one and the same legal entity acts as both a dealer (for his own account and in his own interests) and a broker (on behalf of a client and for the latter's account), that is, combines broker and dealer activities, the Law stipulates that the transactions conducted on behalf of a customer have priority over the dealer operations conducted by the broker on his own behalf. In addition, should a broker have an interest preventing the fulfilment of the client's instructions on more favourable terms, the broker should immediately make this known to his client. Otherwise, if a conflict of interests, which the broker had not reported, harmed the client's interests when his instruction was fulfilled, the broker must cover such losses at his own expense in accordance with the procedure established by civil law (Article 3. Brokerage).

A similar requirement designed to protect investor interests is imposed on securities market players who are engaged in asset management. Should a conflict between the interests of the manager and those of his client or between those of the various clients of one manager, about which all the parties were not notified in advance, harm the client's interests, the manager must cover any such losses at his own expense in accordance with the procedure established by civil law.

To prevent any infringement of investor rights as a result of one person simultaneously conducting different kinds of professional activity in the securities market the Law imposes a series of restrictions on such practices, prohibiting a person, for instance, from keeping a register and at the same time conducting other professional activities in the securities market.

This ban is very important for the Russian securities market with its high registrar's risks. The essence of the problem has been that investors often noted cases of abuse by registrars, who, acting in the corporate interests of the issuers, refused to register the assignment of property rights to securities. The Law made the registration and assignment of rights to securities the competence of the depositary (a professional participant in the securities market conducting depositary activities), leaving to the registrar (a professional participant in the securities market, keeping a register of securities holders) the only function of keeping the register of owners and informing the issuer.

In addition, the Law contains provisions aimed at protecting the interests of investors and professional securities market participants from abuses by persons in the latter's employ. Specifically, to prevent any bias on the part of the stock exchange employees in conducting operations the Law stipulates that the stock market employees must not be founders of or participants in the securities market. This is particularly important in the cases when the exchange rules provide for the services of market-makers.

The Law also regulates the activities of advertisers, who are professional participants in the securities market, and bans the use of inside information in transactions and the transfer of inside information in transactions of third persons. These provisions protect the interests of the clients and counterparties of the professional participants and prevent conflicts between the interests of professional participants and those of their clients as well as those of persons in the employ of the professional participants.

Conflict regulation procedures are also contained in some other laws. Thus, the Federal Law on Joint-Stock Companies and Federal Law on Non-Profit Organisations identify the cases in which conflict between the personal interests of the employees of a joint-stock company (non-profit organisation) and the joint-stock company (non-profit organisation) may arise and the measures that should be taken to settle it. Conflicts of interests may arise when a group of people, defined in the laws, is interested in having a company (organisation) take some action, including a particular transaction. The law establishes the procedure for, and the cases in which, such transactions may be made.

In addition to legislative regulation and government control of the relations in the financial markets, an important role in protecting the interests of their participants and ensuring safety and stability of their operations and preventing possible abuses in the market is played by the self-regulating organisations (SROs) founded by the professional participants in the securities market (among such organisations in Russia are NAUFOR, PARTAD, NAURAG, AUVER and others).

The objective of such voluntary associations of professional securities market players, who adopt uniform rules and ethical and other standards, is to protect the interests of the securities holders and other categories of clients. By unifying rules and standards of conducting operations with securities, SRO members also aim to ensure effective performance of securities market services.

However, many questions related to fair play in the financial market are not yet regulated by law, or not adequately identified or reflected in any generally accepted principles of doing business in the financial markets. Although the applicable legislation prohibits price manipulation, it fails to define "price manipulation" and, consequently, to regulate it; there is no list of prohibited transactions; consulting business is not regulated; there is no procedure to detect and prevent insider deals (transactions involving the use of inside information); there is no clearly defined system of penalties for violations of the law, there is no clarity about the scale of and procedure for administrative inquiries and for bringing charges against dishonest financial market players, and so on.

In addition to these and other flaws in the existing legislation regulating the relations in the financial market, a major impediment to its further development is the absence of an effective system of control over compliance with this legislation by the professional securities market participants.

As operations in the financial market are being diversified, the number and size of transactions increase and new, electronic technologies are introduced, the Russian financial market faces an acute problem: violations of the securities market legislation, such as price manipulation, insider deals and the failure to disclose information are on the rise.

Such violations are usually committed, wittingly or unwittingly, by persons in the employ of the professional financial market participants, but it is the professional market participants that are penalised as a result and this practice may lead to big financial losses and seriously harm business reputations.

This problem is not unique to Russia -- all advanced financial markets face it. Although external control (by the government and SROs) over the observance of the applicable legislation by all market participants is necessary, Russia's experience serves to show that it is beyond their power to solve this problem. We believe that it is necessary to enact uniform rules of mandatory internal control over the compliance with applicable legislation of financial market operations conducted by individual professional market players. This means that the regulatory authorities should establish only the basic requirements with which such internal control system should comply, while the professional financial market participants must be required to organise internal supervision in accordance with their own criteria of its adequacy.

As a body in charge of banking supervision and regulation of the credit organisations, the Bank of Russia is currently drafting, in collaboration with other agencies concerned, Provisions on the Internal Control System in Credit Organisations (hereinafter referred to as the Provisions). This document is being elaborated in accordance with the applicable legislation and it further develops this legislation, taking into account international experience in the field of supervision of professional activities in financial markets worldwide.

The principal objective of the internal control system is to protect the interests of investors and credit organisations in the financial markets by preventing conflict of interests and minimising the risks and possible losses of credit organisations as a result of violations by employees of these organisations of the applicable legislation, rules and standards regulating professional activity.

To this end, the Provisions will establish the procedure for credit organisations to set up internal supervision systems and provide recommendations and set requirements on ways to organise the internal control of the main activities of a credit organisation and recommendations on the structure, functions and methods of work of the internal control service.

One of the sections of the Provisions will set standards to regulate the operations conducted by employees of credit organisations, professional participants in the financial markets. These standards will embrace the following range of issues:

- control of the flows of information (banning the transfer and use of inside information and restricting the exchange of inside information between various units of a credit organisation -- the so-called Chinese Wall rules; conflict of interests and the methods of settling such conflicts; requirements to credit organisations' advertisements and publications related to the securities market;

– preventing price manipulation (the definition of manipulation and its types);

– relations with customers (the main principles of relations between credit organisations and their customers in conducting operations in the financial markets, especially the meaning of the "best execution rule", the procedure for providing consulting services for customers, the observance of the client's-interests-come-first principle, and the procedure for reporting and certifying client's operations);

– preventing legalisation (laundering) of illegal incomes (detecting illegal income legalisation activities, establishing the procedure for reporting suspicious operations and monitoring compliance with the regulations on the prevention of legalisation of illegal incomes).

The rules regulating the operations of employees of credit organisations, professional financial market participants (hereinafter referred to as the Rules) set a number of standards designed to protect the rights and interests of the clients of credit organisations, professional financial market participants, and the credit organisations per se and settle the conflicts of interest that may arise.

For example, to protect the interests of the customers and partners of a credit organisation from abuse of inside information by its employees acting in their own interests or in the interests of the credit organisation, the Provisions will impose restrictions on the exchange of inside information between the various units of the credit organisation. The following measures are recommended to prevent unsanctioned disclosure of inside and confidential information between the internal units of a credit organisation:

– the employees of a credit organisation will be required to commit themselves in writing not to divulge any confidential information;

– steps will be taken to organisationally and technically separate the corresponding internal units (specifically, adjacent units will be denied access to one another's computer networks);

- every employee of a credit institution will be denied access to various levels of information;
- different functional units of a credit organisation (the units conducting operations in the financial markets and the units formalising and registering such operations, for example) will have their own systems of subordination;
- employees and documents will be territorially isolated.

The heads of the corresponding units and the internal control service should jointly ensure control over the observance of the information flow division rules by all employees of the credit organisation, involved in operations in the financial markets.

Inside information may be passed from one unit of a credit organisation to another only if this is absolutely necessary and in accordance with the established procedure. There must be permission for that from the head of the unit and its internal control service and any such passage of inside information should be registered.

Conflict of interests may also arise between a credit organisation operating on the financial market and its customers, between employees of a credit organisation and the credit organisation and between its customers.

To settle conflicts that may arise in a credit organisation the Provisions will set two priorities of interests. The first one will be the priority of the interests of the customers of a credit organisation over those of the credit organisation. In accordance with the Provisions, the transactions on behalf of the clients should always have priority over the broker's dealer operations when a credit organisation acts as both broker and dealer.

The employees privy to information about clients' instructions must not conduct any trade operations for their own account sooner than these instructions are fulfilled, except for the cases when such operations are necessary to facilitate the fulfilment of clients' instructions and when it does not run counter to the obligations of the credit organisation to fulfil its client's instruction in accordance with the best execution rule and applicable legislation.

The second priority is the priority of the interests of a credit organisation and its clients over the personal interests of the employees of the credit organisation operating in the financial markets. To prevent conflict of personal interests of employees of a credit organisation and conflict of interests between a credit organisation and its clients the employees of a credit organisation are not allowed without the internal control service's permission to participate in a deal, in which an employee of a credit organisation may be considered an interested party.

In accordance with the Provisions, an employee of a credit organisation is considered an interested party in a transaction conducted by a credit organisation in the financial markets if this employee:

– is a party to the deal;

– holds independently or as a member of a group 20 per cent or more of voting stock (shares, stakes) of a legal entity which is a party to the deal or participates in it as an agent or intermediary;

– holds any position in the executive structures of a legal entity which is a party to the deal or participates in it as an agent or intermediary;

– if the relatives (husband [wife], parents, children, brothers or sisters) of this employee:

– are a party to the deal or participate in it as an agent or intermediary;

– hold independently or as a member of a group 20 per cent or more of the voting stock (shares, stakes) of a legal entity, which is a party to the deal or participates in it as an agent or intermediary;

– holds any position in the executive structures of a legal entity, which is a party to the deal or participates in it as an agent or intermediary.

Any employee conducting operations on the financial markets must report to the management of the unit and internal control service the transactions he has conducted or intends to conduct, in which he may be considered an interested party.

Yet another sphere of regulation which has not been duly elaborated in the applicable legislation is the relations arising when a credit organisation provides consulting services in the financial market. In accordance with the Provisions, the employees of a credit organisation conducting operations in the financial markets on behalf of their clients must inform the clients before the deal about all possible risks they know, ensuring that the credit organisation is convinced that its client understands the essence and terms of the projected deal and realises the risks involved in it.

Recommendations given to a client by employees of a credit organisation on questions related to the purchase and sale operations on a financial market must be based on an adequate and credible analysis of the available information about this market. The employees of a credit organisation are not allowed:

- to give clients recommendations on operations in the financial markets in order to create favourable conditions for the implementation of operations in the interest of the credit organisation or in their own interests, if these recommendations do not accord with the interests of the clients of the credit organisation or violate the applicable legislation, regulatory rules and professional practice standards;
- to make deals for their own account by using information obtained from clients' instructions, which may incur losses to the clients.

To prevent conflict of interest between a credit organisation and its partner the Provisions prohibit credit organisations operating in the financial market from manipulating prices. They define price manipulation and describe the practices which constitute price manipulation:

- simultaneously bidding for and offering securities in the organised market at prices that definitely differ from market prices in order to change the latter in one's favour or derive some other profit;
- a collusion between two or several traders or their employees on the purchase/sale of securities in the organised market at prices that are definitely different from market prices;
- making a one-off purchase/sale of large blocks of securities in the organised market without prior agreement with an agent on an operation plan to prevent a possible destabilisation of the market and without obtaining the corresponding permission;
- providing intentionally false information about securities, securities issuers and securities prices, including information

placed in an advertisement in order to persuade another securities market participant to make an erroneous investment decision.

Control over the compliance with this requirement must be exercised by the management of the corresponding units and the internal control service of a credit organisation.

Such are some of the principles of settling conflict of interests and protecting investor rights, established by the Provisions.

Every credit organisation must set up an internal control service to regulate the operations conducted by employees of credit organisations that operate professionally in the financial markets, ensure the implementation of other rules and recommendations formulated in these Provisions and set in motion the mechanism of internal control over the compliance by employees of credit organisations with legislation, regulatory rules and professional and ethical conduct standards.

The aims, functions, rights and duties of the internal control service, the requirements made to its employees and the procedure for co-operation between the credit organisation's employees and internal control service are established by the Provisions and the internal control service's own rules and regulations, which are approved by the highest executive body of the credit organisation.

The Bank of Russia approves the procedure and deadlines for submitting information by the internal control service of a credit organisation.

These are the Bank of Russia plans with regard to the creation in credit organisations of a system of internal control over the compliance by employees of credit organisations with the applicable legislation, regulatory rules and professional activity standards. We hope that this system will help resolve a number of problems of the Russian financial market. As for the time when this system will be put in place and how effectively it will function, this depends not only on the regulatory bodies, but also on the professional financial market participants.

Information disclosure

In 1995 the Bank of Russia became the first government agency to implement a programme for the disclosure of information about bank securities and their issuers.

Since there were no federal laws on the disclosure of information at that time, the Bank of Russia issued a departmental instruction establishing the procedure for disclosing information by the credit organisations issuing securities and determining the amount of such information.

The Bank of Russia was guided by the thesis that any investor who has bought or intends to buy bank securities should have the opportunity to receive open information necessary for making an investment decision.

By that time the Bank of Russia had organised a system of centralised collection of the documents accompanying the issue of securities by banks and the corresponding reports in electronic form and in standard formats.

The use of the Bank of Russia technical facilities made it possible to organise a system of information disclosure without additional financial and organisational expenditures by the issuers.

This system works as follows. The issuing banks send the required documents to the Bank of Russia by telecommunications networks. After being checked, corrected, if necessary, and registered, these documents are passed by the Bank of Russia in accordance with the established procedure and free of charge to the official distributors of information, with which the Bank of Russia signs special contracts.

Any organisation may become a distributor; the only condition is that it should specialise in processing information or providing information or consulting services. The main provision of the contract is that the distributor must not make any changes in the information he receives and must pass it to consumers unchanged and for a fee that must not exceed the cost price of this service. It is a non-profit operation for the distributor, but he may use the information he receives to make his own information and analysis products, such as surveys, reports, search systems, etc. There are more than 50 such distributor organisations in Russia today.

The implementation of this programme provided investors with full information about each new securities issue by each bank and their parameters and that became a major factor of protection of the rights of small shareholders. Previously, big shareholders sometimes sold new shares to a small group of persons, because small shareholders were informed about the sale too late to apply by the established deadlines.

In addition, implemented nation-wide, this programme made it possible to increase the number of potential investors in specific bank securities and stimulated inter-regional capital flow.

Now that Federal laws regulating information disclosure in the stock market have been passed and the Bank of Russia and Federal Securities Commission have refined their regulatory rules a further development of the information disclosure programme proceeds in two directions.

The first is connected with adaptation of the system's software and organisational structure to the requirements of the new regulatory rules. The system of information collection, for instance, has been changed so that it now makes it possible to receive quarterly reports of joint-stock banks and messages on major actions undertaken by a securities issuer.

The other direction is towards integrating the Bank of Russia information disclosure system with the other systems that are being developed in order to create a single federal stock market information disclosure system. Specifically, Bank of Russia representatives are participating in the efforts by a Federal Securities Commission working group to set up a Federal Information Disclosure Centre.

Chapter 9

CORPORATE SECURITIES MARKET DEVELOPMENT IN RUSSIA

by
Alexander Radygin
Institute for The Economy In Transition (Moscow)

1. Development of the corporate securities market 1996 - 1997

1.1 Major quantitative indices of market development

The major type of corporate securities traded in the Russian market is *common stock* of such issuers as the joint- stock companies founded in the process of privatisation of state- owned and municipal enterprises. Despite remaining investment risks, the rate of the Russian stock market's development in 1996- 1997 was fairly swift.

According to data from the International Financial Corporation (IFC), in 1996 there was a 153 per cent increase in the Russian stock market index, leaving far behind the closest (with respect to growth record) competitors: Venezuela with 114 per cent and Hungary with 97 per cent. Thus, in 1996 the Russian corporate securities market showed the maximum growth rate among all the emerging markets worldwide. According to the data from the "Skatepress" agency, investors' return from holding Lukoil stocks during 1996 was 163 per cent annualised in hard currency equivalent, while Mosenergo' stocks yielded a return of 367 per cent, and those of Surgutneftegas 440 per cent.

On the whole, for the period of 1996- 1997, apart from some notable fluctuations, the market was characterised by a clear rising trend, manifested both in the dynamics of the Russian stock market indices (see Charts 1-2) and in the growth in capitalisation of the Russian market.

Chart 1. **Stock market index for the companies traded in the RTS-1**
1995-1997

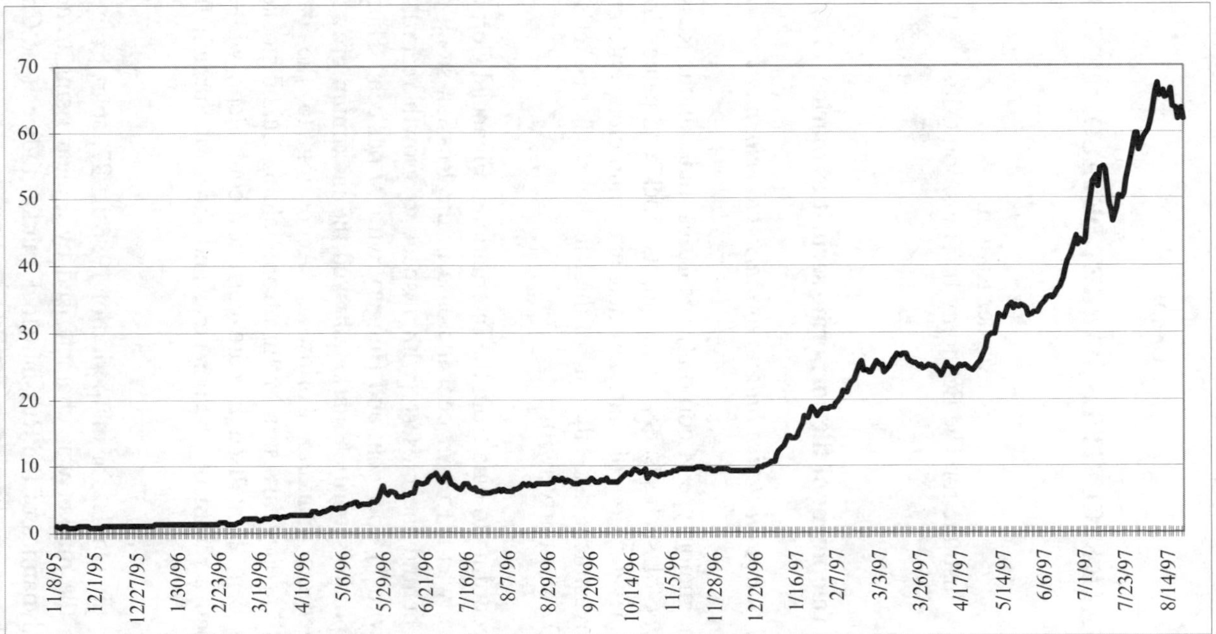

Source: Russian Trading System.

Chart 2. **Volume of trading in the RTS-1 in 1995-1997**

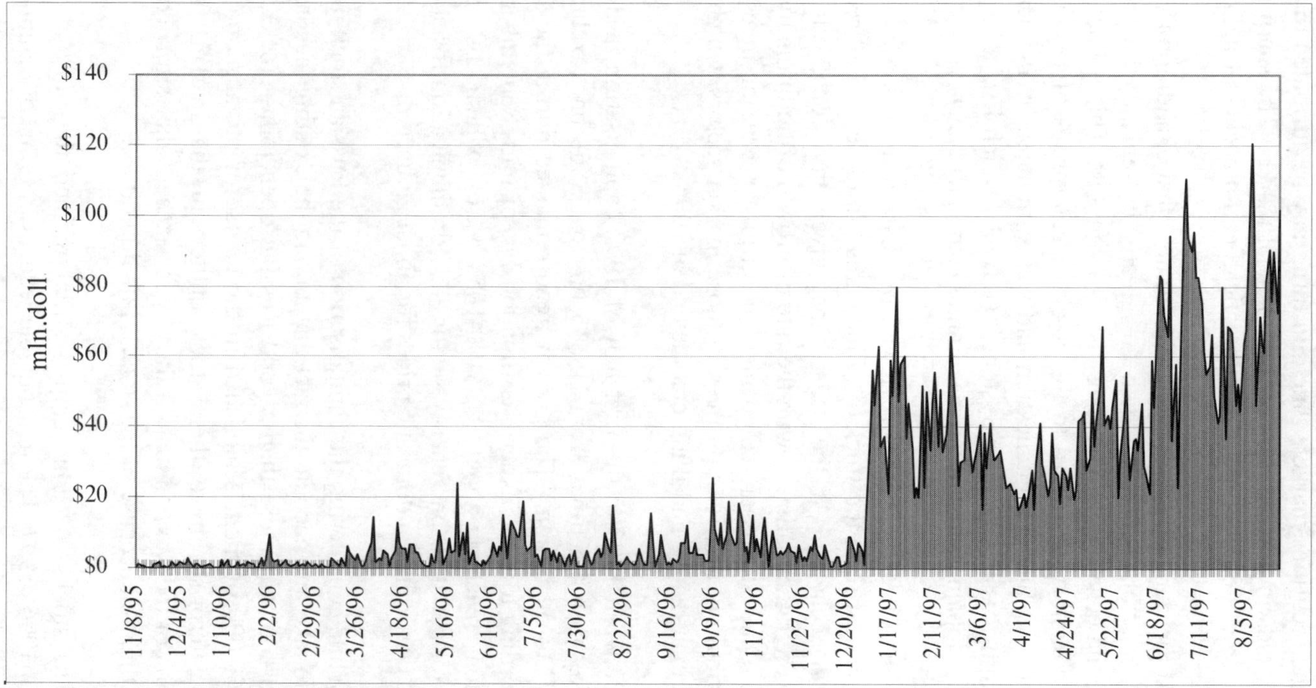

Source: Russian Trading System.

In 1997 a significant rise in price quotations of practically all the most liquid securities of Russian issuers was observed. This was mainly brought about by the entry of new groups of Russian and foreign investors to the corporate securities market, which, in turn, may be attributed to the steady decline in yields in other sectors of the financial market. The sharp price rises affected the stocks of enterprises from practically all branches of industry.

At the same time, it is interesting to note that in addition to the highly liquid stock of "blue chips", which are greatly in demand, the prices of so called "second echelon" stocks were also growing fast. This phenomenon was especially notable with regard to the stock of enterprises of regional energy sector companies and communication and was stimulated by the activation of trading within Russian Trading System-2 (RTS-2), which lists a large number of regional companies, including telecommunication and energy enterprises.

Thus, over the period reviewed one can observe a gradual shift of investors' interest from the stock of "blue chips" to those of the "second" and even "third" echelon. At the same time, given that conservative foreign investors were rather satisfied with the rate of growth of traditionally attractive stocks of the largest Russian companies, the inflow of Russian investor capital served particularly to drive up prices in those market sectors, which were still considered unattractive and illiquid at the end of 1996.

Between 1996 to the first half of 1997 capitalisation in the Russian stock market rose 4.5 times from US$15 bn. to US$68 bn. (excluding RAO "Gasprom" to 54 billion.) The growth trend remained during the summer of 1997. According to some experts' estimations, as of mid- September 1997, the capitalisation reached about US$100-105 bn.(of which oil companies accounted for about 30 bn., energy sector and communication for about 40 bn. and RAO "Gasprom" in domestic prices for about 25 bn.)

While considering the capitalisation of the Russian stock market, it is necessary to take into account the fact that among the existing (according to the data of Goskomstat) more than 50 000 Russian open joint- stock companies, including 30 000 of them established in the course of privatisation, not more than 150 enterprises have their stock quoted in the market. The actual capitalisation of the Russian market thus by far exceeds the estimated level, but it defies estimation because of the stocks' low liquidity.

The stocks of "blue chips" still remained the most attractive for investors in 1996- 1997. The indisputable leaders in terms of capitalisation are found in the following four branches: oil and gas (refining industry inclusive)-

58 per cent of the overall capitalisation, energetics- 28 per cent, communication (telecommunication)- 11 per cent, non- ferrous metallurgy- 2 per cent. At the same time eight enterprises of the said branches account for over 80 per cent of the overall capitalisation of the market (the data as of May 1997): RAO "Gasprom"- 24 per cent, joint- stock company "Lukoil"- 18 per cent, RAO "EES Rossii"- 17 per cent, joint- stock company "Surgutneftegas"- 7 per cent, joint-stock company "Mosenergo"-6 per cent, joint-stock company "Rostelekom"- 6 per cent, joint- stock company "MGTS"-2.5 per cent, joint-stock company "Irkutskenergo"-2 per cent.

As of today, the complete market capitalisation of the Russian market accounts for about 12 per cent of GNP, which is significantly lower than in most developed countries. Nevertheless, it is necessary to take into account the following facts:

Firstly, there has been a notable qualitative progress. According to some estimates, between 1993-1994 the capitalisation of the Russian market was about US$300 mln. Thus, given that over the period between 1996 to the first half of 1997 the rise in capitalisation was 4.5 times, between 1993 to early 1997 the respective index rose by 200 times.

Secondly, as international experience shows, for the majority of the countries with emerging stock markets, a low level of capitalisation is quite natural (in Mexico and Brazil-about 20 per cent of GNP, in Turkey-about 12 per cent of GNP).

Thirdly, the low capitalisation (relative to GNP) is characteristic of practically all transition economies.

It should be expected that the capitalisation of the Russian stock market will be growing in the future. Among the leaders of such growth, apart from " blue chips", one would also expect the undervalued stocks of the "second echelon". It is probable that investors' interest in the stocks of enterprises of the technologically developed industrial and construction branches will grow. Some further large Russian companies should be expected to enter foreign stock markets.

Practically all the experts unanimously agreed that the following major factors constitute grounds for further growth in market capitalisation:

– present significant undervaluation of assets;

- diminishing political risk;

- potential migration of a part of capital from the state T-bill market (according to some estimates, should an inflow of only 10 per cent of the capital from the said market to the corporate securities market occur, it could result in a 100 per cent rise in the capitalisation of the latter);

- rise in investment on the part of the global funds;

- decrease in the risks related to the market infrastructure;

- development of the domestic institutional investor sector.

One of the most dynamic segments of the stock market between 1996 to early 1997 was preferred stocks.

These stocks are a suitable instrument for portfolio investors and individuals who are interested in stable dividends rather than in voting at shareholders' meetings. Until the summer 1996, this market remained non-liquid, since a major share of the preferred stock was owned by enterprises' employees. The regular purchasing of stocks at enterprises has resulted in a significant increase in the quoted prices and liquidity of the preferred stocks. In the course of 1996 prices quoted for preferred stocks grew 6.7 times on average (while quotations of regular stocks grew by 2.5 times). In February 1997 the capitalisation of outstanding preferred stocks was estimated at about US$4 bn.

The first issuer of preferred stocks for which a relatively liquid market has developed, was RAO "Norilsky Nickel". By the spring of 1997, the joint-stock companies "Lukoil" , "Rostelekom" and "Surgutneftegas" accounted in all for over 50 per cent of this market. As was observed with regard to privatised enterprises' stocks as a whole, over 90 per cent of the preferred stocks are issued by firms in the three dominating branches: oil-and gas-extracting industry, communication and energy. The absolute leader in 1996 was the preferred stocks of joint-stock company "Lenenergo", for which price quotations grew by 20 times over that year. The quotations of the preferred stocks of joint-stock companies "Surgutneftegas", "MGTS" and "Lukoil" grew by 10-15 times in 1996.

The admittance of the preferred stocks of a number of issuers to trading in the RTS in 1996 was driven by growing investor interest. In the spring of 1996 preferred stocks of 16 issuers were added to RTS' listings, while another 33 issuers were included in the RTS-2 listing. In February 1997, for the first time, first level ADR were issued on the basis of the preferred stocks of joint-stock oil company "Lukoil".

The price for the preferred stocks of the majority of companies with a liquid market normally ranges between 50-85 per cent of the price for their regular stocks, and the price for the preferred stocks of some regional energy systems is, in fact, equal to the price of their regular stocks. The rise in market price is not the sole indicator of the preferred stocks' attractiveness. The majority of Russian enterprises steadily pay dividends on the preferred stocks. According the data of a survey conducted by the Federal Commission on Securities Market, 84 per cent of the enterprises studied paid dividends on preferred stock on 1995 profits, while only 52 per cent of those enterprises paid dividends on common stock.

Corporate bonds of the Russian joint-stock companies are still unpopular among investors. According to the FCSM's data, of 13, 345 issues of corporate securities in 1994, the share of corporate bonds accounted for only 0.26 per cent, and in 1995 it accounted for 0.68 per cent. In 1994 the proportional weight of bond issues in the nominal value of total issues of corporate securities was 2.0 per cent and in 1995 0.7 per cent.

Although the ability to maintain corporate control in the hands of existing shareholders is a clear advantage of the issue of the corporate bonds (non-convertible bonds) as compared to equity, the issuer has to assume certain obligations relating to the repayment of the bonds as stipulated in the conditions set out in the terms of issue. However, only companies which have a steady, high profitability can afford this. In addition to the above, in order to maintain the securities' attractiveness to investors, the conditions of the issue must not be less attractive than those offered by other bond issuers(including the government).

In general terms, between 1992 to 1995 the RF Ministry of Finance registered 177 issues of non-bank corporate bonds, the overall nominal value of which amounted to RUR 1.15 trillion. Stable growth in the number of issues as well as in the average size of corporate bond issues became characteristics of the said period. At the same time the clear decrease in the both aforementioned indicators were noted in 1996 (18 issues), which the experts attribute to the specifics of the political situation in Russia in 1996. In terms of regions, the major volume of sales of corporate bonds in 1996 (over 90 per cent) was registered in Moscow.

Despite the general positive qualitative developments, one cannot at present regard the corporate bonds issued as " classical" securities, *i.e.* meeting international standards, at least, from the formal viewpoint. Thus, among issues in 1996 it was the securities of RAO "Vysokoskorostnye Magistrali" which were the absolute leader in the stock market (where over 95 per cent of the overall volume of trade in corporate bonds takes place). At the same time, it is hard to classify these securities as pure corporate bonds. Between 1994-1995 the biggest volume of corporate bonds was issued by firms in the branches of communication, oil and gas extracting and housing construction. The obligations were mostly "goods-linked" (installation of telephone line, etc.) or linked to housing projects.

The instances of an issue of corporate eurobonds and convertible securities by non-banks are still rather rare. Among issuers, who expecting to issue their own eurobonds, one can single out joint-stock company "Mosenergo", joint-stock company "MGTS" (Moscow City Telephone Network), RAO "Gasprom", oil company "Rosneft", joint-stock company "Rostelekom". The best known example (if not the only one) of an issue of corporate convertible securities is the issue of convertible bonds by joint-stock company "Oil Company "Lukoil", which was made in compliance with the specially adopted normative documents.

In the majority of cases, according to FCSM's data, non-bank corporate bond issues were undertaken by joint-stock companies with a number of employees over 3000, *i.e.* by relatively large companies. In addition, joint-stock companies with government or municipal ownership in excess of 25 per cent (usually-38-51 per cent) were issuers of this type of corporate securities. This is related to the legislative restrictions in Article 28, p.4 of the Law "On Joint-Stock Companies", which states that a joint-stock company does not have the right to issue additional stocks (for example, for the purpose of attracting investment), if the share of the government ownership exceeds 25 per cent, without keeping the amount of the government/municipal share unchanged. In such a situation, the joint-stock company has an opportunity to attract capital through bond issues.

1.2 Major qualitative characteristics of the current stage.

a) Macroeconomic and political situation

The relative stabilisation of the rouble and slowdown of the inflation rate and the concomitant decline in the GKO yields observed between 1995 to 1997 have decreased the attractiveness of the usual investment choices for the agents of the Russian financial market (see Charts 3-4). That is why one should expect -- other conditions being equal -- a growing inflow of capital to the corporate securities market. This allows one to draw three important conclusions:

Firstly, the on-going migration of financial resources between the two largest segments of the market says something about the market's growing integration, which manifests itself, among other things, in closer correlation between GKO yields and quotations of the most liquid stocks. At the same time it means that the corporate securities market increases its focus on domestic realities and not only on Western investors.

Secondly, on account of the relatively restricted supply of liquid securities in the present market, the growing demand on the part of both foreign and Russian investors establishes a relatively firm basis for further rises in stocks' price quotations and the market's capitalisation as a whole.

Thirdly, the stocks of different enterprises are becoming the object of investor attention as a short term financial instrument (and not only as an instrument for establishing control).

It should also be pointed out that the state of affairs in the market is still strongly influenced by the political situation in this country. There have been some recent situations in which the price of a specific company's stock rose at a point in time when -- simultaneously -- both favourable political news and negative data on the company's financial status arrived. The opposite viewpoint, according to which in 1997 the Russian security market became indifferent to political events, is sometimes heard, however.

b) Legislation

The adoption of several fundamental legislative acts between 1995 to 1996, namely, the Civil Code of the Russian Federation, Federal Laws " On securities market" and "On joint-stock companies" have had a positive impact on the development of the market.

The current legal base for regulating the market and protecting investors' rights also comprises a number of the Presidential Decrees (Complete programme of the measures on protecting the investors' and shareholders' rights approved by the Decree of the President of RF # 408 of 21 March 1996; the Concept of the development of the securities market in the Russian Federation approved by the Decree of the President of RF # 1008 of 1 July 1996, etc.) normative acts of the FCSM of Russia, the Central Bank of the Russian Federation and other bodies.

In general terms, by the autumn of 1997, the normative basis for the securities market has already been established. At present the priorities are perfection and concretization of this basis as well as efficient co-ordination between legislature and policies implemented by different authorities.

c) State of the market and infrastructure

The Russian market is still dominated by large-scale institutional investors, who operate with significant capital and large portfolios. Although the current restrictions for small-size investors hamper liquidity, a market of large professionals is more stable.

According to some estimates, in 1997 private foreign capital (investment banks and funds) and Russian enterprises-issuers of stock play the major roles as investors. The role of the Russian commercial banks is growing in importance although it is still fairly insignificant in the investment process (Starostenkova, 1997).

The predominance of "over-the-counter" (OTC) trading is typical. It manifests itself both in the course of market transactions (within the framework of RTS and in the "telephone" market), and via direct transactions with significant blocks of shares upon the parties' mutual agreement, which are not recorded in trade and information systems. At the same time one can also talk about some renewal of the stock-exchange trading: trading with corporate securities has been commenced on the Moscow Interbank Currency Exchange (MICEX), and the Moscow Stock Exchange was established and has started operating.

Chart 3. **Weekly consumer price index for 1995-1997**

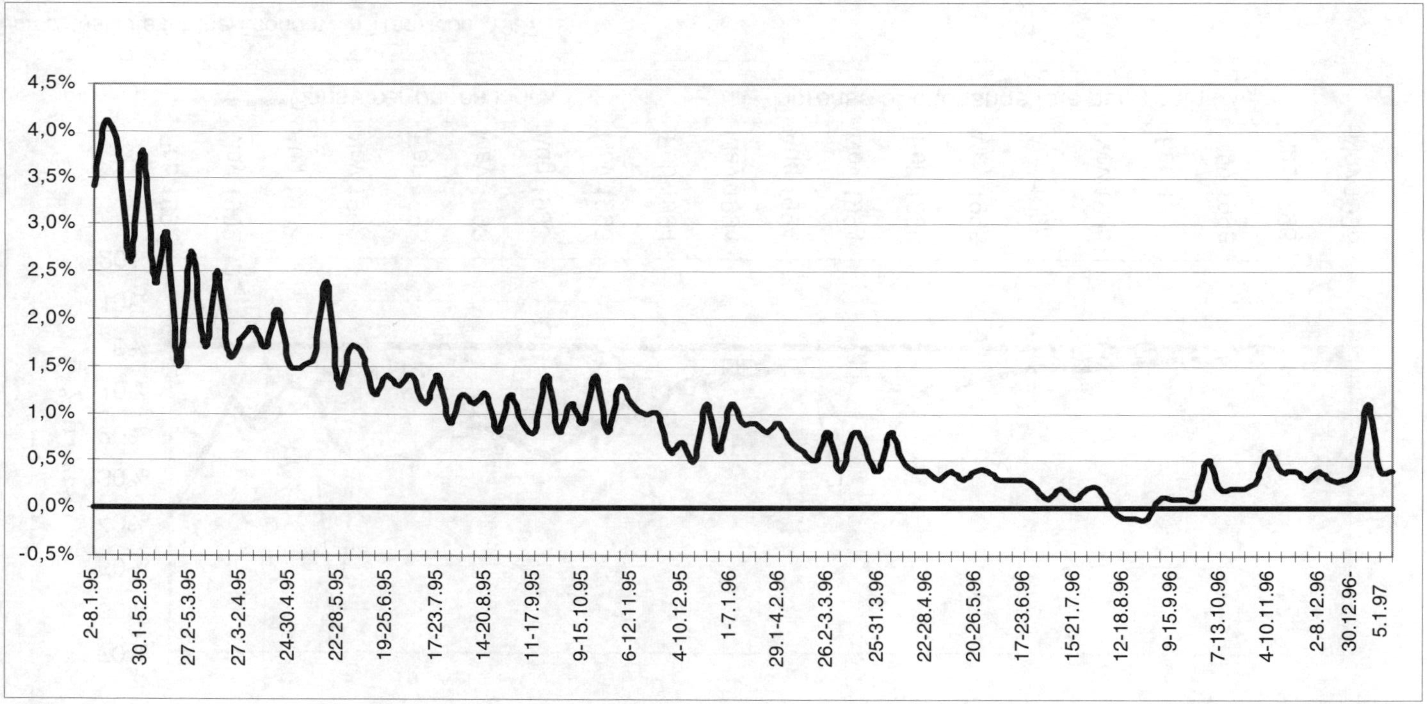

Source: Institute for the Economy in Transition, 1997

Chart 4. **Consumer prices index and increase of official US$ exchange rate per month**

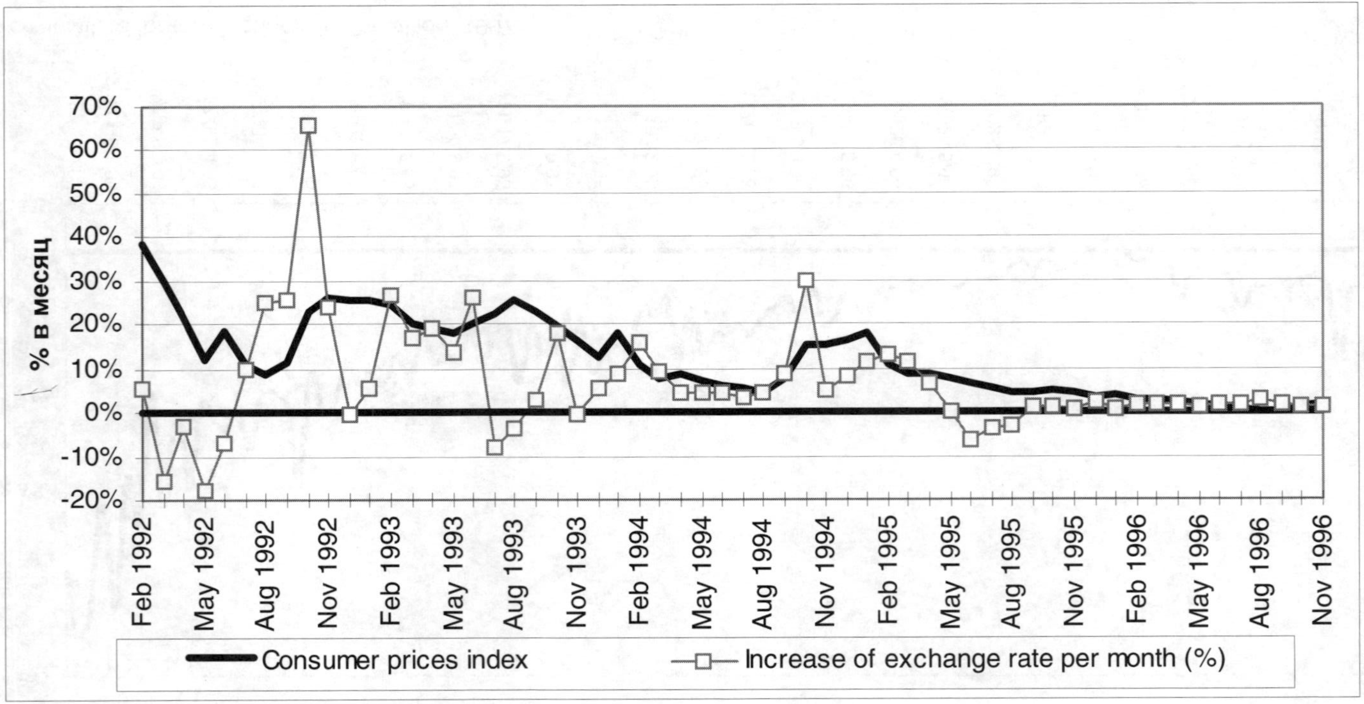

Source: Institute for the Economy in Transition, 1997

A major share of market turnover is accounted for by strategic investors' purchasing controlling blocks of privatised enterprises' stock. At the same time the rise in foreign portfolio investors' interest in the Russian stock became a characteristic of the period between 1996-1997. Although the interest is still concentrated on the most liquid blue chips, there is a clear expansionary trend in professional agents' interest in the stock of "second echelon" companies.

According to some current estimates, in 1997 investors are showing preference for these "second echelon" stocks, which receive high marks according to major criteria such as: investment attractiveness, the level of transparency, quality of the services provided by the depository (custody, registrar); the ownership distribution of the authorised capital (if the structure is stable, this often decreases investor interest in the company), the attitude of the company's executives towards outsiders as shareholders, the level of the local market's development, acceptability of the financial and economic prospects.

The degree of transparency provided by the issuer is considered to be the most crucial factor. As a rule, the company with a favourable score in this respect, is positive to outside investors. Thus, many regional energy and communication companies have foreign shareholders on their lists. At the same time the regional communication companies' relationship with their controlling owner -"Svyazinvest holding"-is often problematic (Volkova, 1997).

In general terms one may note the following trend: given that previously investing was made "into Russia", in 1996-1997 investors paid more attention to specific firms' concrete prospects. This means that, firstly, there is a significant basis for further extension of the Russian market's liquidity and, secondly, it is the concrete information concerning the corporations' activity (profit, joint projects, issue of ADRs, etc.), which becomes important for the development of the market for their stock.

Positive shifts have taken place in the market infrastructure. Some specific risks notably decreased, especially with regard to the running of registers and protecting shareholders' rights in the course of additional issues of stocks. By the summer of 1997 there were about 200 licensed registrars, 6 licensed depositories, the formation of the system of self-regulating organisations of market participants is under way. The Russian Trading System was the first trading system which obtained a license from the FCSM of Russia. As of early March 1997, the RTS listing comprised common stock of 58 issuers and preferred stock of 16 issuers, while in the RTS-2 listing there were, respectively, 60 and 33 issuers. This has contributed to the rise in liquidity of corporate securities. The preparation for the establishment of a central depository is under way, though there are some conflicts around this process.

d) International recognition and foreign investors.

The actual volume of foreign investment into Russian companies' stock cannot be precisely estimated. Suffice it to refer to the data of Goskomstat of the Russian Federation and expert estimates by participants in the market (the latter are undoubtedly more realistic) presented in Table 1.

Table 1. **Some estimations of the volume of foreign investment to the Russian companies' stock**

	Goskomstat of RF	Estimations of the participants in the market
1994	0	US$1.5-2.5 billion
1995	US$30 mln.	US$1-1.5 billion
1996	US$45.4 mln..	US$1.5-2 billion.
1997	-	US$3-4 billion (estimated)

The most important qualitative distinction of the current stage of the market development is the growing international recognition of the Russian market with parallel increased access for various categories of Russian issuers to international financial markets. Among the most important events in this field, one should note Russia's joining the International Organisation of Security Commissions (IOSCO), simultaneous receipt of the Moody's, Standard & Poor's and IBCA's ratings, successful issues of "eurobonds", publication of the IFC Global Russia Index, issues of ADRs/GDRs performed by a number of companies (as of early March 1997, ADRs and GDRs were issued on the stock of 14 Russian companies and another 10 ADR issuing programmes were under way), a Russian company's entering the listing of the New York stock exchange, US SEC's recognition of some Russian banks as " reliable foreign depositories" etc.

All the above has resulted in an inflow of "fresh" foreign capital to the Russian stock market in 1997 (importantly, from conservative investors, as well). At the same time, the situation in the stock market is still heavily dependent on foreign investors' orders, since the latter are strongly focused on the securities of certain enterprises. The global funds' portfolio investment, is in turn cyclical, depending on the term and volume of the capital earmarked "for Russia" and the political juncture. Thus, for example, a sharp rise in Russian blue chips' price quotations in July 1997 was directly related to the fact that the global funds had concluded a half-year reporting period of their activity and proceeded to increase their limits for investment in one of the world's most dynamic emerging markets. Nevertheless, it is worth noting that the steady rise in price quotations in the first 8 months of 1997 practically for the first time may be attributed to the inflow of "free" Russian money.

According to a survey conducted by the FCSM with 200 executives of managing companies of Western investment funds, which invest in emerging markets (January 1997), during the course of 1996 the structure of ongoing and planned portfolio investment changed in favour of long-term investment. This reflects a substantial change in investors' incentives. According to the FCSM's estimates, over 2/3 of foreign investors investing in Russian securities or planning to do so within the forthcoming 6 months, target investments for a term of over two years. By today, the short term speculative focus of investment in Russian securities is characteristic for less than 1/3 of foreign investors, while between 1994 to 1995 it was that group of investors which provided the overwhelming part of the foreign portfolio investment in this country.

The geographical diversification of the interest in Russia on the part of foreign investors showed itself in the fact that among current and potential investors the share of European financial institutions, especially British and German ones, has grown very significantly. The latter seems of particular significance, taking into account the traditional conservatism of the German financial institutions.

2. Struggle for control, insiders, and their impact on market development.

With some reservations one may single out at least the following three major stages of redistribution of property in the industrial sector of Russia's economy since the beginning of "perestroika":

- the spontaneous period from 1988 to 1991: at that time, when the USSR Law "On state-owned enterprises" came into force, with a temporary leasing and co-operative boom, state-owned enterprises' assets in one form or another were very actively transferred to the private sector;

- the "mass privatisation" stage between 1992 and 1994: at that period of time, using a voucher scheme, insiders and outside shareholders gained control over a large part of equity and private ownership rights were established for the thousands of joint-stock companies operating in Russia;
- the stage of the struggle for control over newly formed joint-stock companies, including redistribution and concentration of newly acquired property rights, which began in 1993-1994 and continues to this day. [1]

As a result, by today a certain structure of ownership of privatised enterprises' stock has taken shape, which, so far, may be characterised as "intermediary" and relatively unstable (see: Radygin, 1996a-b).

Among the typical forms of this redistribution arising over the period 1993-1997, the following were notable:

1. the aggressive or " agreed-upon" purchase of stocks at secondary market (from employees, investment institutions, brokers, and banks);

2. active lobbying for transactions with blocks of stocks which so far remained in control of Federal and regional authorities;

3. voluntary or administrative and compulsory involving holding companies or financial-industrial groups.

The common methods most characteristic of the 1993-1995 period of post-privatisation redistribution of equity were connected to transactions (quasi-deals) in primary and secondary markets (naturally, with correction for "specifics" of the transitional economy and the "specific" role of the state). Although it is still not possible to claim any significant progress regarding the protection of shareholders' rights in 1997, it was during this period, between 1993-1995, that violations of corporate law, resulting from the struggle for control, acquired their "wildest" forms (dilution of "alien" shareholders' stocks, etc.).

In essence the basic conflict of those years was one between old managers fighting desperately to keep their positions and potential "occupants" seeking control. The majority of Russian enterprises were involved in this struggle, for different reasons: financial flows and profit generation, book-keeping, export orientation, land and other real estate, market segments or branch specialisation which are of interest for a foreign company of the same profile, etc.

The clash of interests manifested itself in the discrimination of certain rights of investors stipulated in the respective Russian legislation. It is possible to single out typical scenarios of violation of investors' rights as follows:

- dilution of the equity owned by the investors " from outside";
- violation of the right to receive dividend payments (for example, the dividends which were announced and approved at the meeting of the shareholders of a joint-stock company, are not paid or the general meeting of shareholders makes a decision to pay dividends only to a part of shareholders (usually the employees in the same joint-stock company);
- the shareholders are not notified at all, or are notified in an untimely fashion (in contrast to what is stipulated in the Law in this respect), or they are not notified of the substantial issues of the meeting's agenda;
- the board of directors, which was approved in the course of the incorporation of the joint-stock company, is not re-elected at the general meeting, as would have been required by the respective legislation;
- investors-outsiders are not allowed, under various pretexts, to join the board of directors;
- the company resists an independent audit of the joint-stock company's activity, demanded by the investors-outsiders;
- the procedural requirements for voting at general meetings are observed.

It also frequently occurs that managers of joint-stock companies engage in an uncontrolled "pumping-out" of the companies' resources to their personally owned companies or to their bank accounts in Russia and abroad, or, at best, pay themselves extremely high salaries (while, at the same time ordinary employees-shareholders remain with their salaries and wages unpaid for many months and/or dividends are not paid out). This practice may also be described as a violation of shareholders' rights. The reason for such practices is first of all the unstable situation in the field of corporate governance, which encourages the management to arrange for such "golden parachutes".

Some data on violations of existing legislation committed by major issuers, whose stocks' circulation has a significant impact on the development of the market, are presented in Table 2.

Table 2. **The issuers' violation of existing legislation as a percentage of the number of issuers**
(according to the FCSM' inspections)

	107 issuers		52 issuers	
	Sept. 1994	Dec. 1995	Dec. 1995	Dec. 1996
Violations of dividends payment obligations	54	50	36	69
Discrepancies between the register of shareholders and primary distribution	24	22	10	19
The register kept by the issuer with a number of shareholders exceeding 500	22	21	7	13
Violations related to the execution and issue of the documents proving ownership rights	21	20	14	27
Keeping the register with violations of the stated term	19	18	5	10
Violations connected to assignation of keeping the register	19	18	16	31
Violations connected to the issuer's redemption and purchase of his own stock	16	15	11	21
Violations of procedure for holding the general meeting of shareholders	10	9	10	19
Violations of procedure relating to additional issue and registration of shares	6	6	6	12

Source: Federal Commission for the Securities Markets.

The specific problem is the impact of the emerging ownership structure of equity resulting from the mass privatisation on the development of the Russian stock market. The obvious driving force behind the transformation of ownership structure is the ongoing struggle for control in joint-stock companies, which is observed at many Russian enterprises. According to current estimates, the struggle for control has ended only in some 30 per cent of Russian privatised enterprises. The growing "invasion" of outsiders and concentration of ownership will remain as major trends for a typical privatised enterprise even after the year 2000.

In general terms, the processes described above to a large extent affect the stock market's development, by intensifying the current numerous problems:

- the processes have a dual effect on the liquidity of the market of specific enterprises' stock
- (on the one hand, the liquidity, though a one-sided one, is growing as the struggle for control intensifies, but, on the other hand, the stock market's liquidity may drop sharply, as this struggle ends, since both the interest in stock remaining in circulation and, by definition, the market disappear;
- they hamper the development of market infrastructure (for example, unwillingness to submit the registers to independent registrars, non-acceptance of the institution of nominees);
- they provoke mass violations of shareholders' rights, especially those of small-size and "outside" shareholders, which strengthen and accentuate the general problem of protecting shareholders' rights, both in legal terms and in terms of direct interference by authorised bodies of the state;
- they preserve the lack of transparency of the market (in terms of issuers and transactions), due to the fact that managers reluctantly disclose information on joint-stock companies;
- they, accordingly, form an obstacle (among other factors) to the introduction of international standards of book-keeping;
- they lead to the absolute domination of the OTC market, since it is seen as most disadvantageous for both brokers and their clients to disclose prices and other information;
- they are a cause of the lack of serious interest in new issues of stock.

Many of the aforementioned problems are of an objective nature and probably relatively long-lasting. This is related primarily to the fact that in many enterprises the process of the struggle for control has not yet ended, with all the resultant consequences for the stock market. At the same time progress in overcoming many of these problems to a large extent depends on the amount and detail of state regulation of the market.

3. Providing transparency and protecting shareholders' rights.

The legislation of the period 1991-1995, relating to disclosure of information on companies-issuers, required a relatively small volume of information on enterprises. However, "The concept of the development of the security market in the Russian Federation" approved by the Presidential Decree # 1008 of 1 July, 1996, states that one of the government's crucial tasks in promoting the development of the stock market is to increase the degree of market transparency.

Meanwhile, the basic documents setting out the requirements with respect to disclosure of information now are the above-mentioned two Federal Laws "On joint-stock companies" and "On the securities market". In compliance with Article 30 of the Law "On the securities market", the disclosure of information is understood as "ensuring its accessibility to all parties concerned, regardless of the purpose of obtaining such an information, under a procedure , which guarantees its location and receipt."

In compliance with Article 92 of the Law "On joint-stock companies", the joint-stock company is liable to publish every year in mass-media accessible for all the shareholders of the said company, the company's annual statement, its balance sheet, and its profit and loss account.

The Law "On the securities market" contains detailed requirements with respect to the following matters:

- the decision concerning the issue of securities;
- certificate of securities;
- prospectus of issue;
- information subject to disclosure due to the issue of securities;
- final report on the issue of securities.

The Law also comprises (Chapter 7) the general requirements for all the cases of the disclosure of current information on the part of the issuer of securities, owner of securities and professional participant in the market. In compliance with Article 30 of the Law "On the securities market", the quarterly report (including the financial report for the last three financial years and as of the end of the current complete quarter) must be forwarded to the FCSM of Russia or a government body empowered by the Commission. This report must be also presented to owners of the issuer's securities upon their request. The charge for this service must not exceed the costs of producing such a brochure.

In compliance with the said Article of the Law, the issuer is liable to submit to the FCSM of Russia or the government body empowered by the Commission, as well as to disclosing in printed media statements concerning any significant events and activity relating to the issuer's financial and economic activity (reorganisation of the issuer, information on an issue of securities, paid dividends on securities, changes in the list of the shareholders owning 20 per cent and over of the authorised capital, etc.).

In compliance with the Article 16 of the Law " On book-keeping" (#129-FZ of 21 November, 1996), open joint-stock companies, banks and other credit institutions, insurance companies, stock-exchanges, investment funds and other funds established on the basis of private or public capital contributions, are liable to produce an annual statement of accounts not later than by 1 June of the year following the accounting year. At the same time the publicity of such a statement of accounts is understood as its publication in magazines and newspapers available to users of such statements of accounts, or as the distribution of brochures and other kinds of publications, which may contain such statements of accounts, among the said users.

The specific mechanisms of disclosing information are regulated by other normative acts, primarily by the Resolutions of the FCSM of Russia.[2] The main direction of the FCSM's policy in this field has been to extend the amount of information, which is subject to publication in the prospectus of issue for the public placement of securities, in order to attain international standards. At the same time a crucial task for the FCSM must also be to improve the quality of information provided, in addition to increasing its availability.

At the same time introducing Western practice of compulsory disclosure of information has proved a double-edged weapon for the market. Such compulsory disclosure of information sharply restricts the right to retain privacy and commercial secret. In particular, in the securities market the disclosed information has often turned out to be used rather for competitors' scrutiny than for investors' analysis. Due to this fact, it is important to keep a sensible balance between commercial secret and necessary amount of disclosed information when the respective regulating norms are being introduced.

In March 1997 the decision was taken that the most rigid requirements for the disclosure of information, primarily with regard to financial and economic data and advertising of the issues, will be imposed on the 202 largest Russian issuers. At the same time, the secondary issues of the said companies will be registered not by the Ministry of Finance, but by the FCSM (in the department of regulation of issuance and circulation of securities and by the FCSM's regional divisions), while other enterprises' issues will be registered by the territorial branches of FCSM.

As to information on transactions in securities, between 1993-1995 the majority of securities were sold and bought on the OTC market, without any published information nor technical means for announcing quotations for sales and purchases. If quotations were ever listed in any system, they were at best indicative (informational). The establishment of RTS in May 1995 (and the introduction of firm quotations) has resulted in a growth in volume of information, especially notable in the recent period. However, this has not been sufficient to keep up with market growth. Certain improvements in this area may be realised, when the Technical Center for the Disclosure of Information, provided for by the Resolution of the FCSM, starts to operate.

In compliance with the Law "On securities market" (Article 7), professional participants in the market must, in the course of offering and/or announcing the bid and/or offer price for issued securities, disclose all the general information he possess, which is subject to disclosure on the part of the issuer of the said securities. Alternatively, the said participant is liable to report the lack of such information if not at his disposal. As to the requirements for market participants to produce price quotation reports or reports on transactions (with the exception of large volume transactions in the same type of securities), nothing is stipulated in the Law in this respect.

Transactions with large volumes of the same type of securities will be subject to regulation on the part of the FCSM and self-regulating organisations of professional participants in the market. At the same time, in compliance with the Complex Programme of Measures for Securing the Rights of Depositors and Shareholders (approved by the Presidential Decree # 408 of 21 March 1996), without membership in any licensed self-regulatory organisations (SRO), it is impossible to obtain the obligatory license for the conduct of professional activity.

In general terms, one may state that the informational environment has been improving between 1996-1997. In particular, for past meetings of shareholders, issuers have been compelled to report at least a summary of decisions taken. As to enterprises, the main incentive encouraging them to disclose the required information is their gradual understanding of the role of transparency in attracting real investment.

Nevertheless, the problem of lack of transparency is still very acute. According to the FCSM's survey of the executives of Russian privatised enterprises conducted in 1996, 15 per cent of enterprises endeavour not to distribute any information concerning themselves, 25 per cent provide information to creditors and publish it in the press, 87 per cent provide it to shareholders, and only 2 per cent of enterprises provide their information to all the parties concerned.

Responding to the questionnaire, the users of information from outside also emphasised that obtaining financial information directly from enterprises is very problematic, while at the same time almost half of the surveyed investment institutions acknowledge the fact that the financial statement is the most crucial factor in their investment decisions (for reference: less than 1/3 of them put the results of their own research in the first place, and only very few of the institutions prefer to consult publications in the press).

However, the respondents note that the statements are not available and enterprises are reluctant to provide even their annual reports, to say nothing about quarterly reports. This problem arises even with regard to obtaining financial information from the enterprises whose stocks are traded within the RTS. To the extent that enterprises do not reveal the information on themselves, the investment institutions use data from Russian and foreign information agencies ("AK&M", Reuters, Skate , Interfax, "Prime"). The overwhelming majority of investors emphasise that the quarterly reports are unavailable, thus leaving them no opportunity to follow the enterprises' development during the course of the year. Another problem, according to the investors, is that the information is non-operational, in the sense that even if financial accounts do appear in the press or in an information agency's data base, it happens with too long a delay.

The link between this problem and development of market liquidity is obvious. It is known that the degree of liquidity of an issuer's securities indicates both the general level of the enterprise's development, as well as its management's commitment to the disclosure of information on the enterprise's production and financial activity. This includes the regular conduct of financial and production audits, preparation of quarterly reports concerning the enterprise's activity, maintenance of accounts in accordance with international standards, etc.

All the above undoubtedly assists in improving the rating as well as the liquidity of the enterprise's stock. However, this only constitutes a necessary condition for the establishment of liquid security markets, but not a sufficient condition (as the example of such issuers as joint-stock company "Krasny Oktyabr" or "joint-stock company "GAZ", shows : they are among the most open companies in the Russian market in terms of information, but at the same time the level of their stock's liquidity is relatively low).

Among other policies favourable for both investors and professional participants in the market one should also mention the following:

- establishment of independent registrars;
- simplified procedure for re-registration of ownership rights to securities (*e.g.* the branch network of transfer-agents under the registrar, or the system of remote terminals, reasonable tariffs for the recording of changes in ownership rights for securities in the register of shareholders, etc.);
- absence in the Statute of the joint-stock company of any restrictions imposed on potential investors or on the share of their contribution to the authorised capital, which to certain extent may result in the decrease in the securities' market liquidity;
- issuer's active policy with regard to potential investors;
- promotion of securities in foreign financial markets, primarily in the form of the issue of depository receipts on the basis of underlying Russian securities (ADR, GDR, RDC).

One may also give examples of the direct negative influence of the scarcity of information on Russian issuers, both on the development of the market and on shareholders' rights. Thus, the determining factor of the preferred stock's market value is the expected monetary flow (dividend) on the stock, which, in its turn, depends on the issuer's current and future profitability. The lack of true financial information concerning the issuer (in particular, current information) increases the risks of investing in these securities and, consequently, decreases the stock's quotation value and extends the spread between the bid and offer prices for the stock, which has a negative impact on the stock's liquidity.

The potential of acquiring voting rights on the preferred stock may have a significant impact on its market quotation. If the board of directors take a decision concerning non-payment or partial payment of dividends (the meeting of shareholders does not have a right to increase the dividend proposed by the board of directors), a change in the balance of forces with regard to the owners of voting stock may result.

This fact can be well illustrated by the situation at the former subsidiary of "Surgutneftegas" oil company -joint-stock company "Nefto-Kombi". The meeting of the company's shareholders decided not to pay dividends on the preferred stock for 1995.[3] In compliance with the Law, the preferred stock thus received the status of voting stock. The balance of forces among the owners of the voting stocks had changed, and in August when the new meeting of shareholders was held, a decision concerning a new issue of stocks was taken. This issue decreased the share of "Surgutneftegas" from 38 to 11 per cent. Another example is an attempted private placement of shares of joint-stock company "Surgutneftegas" which could have resulted in the parent company buying all of the issue (The stocks were purchased at their nominal value, which is approximately 2.5 times lower than the respective quotations in RTS). According to some analysts, the reason for such an attempt was the concern that the company would not be able to announce dividends on the preferred stock, and the latter would be transformed to voting stock. Thus, the voting preferences of preferred stock owners may become an important factor in the running of a company.

4. Conclusion

Further development of the security markets in Russia is a vitally important condition for enterprises' obtaining access to investment resources. Without progress in the sphere of securities markets, the further advancement of the Russian economic reforms may be put in jeopardy. In general terms, the significance of the securities market as a mechanism for the mobilisation of investment resources will be growing in tandem with qualitative shifts in the development of the market itself.

According to some estimates (see Table 3), by the year 2000 the aggregate capitalisation of the Russian market may reach US$150-200 bln., and the securities turnover in the secondary market -- US$30-80 bln. Over this period the role of the corporate segment of the market will be growing at the expense of the state securities market, the scope for issuing corporate securities and secondary issues will be increased, and a stable group of first-class issuers-Russian "blue chips" will take shape. Nevertheless the Russian securities market will need a long time to turn into a reliable, stable and transparent financial mechanism. Even in countries with highly developed markets the regulatory bodies constantly face problems related to new financial products and experience the need for improving market regulation in the direction of efficiency and impartiality.

Table 3. **General forecasts for the market for corporate securities: quantitative characteristics**

Characteristics (year end)	1995	1996	2000
Securities turnover in the secondary market, billion $	5	5.5	30-80
Aggregate capitalisation of joint-stock companies operating in the market (minus banks), billion $	10-12	35-50	150-200
Securities in active commercial turnover, billion $	5	5.5	25-50
Net foreign portfolio investments, billion $	1	1.5	10-11
Ratio of deals settled inside Russia (A) and outside it (B): A/B	1/3	1/3	10/1
Number of privatised enterprises -open joint-stock companies, (thousands)	25	28-30	30-32
Share of 200 major enterprises in industrial output, percent	70-75	70-75	70-75
Number of privatised enterprises where the "struggle for control" is over, percent of the overall number of privatised enterprises	20	25-30	50

Source: FCSM, author's estimate.

Important conditions for further development are:

- a favourable general macroeconomic and political climate;
- decrease in the yields on government securities;
- elimination of various problems relating to currency transactions in connection with foreign portfolio investment;
- continued reform of enterprises (governance of the state-owned portfolios, residual privatisation, etc.)
- implementation of effective bankruptcy procedures;
- change in the taxation system with regard to investment in securities and other transactions with securities.

NOTES

1. Between late 1995-1997 the new phase of the post-privatization redistribution of property was taking shape. By the initiative of the largest financial groupings and with the active government assistance the largest or the most "interesting" Russian companies became its major objects. This stage is also characterized by usage or at least elaboration of non-trivial technical schemes (loans-for-shares auctions, legalized dilution of government stocks, conversion of debts into securities, sales of debtor debts, trust schemes, purchase of promissory notes, manipulations with dividends on preferred stock, etc.). The core conflict during this stage is obviously the clash of interests between old (in a new corporate "shell", though) natural monopolies, large industrial and extracting structures and new financial and industrial groupings whose expansionist interests became intersected in the course of the redistribution of property (See: Radygin, 1997).

2. Thus, for example, the Resolution of the FCSM of Russia #9 of 7 May 1996 defines the information, which is subject to annual publication by the open joint-stock company in addition to the requirements stipulated in the Article 92 of the Law "On joint-stock companies": the ratio between the value of net assets and the volume of authorized capital, number of shareholders and information on the registrar. On the basis of the experience related to the first issues of the securities performed by the Russian enterprises, the new format of the prospect of the issue of stocks and bonds was designed and approved. In September 1996 with the Statute of the FCS #19 the new "Standards of the issue of stocks in the course of founding of joint-stock companies, additional stocks, bonds and the prospectus on their issue" were approved. In February 1997 with the Statute #8 the "Standards of the issue of stocks and bonds and prospectuses on their issue in the course of reorganization of commercial institutions" were approved. The latter document replaced the Instruction of the Ministry of Finance #2 of 3 March 1992 "On the rules of the issue and registration of securities in the territory of the Russian Federation".

3. According to the data of the survey conducted with the FCSM's Group of Stock Market Monitoring (186 issuers in 55 regions), upon making the decision concerning the non-payment of dividends on the preferred stocks for 1995, voting rights were received by the owners of preferred stock of 13.8 per cent of issuers.

BIBLIOGRAPHY

FCSM (1995): "Problems of the Development of the Securities Market in Russia". Report of the Federal Commission on Securities and the Stock Exchange under the Russian Government. M., July 1995.

FCSM (1997): "Development of the Securities Market in Russia". Report of the Federal Commission on Securities Market. M., June 1997.

GOSKOMSTAT RF (1997): "Social and economic situation in Russia. January-May 1997". Moscow.

IET (1997): "Russian economy in 1996. Trends and outlooks". Moscow, Institute for the Economy in transition.

RADYGIN A. (1996a): "Residual Divestiture Following Mass Privatisation: the Case of Russia". OECD Advisory Group on Privatisation, Ninth Plenary Session, Berlin, 6-7 May 1996. Room Doc. AGP 9/6, pp.1-22.

RADYGIN A. (1996b): "Securities Markets Development and its Relationship to Corporate Governance in Russia". Paris, OECD: DAFFE/MC/EW (96)25, 1996, pp. 2-79.

RADYGIN A. (1997): "Corporate Governance Through the Banks: The Experience in Russia". OECD Advisory Group on Privatisation, Eleventh Plenary Meeting "Banks and Privatisation". Rome, September 18-19, 1997

STAROSTENKOVA E. (1997): "The experts make a prognosis for the stable growth of trading at the stock market". Finansovye izvestya, N 12.

VOLKOVA V. (1997): "Shares of the regional issuers". Ekonomika i zgizn, N 21.

Section III

INSTITUTIONAL AND RETAIL SECTORS AND THE DEVELOPMENT OF NEW INSTRUMENTS

Chapter 10

INSTITUTIONAL INVESTORS, PENSION REFORM AND EMERGING SECURITIES MARKETS

by
Hans J. Blommestein
Head of Financial Affairs Division, OECD

1. Introduction

Institutional investors have been growing in size dramatically over the past decades. Total assets under management of OECD institutional investors rose from 38 per cent of GDP in 1981 to around 106.5 per cent in 1995. The increasing importance of institutional investors as holders of financial assets means that their impact on the functioning of financial markets is steadily growing. Vice versa, their reliance on well-functioning of financial markets has also increased. In most OECD countries, institutional saving institutions -- in particular pension funds -- now play a key role in domestic financial systems[1].

The involvement of institutional investors in capital market transactions is increasing in tandem with their growing financial clout. A strong community of institutional investors seems to be a precondition for the development of liquid securities markets with sophisticated financial vehicles. In view of the growing influence that institutional investors exert on the structure and *modus operandi* of capital markets, the importance of capital markets for the real economy, corporate finance, and income security, it may be necessary for policy makers to take a closer look at the functioning and the regulation of these institutions. A full analysis would include the functioning and regulation of the fund management profession, the impact of changes in demography and the regulation of pension schemes on the efficiency of the allocation of savings, the influence of the international portfolio diversification of institutional investors, and the impact of tax regimes on the behaviour of institutional investors. Also the consequences of investment practices of institutional investors for the functioning of financial markets may need to be analysed.

Also in emerging financial markets the importance of institutional investors (both foreign and domestic ones) is steadily increasing. In particular pension reform has been an important factor in developing a domestic institutional sector in emerging market economies. This in turn has been a major force in the further development of securities markets. However, there is still considerable scope for promoting the growth of securities markets through the development of insurance companies and domestic mutual and pension funds. The paper will discuss the range of factors that can stimulate the further development of the domestic institutional sector, in particular through pension system reform measures. In doing so, the development of the institutional sector in emerging market economies will be compared with the experience in the OECD area, focusing in particular on the key factors that have been (and are) driving the growth of OECD institutional investor activities and the impact of institutional investors on securities markets.

In addition, the paper will identify obstacles in the development of the institutional sector in emerging markets and suggest policies to deal with these problems. It will be argued that these policies are also beneficial for the growth of the securities market. However, this is not sufficient. The efficient operation of institutional investors such as pension funds, requires the presence of a supporting securities market infrastructure. The paper will outline the key infrastructural elements and the associated financial policies, at both the micro and macro levels. In addition, attention will be paid to the more general conditions (macroeconomic stability, tax regime, property rights laws, bankruptcy legislation, privatisation of state-owned enterprises) that can be expected to promote the development of securities markets.

The paper is organised as follows. An overview of the development of institutional investors in the main OECD regions and countries is given in section 2. Section 3 will discuss the development of the institutional sector in emerging market economies in Latin America, Asia and the transition countries in Eastern Europe and the former Soviet Union and its impact on the growth of the securities market. These developments will be compared with the experience in the OECD area by focusing on the key factors that have been (and are) driving the growth of OECD institutional sector activities and the impact of the institutional sector on securities market development. Obstacles in developing an institutional sector in emerging market economies will be identified in section 4. Policies on how to deal with these obstacles will also be suggested, in particular through a programme of pension system reform. Section 5 outlines the key infrastructural elements of a well-functioning securities market and the associated financial policies. In addition, the more general conditions that can be expected to promote the development of securities markets will also be identified. The final section presents policy conclusions.

2. Overview of the growth of the institutional sector in the OECD Area

The importance of institutional investors is steadily increasing. Total institutional assets of the main regions in the OECD area rose from $3.2 trillion in 1981 (*i.e.* 38 per cent of GDP), to $16.3 trillion in 1991 (90 per cent of GDP), to more than $24.3 trillion in 1995 (106.5 per cent of GDP). In the period 1990-95, average annual growth of holding by all categories of institutional investors has been spectacular (see Chart 1).

Chart 1. **Annual average rate of growth of Institutional investors in OECD regions, 1990-1995**

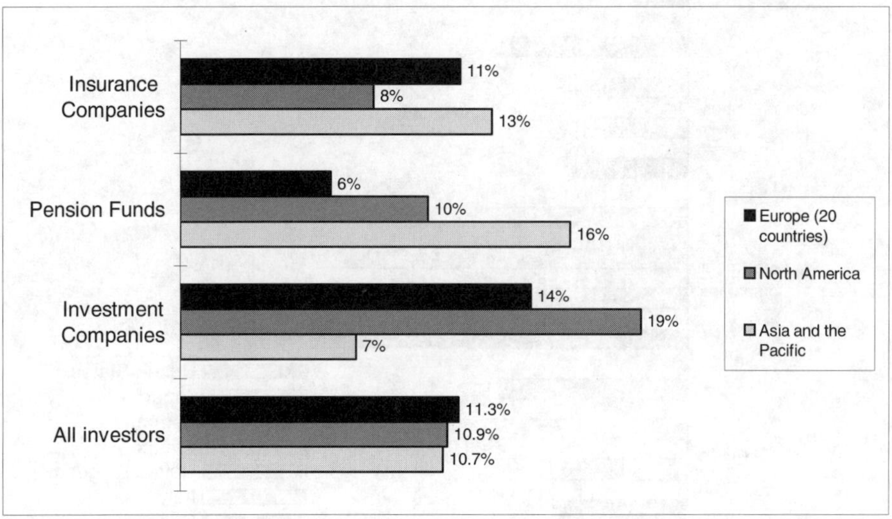

Source: OECD/DAFFE.

Pension funds, insurance companies, and investment companies in the Group of Seven countries had close to $17.5 trillion in assets under management in 1995. In comparison, the global equity market in 1993 amounted to $14.1 trillion, and the total outstanding stock of government debt in the Group of Seven countries was $9 trillion. In the period 1980 -- 1993, the aggregate assets of institutional investors in the United States, Japan, Germany, United Kingdom and Canada have increased by more than 400 per cent and have more than doubled as a percent of GDP ; at the end of 1995, aggregate institutional assets in the G-5 countries were around $20.4 trillion or 119 per cent of GDP. G-7 aggregate institutional assets stood at $21.3 trillion at the end of 1995 or 113 per cent of GDP, while recording strong growth for all categories of institutional investors (see Chart 2). Other OECD countries have recorded similar changes in total assets under management.

Chart 2. **Annual average rate of growth of institutional investors in G-7 countries, 1990-1995**

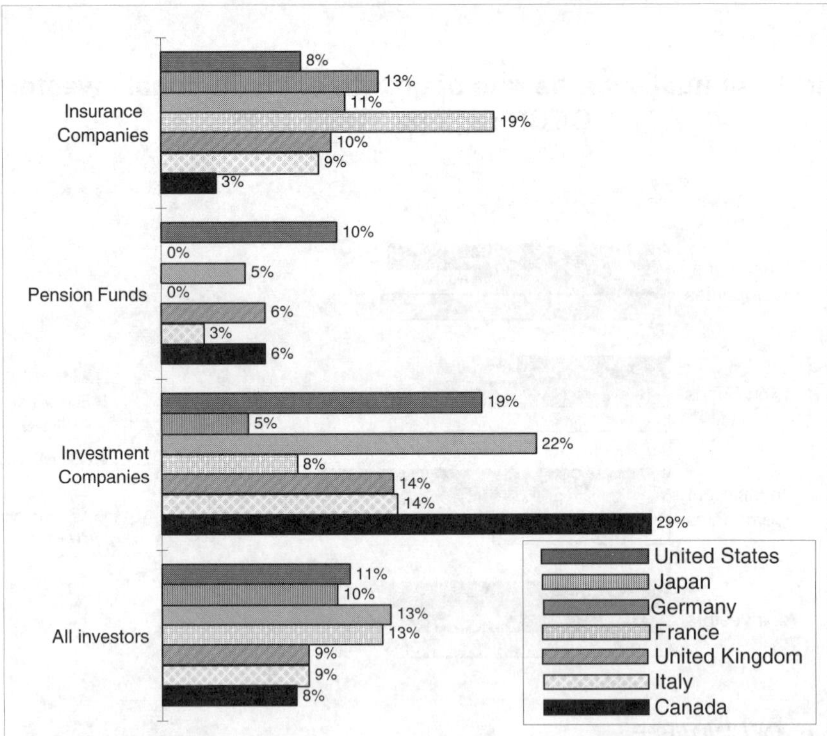

Source: OECD/DAFFE

Chart 3

Change in asset holdings by the different types of Institutional investors 1990-1995

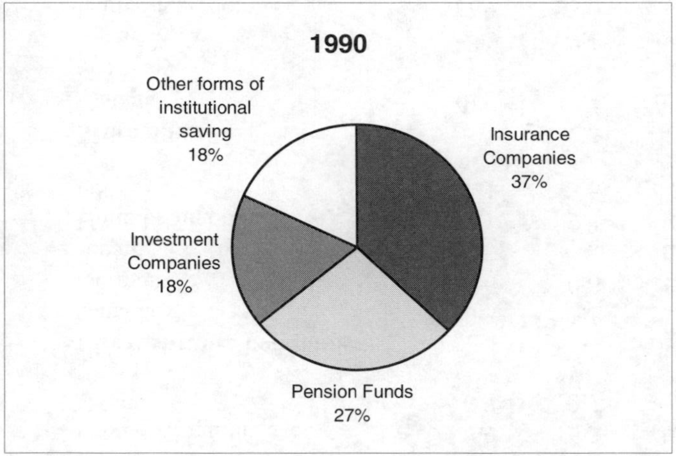

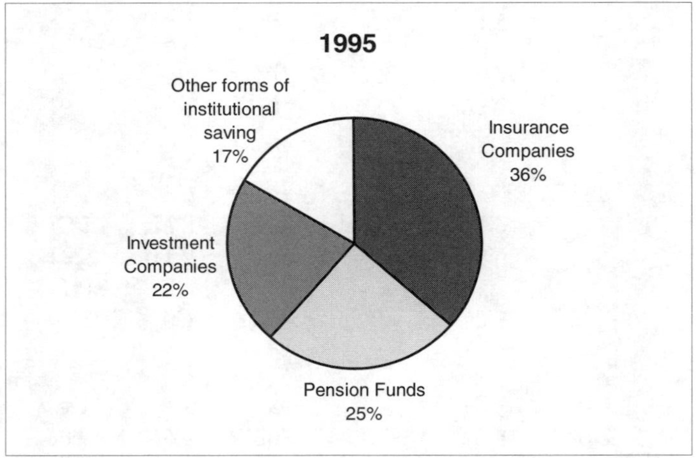

Source: OECD/DAFFE.

Table 1. **Institutional investor's holdings of securities issued by non-residents** (in percent of total assets)

	1980	1988	1990	1991	1992	1993	1994	1995	1996
Pension funds									
Canada[1]	4.6	5.9	6.4	8.6	10.2	11.6	12.9	13.4	..
Germany[2]	..	3.8	4.5	4.5	4.3	4.5	5.0[3]	..	7.7
Japan[2]	0.5	6.3	7.2	8.4	8.4	9.0	..	..	14.9
United Kingdom	7.9	16.3	17.8	20.6	19.5	20.0	19.8	19.8	29.2
USA[2]	0.7	2.7	4.2	4.1	4.6	5.7	..	..	10.4
Life insurance companies									
Canada[1]	0.3	1.5	1.1	1.2	0.7	0.5	0.5	0.3	..
Germany[2]	0.6	0.6	1.0	1.0	..	..	..	..	..
Japan[4]	..	..	13.5	12.5	11.4	9.0	6.7	6.9	..
United Kingdom	4.1	9.4	10.7	12.2	12.4	13.3	13.5	14.2	..
USA[2]	4.1	3.6	3.6	3.6	3.7	..	..	..	5.8
Mutual funds									
Canada[1]	19.9	19.4	17.5	16.1	17.0	20.4	23.6	23.4	..
Germany	..	..	..	..	..	24.8	20.3	20.2	..
Japan[2 5]	..	9.1	7.9	13.0	9.9	..	..	..	..
United Kingdom	17.9	33.0	31.0	34.3	35.2	35.8	36.4	34.5	..
USA[2]	..	..	6.6	..	10.1	..	..	..	..

1. Non-resident investment
2. Source: International Capital markets, IMF, Washington D.C., 1995
3. Source: EFRP
4. Only bills & bonds
5. Investment trusts

Sources: Statistics Canada, Deutsche Bundesbank, Bank of Japan, Office for National Statistics, and OECD staff estimates.

Pension funds and insurance companies have traditionally been the most important institutional investors in OECD capital markets. Although they still control very sizeable (and still growing) asset portfolios, the asset growth of investment companies has been even more spectacular. It is estimated that mutual funds alone accounted for about $3.3 trillion in 1994. Investment companies assets have increased at a much faster pace than have the assets of other institutional investors. Assets of investment funds amounted to $5.2 trillion in 1995, a growth of 19 per cent over the 1990-1995 period; the total share of assets under management of investment funds increased from 18 per cent in 1990 to 22 per cent in 1995 (see Chart 3). Total assets under management of hedge funds stood at an estimated $75-100 billion in 1994, a doubling since 1991, and have further grown to an estimated $236 billion in 1995.

Another noteworthy trend is the changes in the share of foreign securities in the portfolios of institutional investors. There is a gradual but clear trend toward internationally diversified portfolios of pension funds. The behaviour of life insurance companies and investment companies is less clear. In fact, their international diversification shows some decrease in the 1990s. The portfolios of insurance companies are less diversified than those of pension funds. There are important differences in the share of foreign securities in the portfolio of OECD investment companies: *a)* the portfolios of mutual funds in Canada, Germany and the United Kingdom are more internationally diversified than in the United States and Japan; *b)* possibly related to the previous point, US mutual funds show a clear trend toward increased international diversification, while in other countries this trend has levelled off or even declined somewhat; *c)* mutual funds in the larger OECD countries are significantly more diversified than insurance companies and pension funds.

Increasing institutional and functional overlaps

The analysis of these general trends and developments is complicated by the fact that increasingly there are a number of institutional and functional overlaps between the different categories of institutional investors. World-wide deregulation in the financial sector industry and revolutionary technological developments have eroded the statutory and physical barriers between banks, other financial intermediaries and the securities industry. The same forces that are contributing to financial sector integration are also increasingly affecting institutional investors. The process of integrating institutional investor operations into the more "traditional" financial sector activities is being strengthened by the growing influence of the professional fund managers[2].

Firstly, the links between banks and institutional investors have grown stronger over time. Banks have moved on a wide scale into the investment fund business, also in OECD countries with non-universal banking systems. Secondly, deregulation and the liberalisation of the rules governing the operation of financial institutions have encouraged the formation of financial conglomerates in which banks and insurance companies offer the widest possible array of services. This integrated financial activity is often called *bancassurance*. Not all OECD countries allow such integration. For example, in the United States' and Japan's regulations, separating banks from insurance companies is still intact, although bank sales of insurance products have expanded rapidly in recent years in the United States. Thirdly, larger insurance companies that can afford the services of large professional asset management teams are increasingly moving into the investment fund business, either by developing "unit-linked" insurance products or by launching investment fund companies that offer financial products also to clients that are not necessarily insurance policy holders. Another development is the so-called alternative risk transfer market, where insurance risk is transferred on investment instruments such as catastrophe futures. Fourthly, even insurance companies and pension funds that cannot afford a full-fledged professional asset management team have usually strong links to the financial sector because they are employing outside teams to invest and manage their assets.

3. Role of the institutional sector in emerging securities markets

Securities markets in emerging market economies are developing at a rapid pace. It is estimated by the International Finance Corporation (IFC) that in 1996 over 60 developing countries have stock markets, compared with half that number in 1985.[3] The combined stock market capitalisation of these countries has increased more than ten-fold over the past decade, from US$171 billion in 1985 to US$1.9 trillion in 1995. The 18 major emerging market economies that constituted the IFC Emerging Markets Index (IFCI) had a combined market capitalisation in 1996 of US$1.4 trillion, 14 times higher than it was in 1985, while the average market capitalisation rose from 7 to 40 per cent of GDP.

The role of foreign institutional investors

Foreign institutional investors have had a major impact on the development of securities markets[4], notably stock markets. There has been a dramatic increase of portfolio flows from institutional investors into emerging markets, with professionally managed investment funds taking the lead. However, this is a relatively recent phenomenon. It has only been since the mid- 1980s that closed-end investment funds (including country funds) began to invest in emerging stock markets. In 1986, there were only 19 emerging market country funds and 9 regional or global emerging market funds. By 1995, the picture has changed dramatically with 505 country funds and 773 regional and global emerging market funds, of which around 50 per cent open-ended. The combined assets of all closed- and open-end emerging market funds increased from US$1.0 billion in 1986 to US$132 billion in mid-1996 [5].

Pension fund investment in emerging financial markets is an even more recent phenomenon. Total holdings of emerging securities markets assets by OECD institutional investors is relatively low. Surveys suggest that US pension funds and mutual funds currently have about 2 per cent of their assets invested in emerging markets. Emerging market exposure of UK pension funds and mutual funds is somewhat higher (3-4 per cent) but Japanese and continental European institutional investors have negligible emerging market assets in their portfolios. All the evidence points to the fact that all types of institutional investors are much less internationally diversified than the world market portfolio. Several reasons for this home bias have been identified in the literature[6]. Some of them are rational (*e.g.* additional risk) or policy-determined (*e.g.* prudential regulations) but—on balance—there seems to considerable scope for increasing the share of emerging securities market assets in the portfolios of OECD institutional investors. In addition it should be noted that the international investment behaviour of pension funds, insurance companies and investment funds differs because of the different structure of their liabilities (this is in large part reflected in the regulatory structure; see ANNEX I for an overview).

Foreign institutional investors have played an important catalyst role in the improvement of the institutional infrastructure of emerging market economies. This has undoubtedly contributed to the most recent development in which **domestic** institutional investors are starting to play an increasingly important role. However, their role is as yet fairly modest and, therefore, there is considerable scope for an expansion of both the domestic institutional sector and the domestic securities market. In order to get a better understanding of the scope for expansion and policies to promote them, a two-pronged approach will be followed. In the remainder of this section the OECD experience will be analysed in order to identify the main factors driving the growth of the domestic institutional sector in the OECD area. This should be helpful to get a first idea about the scope for expansion as well as required policy actions to promote the domestic institutional sector. Against this backdrop, the second step is to examine in the next section the main obstacles to the expansion of the domestic institutional sector.

Forces shaping the role, structure and modus operandi of OECD institutional investors

The overview in the previous section shows very clearly that OECD institutional investors as a group have vastly expanded their economic sphere of influence. Yet, institutional investors are by no means a monolithic group, since they have different investment objectives and fiduciary mandates, operate under different regulatory and tax regimes (see Annex I), and have a different tolerance to risk. The nature of the liabilities of the different types of institutional investors is a key determinant of their behaviour, including their investment activities (Annex I). Nonetheless, it is possible to identify a number of major structural factors driving the growth of institutional investors as a group:

Deregulation of the financial sector

Deregulation of the banking and securities industries since the beginning 1980s has heightened competition between and among banks and other financial institutions[7]. Abolishment of cross-border capital flow restrictions has further increased competition. New capital standards for banks were introduced in the same period. In response to these pressures, banks have massively expanded, or moved into, the insurance and investment fund business in search of new activities that generate earnings in the form of commissions and fees, while they do not necessarily absorb additional capital.

Liberalisation of the institutional sector

Liberalisation of the activities of institutional investors, both in terms of the production and distribution of their respective products and the investment of their assets. An important aspect of the liberalisation process is the relaxation of regulatory constraints on cross-border activities and investments.

Demography, pension systems reform and financial markets

The rising needs for retirement benefits of a rapidly ageing population in conjunction with more sophisticated and wealthier private investors have had a significant impact on the growth of demand by private households for retirement benefit offered by the different types of financial institutions—banks, insurance companies, and investment products funds.

Advances in communications and information technology

Spectacular technological advances in communications and information technology enhanced the capacity of the financial sector, the professional fund managers, and the institutional investor community to use the opportunities offered by the liberalised environment. Advances in technology have enabled funds to be managed at lower costs. More reliable and efficient clearing and settlements systems for securities and payments, the creation and use of complex new financial products for risk management purposes, and the integration of capital markets have been important factors underpinning the spectacular growth of the managed assets of institutional investors, in particular, mutual fund assets.

The role of the fund management industry

The increasingly active role of the fund or money management profession has made important contributions to the transformation and dramatic expansion of the institutional investor industry. The management of funds by these professionals has common, technical features on the operational side, but the exact strategy and specific objectives are adapted to the specific institutional set-up.

When discussing the forces shaping the investment behaviour of institutional investors it is conceptually important to make a distinction between the legal and economic definition of the different types of "institutional investors", on the one hand, and the professional fund managers who develop asset allocation strategies and take investment decisions, on the other. The fund management profession is an important driving force behind the increasing sophistication of the investment strategies of institutional investors. Individual and institutional investors have increasingly delegated the management of their portfolios to professional fund managers. The role of the fund management profession is therefore a key factor in analysing the relationship between institutional investors and financial markets[8].

Financial integration

Financial integration is proceeding at a rapid pace fuelled by financial market liberalisation and modernisation, advances in information and communication technology, and the increase in international diversification of portfolios of the OECD institutional sector. In addition, there are important recent policy initiatives such as NAFTA and EMU that have given a major push to financial integration, first at the regional level and subsequently at the global level There is a dynamic two-way process in which the expansion of the institutional sector is fostering financial integration while at the same time financial integration is having a profound impact on the investment behaviour of the institutional sector.

Scope for the development of a domestic institutional investor base in emerging securities markets

The structural factors behind the growth of institutional assets in the OECD area have hardly started to play a role in emerging markets. Hence, the scope for the development of the institutional sector and the domestic capital market is enormous.

Deregulation and modernisation of the financial sector

Deregulation and modernisation of the financial sector are relatively recent phenomena in emerging markets. The **Latin American** banking landscape has been shaped to a large measure by frequent banking crises[9]. Latin American financial markets are highly volatile. Institutional investors have reacted to financial fragility and volatility by holding short-term assets. Depository institutions, banks and savings institutions issuing deposit-like liabilities, are the major investment vehicles for Latin American **domestic** institutional savings. Chile is the exception, with pension and insurance funds accounting for around 44 per cent of institutional savings[10]. At the end of 1997, 13 private pension funds operating in Chile managed US$33.0 billion in total assets. US$9.4 billion (28.4 per cent) of their assets was invested in the local stock market. AFPs (Chilean private pension funds), as a group, hold roughly 14 per cent of Chile's publicly traded stocks. It is estimated that at the end of the decade assets under management of the Chilean pension funds will reach US$44.5 billion (50 per cent of its GDP)[11]. Moreover, only in Chile are capital-market instruments (including fixed-income securities) a substantial source of funds for the private sector[12].

Central and Eastern Europe and the former USSR are special cases because of their unique initial conditions (chief among them the complete absence in 1989 of both market-based financial institutions and an institutional investor base). Although the transformation of the financial sector is in full swing, many problems remain.[13] It can therefore be expected that continued progress in the restructuring and modernisation of the banking sector (as well as a reduction in macro-economic volatility) will significantly contribute to the involvement of banks in institutional sector activities, including money management services. Moreover, the transformation of the banking sector in transition economies and elsewhere is a *sine qua non* for the emergence of capital markets as important intermediaries of liquid funds to the private sector[14]. Indeed, Latin American experiences provide evidence that building confidence in institutional savings is closely related to building confidence in the banking system.[15] Thus, the further development of a domestic institutional investor base is in large part dependent on success in establishing sound banking systems.

The deregulation and modernisation of the financial sector in emerging **Asian** market economies is in many respects further advanced than in other emerging market areas. Equity and bond markets are relatively well-developed (see Table 2) and have grown strongly in the last decade. For example, in Malaysia and Thailand the share of equity markets in the stock of financial savings increased, respectively, from 49 per cent and 9 per cent at the end of 1985 to 79 per cent and 56 per cent at the end of 1994[16]. Asian bond markets have been growing strongly in large measure in response to the huge infrastructure investment requirements[17]. The increasing supply of long-term capital market instruments is supporting the development of a domestic institutional investor base in emerging Asian economies. Moreover, increased competition among banks have encouraged them moving into capital market activities (including fund management services) to boost fee income. However, turmoil in Asian financial markets in 1997-1998 has demonstrated a number of structural weaknesses in the financial sector, chief among them bank fragility.

The recent downturn in several Asian countries has exposed structural weaknesses in their banking systems[18].

Liberalisation of the institutional sector

Liberalisation of the activities (production, distribution, investment of assets) of the domestic institutional sector has hardly begun in emerging markets. The agenda for liberalisation will be reviewed in section 4 by identifying major obstacles to the development of a domestic institutional investor base.

Table 2. **Securities markets**

As a percentage of GDP unless otherwise stated

	Securities outstanding[1]		Equities				Bonds		
	1990	1994	Capitalisation 1990	Capitalisation 1995	Trading concentration[2]	Turnover[3]	Capitalisation 1990	Capitalisation 1994	Turnover[3]
India	35.0	93.4	12.6	56.9	6.2	24.1	18.5	22.4	57.5
East Asia									
Indonesia	13.5	32.6	7.6	33.9	35.4	29.4	1.6	6.0	10.0
Korea	91.4	105.4	44.0	40.2	12.8	171.6	19.7	24.1[4]	43.0
Malaysia	196.5	352.6	113.8	265.0	13.6	62.3	59.9	51.2	32.6
Taiwan	83.2	134.7	62.3	74.0	23.4	353.5	5.6	13.6	1 840.0
Thailand	37.8	113.8	27.9	85.4	28.0	60.9	9.8[5]	7.0[5]	4.0
Latin America									
Argentina	9.4	30.4[6]	2.4	13.4	47.7	28.1	7.0	18.3[6]	600.0[6]
Brazil	11.9	66.6	3.7	26.2	77.6	83.4			
Chile	54.5	155.8	44.9	109.4	57.7	9.5	9.6	18.4	275.4
Colombia	22.8	34.4	3.5	23.9	52.5	17.8	1.6	4.9	
Mexico	44.6	73.9	14.1	36.3	56.4	46.5	8.7	2.9	32.9
Venezuela	22.4	18.2	17.2	4.9	80.7	20.2	5.2	11.1	
United States	*203.7*	*244.5*	*56.3*	*94.7*	*7.4*	*69.7*	*108.3*	*123.4*	*1 460.0*[5]
Japan	*189.5*	*178.2*	*99.5*	*72.1*	*13.2*	*32.4*	*78.0*	*88.4*	*250.0*[5]
Germany	*88.9*	*132.7*	*21.6*	*23.9*	*61.9*	*97.8*	*70.1*	*85.6*	*2 120.0*[5]

[1]Where available, including short-term money market instruments, government bonds, corporate bonds and equities at market value. [2] Percentage share of the ten most active stocks in the total value traded in 1994. For the United States and Japan, share of total volume traded. [3] Total value traded as a percentage of average market capitalisation in 1994. [4] 1995. [5] Government bonds only. [6] 1993.

Source: Bank for International Settlements, 66th Annual Report, June 1996, BIS.

Table 3. **A summary of Latin American pension system reforms**

	Chile	Peru	Argentina	Colombia	Uruguay	Mexico
Participation	Mandatory	Mandatory	Mandatory	Mandatory	Mandatory	Mandatory
1st Pillar	Public	Public	Public	Public	Public	Public
2nd Pillar	Private Only	Pub/Priv. Option	Pub/Priv. Option	Pub/Priv. Option	Pub/Priv. Option	Private only
Financing						
ER payroll tax	0%	0%	0%	10%/7.5%	na/0%	0%
EE payroll tax	10%	11% or 10%	11% both	3.5% or 2.5%	na/0%-7.5%	6.5%
Gen'l Rev.	Yes	Yes	Yes	Yes	Yes	Yes
Benefits						
Ret. Age (m/f)	65/60	65	65/60	62/57	60	65
1st Pillar: %AvPay	25%	na	28%	55%	na	40%
2nd Pillar: Payout	Lump-ProgWD-Annuity	ProgWD-Annuity	ProgWD-Annuity	ProgWD-Annuity	Annuity	Annuity-ProgWD
Reg. Structure						
Commission Reg.	Yes	No	No	na	No	No
Int'l Invst. OK	Yes	Yes	Yes	na	No	Yes
Minimum ROR	Yes	Yes	Yes	na	Yes	No

Table 3. **A summary of Latin American pension system reforms** (continued)

	Chile	Peru	Argentina	Colombia	Uruguay	Mexico
Transition						
% of GDP	100-80%	27%	na	87%	na	80%
Recog. bond	Yes	Yes	No	Yes	No	No
System Perf.						
Fund (US$)(*)	$28B	$900M	$4.5B	$50M	$25.6M	$3.9B
Fund (%GDP) (*)	41% ('94)	1.5% ('96)	0.7% ('95)	na	na	na
Recent ROR	12.5% ('82-95)	15.5% ('94-95)	19.9% ('95-96)	15.5% ('96)	na	na
No. AFPs(*)	15	6	21	9	6	25
No. Affil's(*)	5.5M	1.5M	5.5M	2.1M	0.5M	11.2M
System Perf. (end 1996A)**						
Fund (US$)	$27.5B	$945M	$5.3B	$879M	$47M	na
Fund (%GDP)	40%	1.6%	1.8%	1%	0.2%	na
System Perf. (end 1997E)**						
Fund (US$)	$32.4B	$1.5B	$8.8B	$1.6B	$167M	$9B
Fund (%GDP)	44%	2.4%	2.8%	1.8%	0.8%	2.8%
No. AFPs	13	5	18	8	6	17
No. Affil's	5.7M	1.7M	6.1M	2.4M	0.4M	10.5M

Source: All data from Mitchell and Barreto (1997) except items with (*) from Superintencia Admn. Privado de Fondos de Pensiones del Peru (1996) and (**) from Private Pension Funds in Latin America; Salomon Smith Barney (1997 update).

Table 4. **Pension funds development in selected transition countries**

Country	Number of funds (end 1996)	Members ('000) (end 1996)	Assets % of GDP (end 1996)	Number of funds (end 1997)	Members ('000) (end 1997)	Assets % of GDP (end 1997)
Hungary	211	300	0.40	228*	500*	0.66*
Czech Republic	44	1 200	0.14	n.a.	n.a.	n.a.
Russia	1 000	n.a.	0.05	260*	n.a.	n.a.
Slovak Republic	0	0	0.00	n.a.	n.a.	n.a.

Note: In the case of Poland the regulation concerning pension funds has been enacted. The licensing process will start in August 1998. It is expected that around 30 pension funds will start operating at the beginning of 1999.

Source: G. Impavido, Pension Funds and Stock Market Development in Eastern Europe: Is There a Link? EIB Report 97/03, Luxembourg except items with * from OECD sources

Demography and pension reform

Demographic developments in conjunction with (the need for) pension reform are perhaps the most important determinants of the (future) growth of the domestic institutional sector in emerging market economies.

During the debt crises of the 1980s, *Latin American* social securities systems experienced major problems: underfunding, falling real pensions, increasing evasion and large social security deficits.[19] In 1981 Chile took the lead in implementing a radical pension reform programme which replaced the PAYG system by a fully funded system based on individual capitalisation accounts. Encouraged by Chile's success, the movement to reform pension systems gained momentum in the region (see Table 3).Among other emerging markets, large funded pension systems exist in relatively few countries. In Asia the pension systems of Singapore and Malaysia are centrally managed by national provident funds. Indonesia and India have funded schemes that are mostly based on company plans. Korea and the Philippines have partially funded public pension systems. Except for Singapore and Malaysia, pension assets in terms of GDP are relatively low in Asia. For example, in Korea they stood at around 3.1 per cent in 1995.[20.]

In the transition economies of Central and Eastern Europe and the former USSR, funded pension systems hardly exist. Only three countries in Eastern Europe have adopted legislation for regulating the activities of private pension funds.[21] Other countries have prepared drafts of new laws or simply have laws allowing the existence of private pension funds but *not* their regulation.[22]

The size of the pension sector in most emerging market economies is very small (see Tables 3 and 4). This reflects differences in some regions (Asia, Latin America) between the demographic structure of these regions and the OECD area. However, transition economies have a demographic structure very similar to the OECD countries.[23] In sum, the relative small size of the pension sector in emerging markets provides a first indication of its scope for expansion through pension reform and the removal of obstacles in other areas (notably the financial sector).[24] Advances in information and communication technology and the role of professional fund managers are key ingredients of a modern capital market infrastructure for supporting a dynamic domestic institutional sector. These factors will be discussed in Section 5.

Financial integration

The pace of financial integration is still gathering speed. Net private capital flows to emerging markets exceeded $265 billion in 1996, nearly six times greater than they were at the beginning of the decade. Private flows are now five times the size of official flows.[25] The driving force behind the portfolio flows of the 1990s has been OECD institutional investors. Among institutional investors, mutual funds led the rapid growth in investments in emerging market equities.[26] However, increasingly it is the expansion of the OECD pension sector that is the main financial muscle behind the continued flow of capital into emerging markets, investing through mutual funds or directly on their own account. Total international investments by pension funds (mostly in the form of portfolio equities) more than doubled from $302 billion in 1989 to $790 billion in 1994.[27]

Integration enhances the depth and efficiency of the domestic financial system, in particular the capital market. This in turn improves the conditions for an expansion of the domestic institutional sector. The pace of change will be especially rapid for emerging economies, given their more insulated financial markets. Structural reforms in emerging markets (privatisation, pension reform, modernisation of the banking sector, etc.), technological change and financial innovations, financial deregulation and major demographic shifts in OECD countries, are major reasons for expecting that rapid financial integration will continue.[28]

The size of the institutional sector and the development of the capital market

The expansion of the institutional sector has an important impact on the development of the domestic capital market.[29] The OECD experience demonstrates how the growth of the institutional sector has contributed to the modernisation of, and a stronger role for, capital markets. An expansion of the domestic institutional sector in emerging market economies will therefore give a similar impetus to the development of the domestic securities market. Important dimensions of this development are the following:

Market liquidity

The growth of the institutional sector has had a profound effect on capital market structure and corporate finance behaviour in the OECD area.[30] Institutional investors are very much interested in market liquidity—*i.e.* the ability to transact in large size without moving the price against them and at low transaction costs. They demand therefore a market infrastructure characterised by specialised wholesale markets which can process large transactions very rapidly and contribute to liquidity.[31] Market liquidity is a key requirement of the larger institutional investors. Institutional trading and investment strategies demand the existence of sophisticated and liquid financial markets. Consequently, the quest for liquidity has changed dramatically the micro-structure of financial markets. Four dimensions of liquidity can be distinguished:

- *width*, determined by the bid-ask spread for a given number of securities;

- *depth*, the amount of securities that can be traded at given bid and ask quotes;

- *immediacy*, the amount of time to carry out a transaction;

- *resiliency*, the time it takes before prices revert to former levels after a large order has been absorbed by the market.

Through sophisticated trading and investment strategies, institutional investors can create additional liquidity in the form of arbitrage activities and diversification of investor portfolios. Liquidity might also be aided by reduction in commissions and other transactions costs, that institutional investors are well placed to press for. Increases in market liquidity should in turn be beneficial more generally to the efficiency of financial markets, and lead to a reduction in the cost of capital.

Liquidity is a form of economy of scale and therefore the larger financial centres have a competitive edge, even with similar technology. Relative liquidity is reflected in transaction sizes. In some countries, the growth of institutional investors—in particular pension funds—has encouraged the development of off-exchange "block trading". This in turn may entail a tiering of markets, with order-driven and heavily regulated domestic markets dedicated to retail investors and small company stocks. Institutional investors have more power than small investors to press for the lowest possible transaction costs, thereby boosting liquidity. Total transaction costs consist of indirect trading costs (determined by the liquidity of the market: the higher market liquidity, the lower indirect trading costs) and direct trading costs (determined by the structure of transaction fees). Institutional investors will seek to minimise total trading costs.

Financial system structure

Institutional investors have also had an impact on the overall structure of financial markets. Countries with large funded pension schemes (*e.g.* United Kingdom, United States) tend to have highly developed securities markets, while capital markets are relatively underdeveloped (in particular the equity market) in countries with small pension-fund sectors (*e.g.* Germany, Italy). Given their focus on real returns, pension funds should be particularly beneficial to the development of equity markets. Although pension funds could in principle also develop by providing loans and investments in real estate, their greatest comparative advantage is in the capital markets. Loans require monitoring, so the customer relationship probably gives banks a competitive edge. In contrast, trading and the pooling of risks are more efficiently undertaken in capital markets, where transactions costs are lower.

The growth of a dynamic institutional sector may contribute to a stronger role of capital market intermediation in so-called bank-based financial systems (*e.g.* Germany, Japan, the Netherlands). In particular, pension funds that are investing significant parts of their portfolios in equities would pressure for changes in laws and regulations of companies that usually can be found in "bank dominated" financial systems. In addition to a modernisation of the capital market infrastructure, pension funds can be expected to push for a move to laws and practices that would better protect the interests of equity holders. These include take-over codes, insider information restrictions, limits on dual classes of shares which seek to protect minority shareholders, as well as equal treatment of creditors in bankruptcy to protect their holdings of corporate bonds.

The resulting modernisation of the capital market might further encourage the larger corporations to shift from bank financing to securities markets. However, similar access to capital markets is not available for the smaller enterprises. This in turn may re-enforce the development that bank lending is being increasingly concentrated in the smaller and medium-size enterprise sector, even in so-called bank dominated OECD countries.

Demand for capital market instruments and innovations

Institutional investors can influence the demand for capital market instruments in several ways: *i)* by increasing the total supply of saving, *ii)* by influencing the personal sector's portfolio distribution between bank deposits and securities, and *iii)* via the institutional sector's own portfolio choices.

Most studies indicate that institutionalisation has a small impact on total personal saving, although some studies suggest a larger effect. Most authors have come to the conclusion that the growth of institutional investors increases the total supply of long term funds, and may reduce bank deposits, but that total savings do not increase or only marginally.

The personal sector tends to hold a much larger proportion of liquid assets than the institutional sector. Institutional investors hold a greater proportion of their assets in the form of long-term assets than households; also, the personal sector's foreign asset holdings are relatively minor. These differences can partly be explained by the following factors:

- Households have relatively short time horizons. Most institutional investors (in particular, pension funds and life insurance companies) have long-term liabilities. They tend therefore to concentrate portfolios on long-term assets such as equity and property yielding higher returns.

- Institutional investors have a comparative advantage in compensating for the increased risk of holding domestic and foreign equities, by pooling across assets that are imperfectly correlated.

The institutionalisation of savings implies therefore a shift in composition of the portfolios of the household sector. The demand for capital market instruments by the institutional sector is the outcome of portfolio optimisation—seeking an optimal risk/return profile--taking into account the nature of its liabilities, tax factors and regulatory regimes. It has been suggested that in recent years the biggest impulse to the supply of long-term funds has come from pension funds (part of the growth of mutual funds is due to investments by pension funds and/or the growth of personal pension plans).

These shifts in portfolios imply that securities are increasingly held by large, informed investors. This in turn means that their behaviour should be strongly influenced by relative asset returns, particularly when there are relatively few regulations governing portfolio investments and transaction costs are low. Adjustments to changes in relative returns are relatively rapid. This implies that capital markets are allocating funds more efficiently and are valuing securities more accurately and rapidly. Studies confirm that adjustments to a change in returns are rapid in countries with few regulations on portfolio allocation and somewhat slower in countries with higher transaction costs, more restrictions and poorer information disclosure. Also, adjustments by households and non-financial companies tend to be slower due to higher transaction costs and poorer information.

Analysts have also argued that the increased supply of long-term capital market instruments, attributed mainly to the growth of pension funds and increased comfort with securities investing by individuals, may be leading to a compression of the yield differential between equities and bonds. It has been suggested that this may have a structural impact on the capital market by making the issuance of equities cheaper relative to bonds.

The process of financial innovation has been driven strongly by the growth of the institutional sector. Sophisticated trading arrangements and investment techniques have been developed in response to the needs of institutional investors. The growing importance of institutional investors is generating also an increasing demand for risk-transfer techniques, which enable the investor to choose the desired combinations of return and risk. Such techniques include both securitisation, which enables the investor to transfer the credit risk as well as the market risk, and derivatives, whereby market or price risk is reallocated among participants. A more recent development is credit derivatives, which enable market participants to transfer credit risk separately.

The demand for risk-transfer techniques has been strongly driven by the nature of the liabilities of the different types of institutional investors and regulatory requirements. For example, defined-benefit schemes and strict minimum-funding requirements have stimulated demand for hedging by pension funds. In order to minimise the costs of hedging, pension funds and life-insurance companies have an incentive to immunise their defined-benefit liabilities via an investment strategy of duration matching.

The requirement of a fixed duration for investment instruments has stimulated innovations such as zero coupon bonds, collateralised mortgage obligations, strips in government securities markets and guaranteed income contracts; immunisation strategies have also stimulated the development of markets for index options and futures. Fixed-duration instruments have also spurred the process of securitisation of mortgages in the case of collateralised mortgage obligations and of loans and private placements in the case of GICs (Guaranteed Income Contracts).

4. Obstacles in developing an institutional sector in emerging market economies

It was argued in the previous section that there is considerable scope for promoting the growth of the domestic institutional sector. However, there are a number of major obstacles that are obstructing or delaying the development of a domestic institutional investor base in emerging markets.

Central to the development of an institutional sector is the *legal base* for institutional investor activities, including beneficial ownership, novation and trusts. The second key requirement is the adoption of *investment management legislation* that fosters confidence. This legislation should cover information about investment objectives and risk profiles, definition of prudential and fiduciary standards, regulation of self-dealing, fair valuation procedures, protection of the integrity of the fund's assets.[32]

Unfortunately, these two key building blocks of a domestic institutional sector are missing or only partially in place in most emerging markets. Against this backdrop, we shall briefly review a number of specific obstacles for each category of institutional investor.

Mutual funds

Increased competition between and among banks and other financial institutions in the OECD area has encouraged banks to move en masse into the mutual fund industry. In contrast, the structure of the banking industry in most emerging markets has hampered the growth of mutual funds. Lack of competition has led to situations where banks redirected fund investors into deposits. Custodial arrangements tend to be costly, with only a few institutions, mainly banks, being allowed to act as custodians. A major barrier to the development of mutual funds is the design and prudential regulation of private pension funds.[33] In many OECD countries, mutual funds play an increasingly important role in managing pension fund assets. However, in many emerging markets mutual funds are excluded from the pension fund business.

Life insurance companies

Emerging markets play a very small role in the life insurance business. In 1993, the world market share[34] of developing countries in the life insurance business stood at nearly 7 per cent, of which around 5 per cent Asian countries and Latin America less than 1 per cent. The growth of the insurance industry has been highest in East Asian countries, while the Latin American insurance sector has been expanding at a very low pace (see Table 5).

Among emerging markets, South Korea and South Africa have the highest ratio of life insurance premium income to gross domestic product. The most rapid growth took place in Chile, South Korea and Taiwan, followed by Singapore, Thailand and Malaysia. Significant determinants of the expansion of the insurance industry are real income growth and level of development.[35] Table 6 provides *prima facie* evidence of the proposition that the level of development (and therefore, personal disposable income) is a major determinant of life insurance development. However, there are also policy-induced obstacles such as weak competition and limited product innovation. The growth of the life-insurance sector has also been hampered by an inadequate sectoral infrastructure, including inadequate financial disclosure on the performance and solvency of insurance companies. Very strict portfolio investment rules have resulted in a "debt bias" with most assets in the form of domestic government securities.

Table 5. **Insurance premium development in selected regions, 1971-1990**

(Average annual real growth[a] in per cent)

	1971-1980	1981-1990	1971-1990
East Asia	13.9	19.3	16.6
Latin America	9.3	3.9	6.6
OECD	3.7	6.1	4.7

a) 1985 prices and exchange rates.

Source: Schweizerische Rückversicherungs-Gesellschaft (1992).

Pension funds

Pension funds are underdeveloped in emerging markets.[36] Important obstacles are the design and prudential regulation of private pension funds. In many countries, existing financial intermediaries are excluded from the management of retirement assets. Instead, pension funds must be new and specially licensed to manage mandated retirement funds and guarantee a certain return. In *Latin America*, minimum profitability guarantees are defined in relative terms. The *return guarantee* and regulation of fee structures tend to promote herding behaviour of pension funds (resulting in very similar portfolios), to limit competition among pension asset managers, and to lead to very high operational costs (marketing and fees). The introduction of greater competition is needed. First, by allowing other financial intermediaries (including mutual funds) to compete for the management of retirement savings. Second, by offering greater freedom to savers to choose among different portfolios of approved products. Third, by relaxing portfolio investment restrictions, including the freedom to invest in foreign securities. Minimum profitability guarantees and minimum capital rules (they can be used to restrict market access, thereby limiting competition in the pension fund management business[37] may also need to be reviewed. Pension regulators in Latin America are already taking action in the areas of cost control and fee deregulation (see footnote 37).

Regulation of pension funds in transition countries varies greatly from country to country (Table 7). In many transition economies pension funds have to invest a minimum part of their assets in government securities. However, asset allocation rules differ significantly across countries. For example, Hungary and Poland have (different) quantitative limits on investments in equity, while the Czech Republic employs a "*prudent man rule*". Also *tax regimes* vary a great deal. For example, in Hungary strong incentives exist to stimulate the growth of funded systems, while in the Czech Republic pension contributions, pension investment income and pension benefits are taxed (see Table 7).

Transition countries, like other emerging markets, have obstacles to the development of funded pension schemes in the form of institutional weaknesses such as the shortage of a domestic asset management industry and other inadequacies in the financial market infrastructure,[38] lack of experienced regulators, and insufficient competition among financial intermediaries that can offer investment management services. In addition, there is only a very narrow range of long-term and liquid savings vehicles, while asset prices (equity, real estate) are very versatile. A final institutional obstacle in developing a funded pension systems in most emerging markets is the excessive size of the pay-as-you-go public pension system. Downsizing of the public pension system and rationalisation of benefits are not only needed on fiscal policy grounds but also to leave greater freedom for the creation and growth (and thus competition) of private pension funds.

Table 6. **Life insurance diffusion[a] in selected emerging economies; 1987 and 1994**

Country	1987	1994
South Africa	8.26	10.32
South Korea	7.31	9.10
Taiwan	2.34	3.64
Malaysia	1.49	2.30
Singapore	1.29	2.73
Chile	1.13	1.95
Philippines	1.06	0.63
India	0.81	1.29
Thailand	0.73	1.36
Morocco	0.36	0.56
Mexico	0.33	0.56
Indonesia	0.21	0.43
Argentina	0.14	0.33
Brazil	0.13	0.27
Colombia	0.28	0.24
Venezuela	0.22	0.04
Japan	6.43	10.10
United Kingdom	5.25	7.31
Switzerland	4.45	5.99
United States	3.69	3.63
Germany	2.83	2.80

a) Share of life insurance premium income to gross domestic product.
Source: Sigma (various) and B. Fischer (1998).

Although emerging market economies face similar challenges in developing a funded pension sector, there are also key differences. Demographic and pension system dependency ratio differ significantly.[39]

In fact, the demographic structure of transition countries is very similar to OECD countries. Average pension expenditure (as a per cent of GDP) in transition economies is very close to the OECD average. Projections of demographic and system dependency ratios for a number of transition countries indicate that already large implicit government debt liabilities (given existing entitlement and contribution rates) will continue to grow.[40] Fiscal positions and/or tax systems are generally weaker than in OECD countries. This makes pension reform in transition countries even more urgent than in the OECD area.

Table 7. **Pension funds legislation**

Country	Min. capital requirement	Foreign participation	Taxation[1]	Portability	Investment limits (in percent of total assets)			
					State bonds and cash (min.)	Other state securities (max.)	Listed shares (max.)	Real estate (max.)
Czech Republic	CZK 20m	Unlimited	TTT[2]	Full no fee	free	free	free	free
Hungary	HUF 20m[3]	Unlimited	EEE	Full with fee	10	30	60	30
Lithuania	TBA	TBA	EET	Full no fee	TBA	TBA	TBA	TBA
Poland	TBA	TBA	EET	Full no fee	10	30	30	10
Russia	n.a.	n.a.	TTT	Full no fee	TBA	TBA	TBA	TBA
Slovak Republic	SKK 30m	n.a.	EET	Full no fee	free	free	na	20

1. "T": taxed; "E": exempt. First position refers to contributions, second to investment income and third to benefits.
2. State subsidy for contributions instead of exemption.
3. The minimum capital requirement of HUF 20 million is required for funds established as legal entities separate from the sponsor.

Source: EBRD 1996, Pension funds regulation.

Table 8. **Average comparisons**[1]

Developing Countries	Per Capita GDP ($ppp)	Male retire-ment age	Demographic dependency ratio (per cent)	System dependency ratio (per cent)	Expenditures on: Social security (per cent of GDP)	Education (per cent of GDP)	Health (per cent of GDP)	Pensions (per cent of GDP)
South Asia	1 260	55.2	15.1	11.2	7.0	3.4	1.4	1.8
East Asia	3 210	55.7	15.5	11.6	3.4	2.8	2.2	2.3
Eastern Europe, Baltics and CIS	5 210	60.0	30.0	48.3	12.3	4.8	5.2	8.4
Latin America	5 360	60.8	14.9	21.0	3.4	4.2	2.4	2.0
OECD Countries	19 000	64.4	32.9	39.2	16.3	4.9	5.9	9.2

1. Weighted averages except for the system dependency ration of Asia; Latin America and OECD.

Source: EBRD 1996, Fox 1993, Sachs 1996, The world Bank 1994, IMF, OECD, Local Authorities.

5. Financial market infrastructure and institutional sector

A well-functioning institutional sector requires a stable and efficient financial market infrastructure. The financial infrastructure consists of: the legal framework; the financial accounting system; the regulatory and supervisory framework; clearing and settlement systems; and the micro-structure for trading securities.

The role of *public policy* in supporting the infrastructure of the financial system is fundamental. It includes establishing and enforcing property rights and other laws affecting contracts as well as regulating financial markets and intermediaries. An important challenge for financial policy-makers is how to respond to financial product and financial infrastructure innovations. Government regulatory[41] actions can do much to either mitigate or aggravate the dysfunctional aspects of financial innovations. For example, the government can promote adequate disclosure standards for OTC derivatives by demanding changes in the financial accounting system. Another important example is the role of regulators or supervisors in setting standards for risk management by institutional investors.

These public policy responses to financial innovations are likely to enhance financial stability without hampering the entrepreneurial activities of financial market participants. Likewise, the focus in this section is on the role of public policy in the development of an adequate infrastructure for the promotion of a dynamic institutional sector. The (expected) growth of the institutional sector is having a growing influence on the structure and *modus operandi* of financial markets and institutions. The design of the proper financial infrastructure to accommodate these structural changes and prospects is, therefore, a key policy issue In discussing the role of public policy in developing and promoting this infrastructure, we shall take a closer look at the regulation and supervision of the institutional sector (including the broader legal framework and accounting system) and the financial market micro-structure (including clearing and settlement systems and the organisation and mechanics of trading).

Regulation and supervision

Institutional investors are increasingly dominating the evolution of capital markets and corporate finance. At the same time, a dynamic institutional sector needs well-developed securities markets for the efficient execution of their investment strategies. Three functions of the regulatory framework are critical for well-functioning capital markets.

The *first function* is to ensure an *accurate disclosure* of all material information. Transparency in the market by mandatory public disclosure is an important requirement for institutional investors. Hence, institutional investors shun capital markets with weak disclosure. Differences in disclosure requirements among countries are significant, partly due to different legal systems. In emerging markets, the ability of regulators to monitor and enforce disclosure may be weaker than in more mature markets. For this reason, it seems sensible to be quite specific on disclosure and reporting requirements.

The international community has been working on the harmonisation of disclosure requirements. Both IOSCO and COSRA have published standards for full and fair disclosure. *Accounting standards* are key because disclosure will be effective only if the financial information provided by the company is based on solid accounting principles and practices. Common accounting standards are essential for institutional investors to be able to assess accurately the "value" of investments. In parallel, *auditing* standards and practices also need to be high enough to ensure the reliability of disclosed information.

The *second* critical function of the regulatory framework necessary to develop confidence among institutional investors is to adopt *insider trading* legislation. Emerging markets should not try to eliminate insider trading by relying solely on criminal prosecution. It is more effective to have the full range of sanctions (civil, administrative and criminal).[42]

A *third* function of the regulatory system is to ensure fair treatment of all shareholders, including minority shareholders, and the establishment of effective corporate governance mechanisms for shareholder approval of key corporate decisions. Different legal systems or traditions influence the extent to which investors are protected. Legal protections for shareholders and creditors are strongest in the English common law countries and weakest in legal systems based on France's Napoleonic Code. (France, Italy, Spain and most of Latin America). In between are countries with laws based on the German model (Germany, Japan, Korea and a handful of others) and the Scandinavian countries, which have their own legal tradition.[43]

Laws and regulations are one main component of an effective regulatory framework. The other component is *enforcement* by both official regulators and self-regulation. There are several obstacles in implementing

OECD-style market-based regulatory models, based on disclosure and self-regulation, in emerging markets. Self-regulation and disclosure may, therefore, be problematic. The alternative is to rely more on excessive or draconian regulations by government agencies. However, this may hamper the development of both the capital market and the institutional sector. These considerations indicate that it is not easy for the authorities to strike the right balance. One regulatory "philosophy" is to impose a draconian regulatory regime in countries with a low degree of capital market development and to allow a gradual relaxation of "draconian" rules as the financial and institutional sectors develop. For example, draconian regulations have been justified in emerging markets with underdeveloped capital markets and where private pensions play a major role in the provision of retirement income.[44]

Most emerging markets have made considerable progress in the development of a solid regulatory and supervisory framework, although progress has been uneven.[45] Nonetheless, important weaknesses remain. Many emerging markets have not established the legal and regulatory basis for dealing with compensation funds, take-overs, and insider trading. In addition, many emerging markets have not yet established the legal and regulatory basis for dealing with institutional investors. The *general* picture among emerging markets in the three regions is as follows:[46] in *Asian* countries there is the common problem of excessive regulations that inhibit capital market developments; in *Latin America* under-regulation or the lack of effective enforcement constitutes obstacles for the creation of confidence in financial systems; *Eastern Europe and the Former Soviet Union* need to make further progress in establishing the basic legal and regulatory framework for capital market development.

Financial market micro-structure

The financial market micro-structure has changed significantly in the OECD area as a result of the dramatic expansion of the OECD institutional sector and its impact on: *i)* capital market liquidity, *ii)* demand for capital market instruments and financial innovations, as well as *iii)* the growing influence of the asset management industry on investment strategies and techniques and trading arrangements. Similar structural changes in the financial market infrastructure will (or need to) take place in emerging markets when the domestic institutional investor base continues to expand. In fact, there is a two-way dynamic process whereby a dynamic institutional sector encourages the development of a modern capital market infrastructure, while at the same time the expansion of a market-oriented institutional investor base requires the existence of a sophisticated financial infrastructure.

The growing influence of asset management

Professional fund or asset managers are an integral part of the financial market infrastructure. They have a growing influence on the structure and modus operandi of financial market institutions. The technical and operational demands, in conjunction with growing size, of the asset management industry has had, and is having, a major influence on how institutional investors are operating.

In its most simple form, fund or asset management can be seen as a service involving management of the investment portfolio on behalf of institutional investors. Asset management can be carried out internally or externally. Delegation to an external fund management service -- *e.g.* a bank, insurance company, mutual fund or other independent money management company -- raises principal-agent problems.[47] The asset management profession is an important driving force behind the growing sophistication of investment strategies of institutional investors as well as innovations in securities trading arrangements and investment techniques.

The impact of the institutional sector on trading arrangements and investment techniques

First, sophisticated trading techniques, such as portfolio insurance, place heavy demands on the liquidity in the securities markets. Institutional investors have encouraged innovations in financial products and investment techniques to provide deposit-like characteristics to their liabilities. Institutional investors are able to offer bank -- like deposits by following sometimes complicated strategies of holding and trading appropriate combination of assets, even when their asset composition is not itself substantially liquid. To the extent that such strategies can be carried out with transactions that are as low as bank operating costs, institutional investors apparently can provide perfect substitutes for bank deposits.

If these techniques to bestow deposit-like characteristics to illiquid securities, which include derivatives, could create liquidity in securities markets without generating additional demands for bank credit lines, bank business would decline sharply. However, access to liquidity through the banking system is vital to the delivery of cash associated with the execution of the above mentioned sophisticated trading techniques. This is an important reason why a sound banking system is a *sine qua non* for the functioning of liquid capital markets with a dynamic institutional sector.

Second, with the increase in trading by institutional investors, trading arrangements more suitable to these investors had to be developed. This has resulted in the evolution of special arrangements for the execution of certain types of orders commonly sought by institutional investors: *i)* orders requiring the execution of a trade of a large number of shares of a given stock (block trades), and *ii)* orders requiring the execution of a large number of different stocks at as near the same time as possible (programme trades).

The operational arrangement that has evolved to accommodate these two types of institutional trades is the development of a network of trading desks of the major securities firms and institutional investors that communicate with each other by means of electronic display systems and telephones. This network is called the "upstairs market." This market plays an essential role in the well-functioning of capital markets by *a)* providing liquidity to the market so that such institutional trades can be executed smoothly, and *b)* by arbitraging activities that help to integrate fragmented stock markets, thereby further boosting liquidity.

Institutional investors' needs are also a driving force behind a switch from market maker systems with screen-based displays of quotes with all trading conducted over the telephone, to electronic order book systems which can automatically execute orders entered by or via exchange members. For example, the London Stock Exchange is planning to introduce an order book trading system for FT-SE 100 stocks, partly in response to institutional investors' demands.

Changes in the micro-structure of financial markets to improve the one or more dimensions of market liquidity have lowered indirect trading costs. The search for more efficient ways of trading is also fostering the growth of alternative or non-traditional trading systems -- in particular proprietary trading systems (PTSs). This has resulted in the bypassing of brokers by institutional investors from securities transactions (disintermediation) and pressure on transaction fees, thereby lowering direct transaction costs

Third, in practice, active asset management often lowers returns when transaction costs are taken into account. This is consistent with the so-called efficient markets hypothesis, that states that current securities prices incorporate all available information. Consequently, no net benefit can be expected from spending extra resources on active investment strategies in order to try to beat the "market index". Thus, portfolio indexing can be the optimal investment strategy in situations where securities markets are price-efficient. The amount of institutional funds managed using an indexing strategy has grown substantially. In particular the use of benchmarks tailored to individual pension funds' liabilities has increased. For example, the use of individual benchmarks for UK pension funds has grown from less than 5 per cent in 1990 to more than 30 per cent of the total in 1996. Typically, the benchmarks consist of guidelines for the proportions of a pension fund the manager can invest in particular asset classes. Yet, despite the growing body of evidence that fund managers are unable to outperform systematically the stock market, indexed funds still account for a relatively small part of total institutional stock investments.

Assessment of progress in emerging markets

A modern financial market micro-structure is an essential part of the development of a domestic institutional sector in emerging markets. As indicated earlier, there is a two-way dynamic process. This means that the implementation of policies that promote a domestic institutional investor base -- *e.g.* via pension reform or via the elimination of other obstacles[48] -- will stimulate the development of the capital market. Nonetheless, financial policies that promote the development of a modern financial market micro-structure, are a key part of building a market-oriented domestic institutional investor base. Although progress has been made,[49] the policy agenda remains full.[50]

6. Policy conclusions

A dynamic community of institutional investors is a pre-condition for the development of liquid securities market with sophisticated financial vehicles. There is a dynamic two-way process whereby the growth of a domestic institutional investor base encourages the development of a modern capital market, while the expansion of the institutional sector requires the existence of a sophisticated financial market infrastructure.

The paper discusses the main factors driving the growth of the institutional sector in the OECD area: financial deregulation, liberalisation of the activities of institutional investors, ageing populations and pension reform, technological advances, expansion of the asset management industry. It is concluded that in view of the OECD experience, the potential for the expansion of a domestic institutional investor base is enormous.

Table 9. **Capital market development in emerging markets, 1995**

Country	Subindex Market structure[a]	Market infrastructure[b]	Institutional development[c]	Overall index
Argentina	4.0	8.7	8.2	6.2
Brazil	5.6	9.1	7.5	6.9
Chile	8.4	10.0	6.6	8.3
China	4.1	7.6	3.9	5.0
India	6.1	3.8	5.2	5.3
Indonesia	5.9	8.1	7.5	6.9
Korea	6.7	8.7	7.7	7.5
Malaysia	8.7	8.6	9.0	8.7
Mexico	6.4	8.4	8.8	7.5
Pakistan	4.3	1.0	7.8	4.1
Philippines	8.5	6.3	6.2	7.4
Poland	4.7	7.5	7.3	6.1
Sri Lanka	2.9	7.0	8.2	5.3
Thailand	8.6	8.7	7.1	8.3
Turkey	4.8	9.3	8.0	6.7

Notes: The index ranges from 1 to 10 with higher numbers representing a higher level of marker development. See annex 6.3 in Worldbank (1997), Private Capital Flows to Developing Countries, Washington, DC.

a) Based on a weighted average of market characteristics, including market capitalisation, volatility, market concentration, and level of activity, relative to an industrial country benchmark.

b) Based on measures of efficiency in settlement and post-settlement actions.

c) Based on measures of the quality of financial reporting, protection of investor rights, and market openness.

Source: IPC, Emerging Market Factbook 1996; Global Securities Consulting Service, Review of Emerging Markets and Review of Major Markets.

Policymakers in emerging market economies need to follow a *two-pronged approach*: *i)* the elimination of policy-induced or structural obstacles to the development of a domestic institutional investor base; *ii)* preparing capital markets for a strong institutional investor community.

The paper identified major *obstacles* in developing a domestic institution sector, including an inadequate legal base and improper (or the absence of) legislation for asset or money management. More specific obstacles for each category of institutional investor have also been discussed:

- *mutual funds* (lack of competition; exclusion of mutual funds from the management of pension fund assets);

- *insurance companies* (overregulation; limited product innovation; inadequate disclosure of financial information on the solvency and financial performance of insurance companies; failure to establish an effective system of consumer and investor protection; excessive portfolio investment restrictions);

- *pension funds* (excessive size of public PAYG system; lack of legal framework for private pension funds; absence of professional asset management industry; excessive portfolio investment restrictions; too restrictive licensing policy, leading to cartelisation of the pension fund business; lack of freedom to savers to choose among different portfolios of approved retirement products; high and/or fixed fees of private pension funds).

The combination of the "natural" growth potential of the institutional sector (*e.g.*, through a rise in living standards, the import of modern financial technology, etc.) and the removal of policy-induced obstacles would allow a major expansion of the activities of domestic institutional investors in emerging markets. Modernising the financial market infrastructure would give an additional push to this development.

Urgent action is needed in the following areas:

1. the *regulatory framework* (stricter financial disclosure standards and improved accounting rules; more effective enforcement of these standards and rules; implementation of insider trading rules and investor protection provisions; the "right balance between statutory regulations and self-regulatory arrangements, taking into account the capabilities of SROs and potential conflicts of interest);

2. *the legal system and property rights* (fair treatment of all shareholders; better accountability of management to

shareholders; independent securities registries of ownership records in order to avoid manipulations or outright fraud by management and/or other insiders);

3. *the financial market infrastructure* (development of asset management industry; introduction of modern trading arrangements and sophisticated investment techniques; reliable and efficient clearance and settlement systems, including a well-functioning central depository; efficient and strong large-value interbank payment systems, including a robust and reliable operational infrastructure; a sound banking system).

NOTES

1. H. J. Blommestein (1998), The Impact of Institutional Investors on OECD Capital Markets, in: Institutional Investors in the New Financial Landscape, OECD.

2. H. J. Blommestein (1998), The Impact of Institutional Investors on OECD Capital Markets, in: Institutional Investors In the New Financial Landscape, OECD.

3. Investment Funds in Emerging Markets, IFC, 1996.

4. Private Capital Flows to Developing Countries, World Bank, 1997.

5. Private Capital Flows to Developing Countries, World Bank, 1997.

6. Modern portfolio theory suggests that pooling of securities in a domestic market can eliminate unsystematic risk resulting from the different performance of enterprises and sectors but not, in a national market, the systematic risk resulting from the performance of the economy as a whole. Systematic risk would be minimised by holding the world market portfolio.

   However, all the evidence points to the fact that all types of institutional investors (including mutual funds) are much less internationally diversified than the world market portfolio. In fact, the divergence between the world portfolio and observed portfolios is even larger when one takes into account the very high correlation between the returns to human and physical capital. Reasons for this home bias include:

   Additional risks in the form of exchange-rate risk, transfer risk, settlement risk, and liquidity risk;

   The benefits of international diversification are dependent on the type of asset and the degree of financial market integration. Bond markets are probably more internationally integrated than other asset markets and hence there is less benefit from diversification out of domestic markets. In contrast, equities can be expected to yield higher benefits. Although real estate is a real asset similar to equity, it is more risky because it is less liquid and its value is dependent on sometimes hard-to-acquire and to assess local information. Surveys of internal investment rules reflect this line of argument (equity investments have the highest portfolio limit for foreign assets and property the lowest);

A third possible reason is that the argument for holding the world portfolio is based on the efficiency of markets. If markets are inefficient -- *e.g.* in the form of speculative bubbles -- then the optimal level of diversification cannot be based on the global portfolio. Instead, it needs to be calculated in a different way;

A fourth reason is related to the fact that the investment behaviour of institutional investors is partly determined by the nature of their liabilities. For example, many pension schemes and life insurance contracts have very precisely defined nominal liabilities. In these cases, the preferred investment strategy may be to match domestic liabilities with domestic assets;

Regulatory constraints on foreign investments constitute another reason for the home-bias of institutional investors;

The "benchmark" orientation of fund managers may be an important reason why domestic assets may be "over-represented" in comparison to the predictions of modern portfolio theory;

Finally, there is evidence that downside market movements occur much more in parallel than upside ones. Unfortunately, downside risk matters more than upside risk.

7. H. J. Blommestein (1995), Structural Changes in Financial Markets: Overview of Trends and Prospects, in: The New Financial Landscape, OECD.

8. The following broad picture emerges from an analysis of the links between institutional investors and professional fund managers:

First, fund managers may work in four different basic types of institutional set-up: (1) in the fund or trust departments of banks; (2) in separately capitalised fund (or money) management companies which may be owned by banks or insurance companies; (3) independent money management companies (that is, firms that or not affiliated with an insurance company or bank); (4) the in-house fund management departments of large insurance companies and pension funds.

Second, the total amount of professionally managed funds is larger than the portfolios of the "classic" (regulated) institutional investors. Fund management companies are also involved in the management of portfolios of "high-net worth" individuals, the non-pension fund money of non-financial enterprises, foundations and endowment funds, and non-pension fund money managed by banks, as well as the bank's and securities firm's own portfolios (proprietary trading by banks and securities firms have expanded strongly).

Third, the number of asset portfolio managers is smaller than the number of institutional investors whose portfolios are professionally managed. The smaller insurance companies and pension funds usually give portfolio management mandates to outside fund management teams. In many cases, fund management companies pool the funds of the smaller institutional investors. There is also some evidence that the larger institutional funds have reduced the number of managers investing their assets. Institutional investors are increasingly indexing assets, thereby reducing the need for a large number of asset portfolio managers.

Finally, to the extent that insurance companies and pension funds invest directly in investment fund shares, they reduce the amount of assets that would have to be invested by the fund's own managers in the capital and money markets.

9. R. Hausmann and L. Rojas-Suarez (1996), eds., Banking Crises in Latin-America, IDB.

10. L. Rojas-Suarez and S.R. Weisbrod (1996), Building Stability in Latin American Financial Markets, in: R. Hausmann and H. Reisen, eds., Securing Stability and Growth in Latin America, OECD.

11. Private Pension Funds in Latin America; Salomon Smith Barney (1997 update).

12. L. Rojas-Suarez and S.R. Weisbrod (1996), Building Stability in Latin American Financial Markets, in: R. Hausmann and H. Reisen, eds., Securing Stability and Growth in Latin America, OECD.

13. H. J. Blommestein (1997), Transformation of the Banking Sector in Central and Eastern Europe: Policy Assessment and Next Steps, in: The New Banking Landscape in Central and Eastern Europe, OECD.

14. H. J. Blommestein and M. G. Spencer (1994), The Role of Financial Institutions in the Transition to a Market Economy, in: D. Folkerts-Landau et al., eds., Building Sound Finance in Emerging Market Economies, IMF.

15. L. Rojas-Suarex and S.R. Weisbrod, Building Stability in Latin American Financial Markets, in: R. Hausmann and H. Reisen, eds., Securing Stability and Growth in Latin America, OECD, 1996.

16. The stock of financial savings is defined here as the sum of the stock of deposits in commercial banks and the capitalisation of the stock market.

17. The World Bank has calculated that infrastructure investment requirements in east Asian economies could be as high as $1.5 trillion for the 1995-2004 period. Bond markets are seen as the biggest source of funds [see Financial Times, September 23, 1997, Special section on Asian Infrastructure].

18. See Bank for International Settlements, 67th Annual Report, June 1997; 68th Annual Report, June 1998.

19. World Bank (1994), Averting the Old Age Crisis, Washington D.C.

20. See Institutional Investors, Statistical Yearbook 1997, OECD, Paris, Table 8, p. 28.

21. Hungary (November 1993), the Czech Republic (February 1994) and the Slovak Republic (July 1996).

22. Russia was an example of where pension funds existed but were completely unregulated (see EBRD [1996] Transition Report). Although till May 1998 there was no comprehensive legal framework for pension funds, more than 260 private pension funds were registered in Russia at the end of 1997. On 7th May 1998 the President of the Russian Federation signed a new "Law on Non-State Pension Funds" which is expected to provide a more stable basis for the creation of new pension funds and encourage individuals to participate in private pension schemes. (OECD sources).

23. See Section 4, Table 8.

24. See Section 4.

25. World Bank (1997), Private Capital Flows to Developing Countries: The Road to Financial Integration, Washington D.C.

26. See the section on The role of foreign institutional investors.

27. World Bank (1997), Private Capital Flows to Developing Countries: The Road to Financial Integration, Washington DC.

28. World Bank (1997), Private Capital Flows to Developing Countries: The Road to Financial Integration, Washington DC.

29. H.J. Blommestein (1998), The Impact of Institutional Investors on OECD Capital Markets, in: Institutional Investors In the New Financial Landscape, OECD.

30. Institutional Investors in the New Financial Landscape, OECD, 1998.

31. See section 5 for details.

32. World Bank (1997), Private Capital Flows to Developing Countries: The Road to Financial Integration, Washington DC.

33. See World Bank (1997), Private Capital Flows to Developing Countries: The Road to Financial Integration, Washington DC and below, this section.

34. Market share as measured by accumulated net premium income; see B. Fischer (1998), The Role of Contractual Savings Institutions in Emerging Markets, in: Institutional Investors in the New Financial Landscape, OECD.

35. See World Bank (1994), World Development Report, Washington DC; and F.J. Outreville (1994), Life Insurance in Developing Countries. A Cross-Country Analysis, UNCTAD/OSG/Discussion Paper No. 93, Geneva.

36. See Tables 3 and 7.

37. M. Queisser (1997), Regulation and Supervision of Pension Funds -- Principles and Practices, Paper prepared for the ISSA VII Regional Conference for the Americas, Montevideo, November 1997.

38. See Section 5.

39. See Table 8.

40. D. Vittas and R. Michelitsch (1995), Pension Funds in Central Europe and Russia, Policy Research Working Paper No. 1459, World Bank.

41. H.J. Blommestein and K. Biltoft (1995), Trends, Structural changes and Prospects in OECD Capital Markets; in: The New Financial Landscape, OECD, Paris.

42. See R.D. Strahota (1996), Securities Regulation in Emerging Markets: Some Issues and Suggested Answers, Paper prepared for the SEC International Institute for Securities Market Development, April.

43. R. La Porta, F. Lopez-de-Silanes, A. Shleifer and R. Vishny, (1996), Law and finance, NBER Working Paper No. 5661.

44. D. Vittas (1998), Regulatory Controversies of Private Pension Funds, in: Institutional Investors in the New Financial Landscape, OECD.

45. See table 9.

46. World Bank (1997), Private Capital Flows to Developing Countries, Washington D.C.

47. See H.J. Blommestein, (1998) the Impact of Institutional Investors on Financial Markets in OECD Countries, in: Institutional Investors in the new Financial Landscape, OECD.

48. See Section 4.

49. See Table 9.

50. See Section 6.

Annex I

REGULATION AND SUPERVISION OF OECD INSTITUTIONAL INVESTORS

Insurance companies

Insurance companies are financial intermediaries that undertake to make payments if a certain event occurs. Their principal activity is to bear and manage risk for a price (*i.e.*, the insurance premium). Insurance activities provide protection against the future consequences of: *i)* uncertain events that may or may not occur; *ii)* certain, inevitable events whose date of occurrence is unknown. There are two basic types of insurance activities: life insurance activities and non-life (property and casualty) insurance activities.

The tax and regulatory aspects of insurance activities differ across OECD countries and even within individual countries (*e.g.* in the USA rules and regulations may vary from State to State). Harmonisation of a number of regulations has taken place within the European Union in the form of EU Directives.

Tax and regulatory aspects of life insurance activities

All OECD countries provide some tax concessions for the purchase, maintenance or execution of life insurance policies. In most countries, tax relief is provided for premiums paid. Policies that are primarily survivorship contracts (*e.g.*, endowments and annuities) are more likely to enjoy tax preferences.

The regulatory regime concerning investments of technical provisions is another determinant that influences life insurance investment activities. Each OECD country has regulations with respect to *i)* the types of securities that are eligible for investment, and *ii)* the valuation of these securities for regulatory purposes. All OECD countries, and in the United States, the individual states, have approved lists of investments which insurance companies are allowed to hold. The rationale of these lists is to ensure that eligible investments possess acceptable levels of investment risk. Most OECD countries impose maximum limits on classes of investment: quoted and unquoted domestic shares, foreign securities, real estate, mortgage loans and other loans (Table A1). The general purpose of these maximum levels is to restrict the default and liquidity risks of investments. Maxima are also applied to ensure that there is sufficient portfolio diversification of investment holdings. Although regulatory investment maxima vary widely across OECD countries, the actual investment portfolios of insurance companies do not appear very much constrained by these maxima. Apparently, in many instances the limits that have been set by the regulatory authorities have been higher than what most insurance companies would themselves view as prudent levels.

Another important area of investment regulation concerns the matching of assets and liabilities in terms of maturity and currency. Only five OECD countries (Greece, Mexico, Norway, Sweden and Ireland) have statutory requirement for maturity or duration matching. However, in most OECD countries the regulatory authorities review on an informal basis the time profiles of assets and liabilities as part of the wider assessment of the solvency of an insurance company. A serious mismatch of assets and liabilities would endanger the solvency of life insurance companies which tend to have longer-term liabilities with often implicit interest guarantees. Life insurance companies need therefore to ensure that the duration of their investments are broadly in line with their mainly long-term liabilities, in order to minimise the inherent interest rate risk. One of the main investment risks for a life insurance company is that with many short-term assets it would face a reinvestment risk in market situations with lower interest rates than warranted by the (often implicit) interest guarantees on its long-term liabilities. Moreover, for life contracts with a significant savings component, legal requirements and/or competitive pressures demand that the rates of returns on investment holdings maintain their value in real terms.

In nearly all OECD countries there are statutory requirements for some degree of currency matching. Currency matching requirements are separate from restrictions on foreign investments (Table A2). The latter are based on default and liquidity risk considerations.

In all OECD countries insurance companies are free to use derivatives in connection with the investment of their capital funds. However, a number of countries restrict their use in the investment of technical (mathematical) reserves (Table A3). In almost all OECD countries the use of derivatives is restricted to risk management purposes. In many countries the writing of options is only allowed when they are covered.

Regulatory treatment of the non-life insurance business

Competitive pressures have made the need for price regulation less desirable than in the past. Regulation of prices could even backfire when imposed prices lead to the withdrawal of insurers offering insurance. Regulations governing eligible investments have been imposed to reduce the likelihood of insolvency. In most OECD countries, the same maximum percentages in investment classes apply for non-life and life companies. Differences between life insurance and non-life insurance can be found in Canada, Ireland, Italy, Japan, Portugal, and some states (*e.g.*, Delaware and New Jersey) for the United States (Table A1). In view of the different nature of investment risks in the two sectors, this degree of uniformity is surprising. Practical problems regarding the enforceability of these rules seem to be the main reason why there are no bigger differences.

For non-life companies maturity matching is relatively unimportant, because the duration of technical provisions is shorter than those of life companies and there are no interest guarantees. On the other hand, currency matching is even of greater importance for non-life companies since there is uncertainty about the timing of claim payments.

Pension funds

In all OECD countries pension funds have become major institutional investors and important players in the capital markets due to the following factors:

- income and wealth have grown steadily since World War II, providing households with more funds for long-term savings;
- people are living longer and have larger financial needs during longer retirement periods;

– pension claims are tax free until after workers retire and income from employment ceases.

Pension fund schemes can be classified into the following three categories:

1. Public managed pension schemes with defined benefits and pay-as-you-go finance, usually based on a payroll tax. They are mandatory for covered workers. In most OECD countries coverage is (near) universal.

2. Occupational pension funds that are privately managed and offered by employers to employees. Thanks to tax advantages not available to personal pension plans, coverage grew in most OECD countries. Currently more than one-third of the working age population (or more than 40 per cent of the labour force) is covered in OECD countries. Within this category of funds there is a trend in OECD countries from defined benefit and partially funded schemes toward defined contribution schemes.

3. Personal pension plans in the form of saving and annuity schemes. These schemes are normally voluntary and based on fully funded defined contribution plans. In some non-OECD countries (*e.g.*, Singapore and Malaysia) there exist publicly managed, mandatory schemes that are fully funded and based on defined contributions, known as provident funds. Tax incentives encourage the development of these plans, although at present their share of total income in old age is relatively small.

An overview of the structure of pension provisions in a sample of OECD countries is given in (Tables B1 and B2).

Tax treatment of pension schemes

Unlike other types of institutional investors, pension funds in most OECD countries benefit from tax deferral: contributions and accumulated interest and capital gains are tax free; tax is paid on receipt of a pension after retirement. Reasons for the favourable tax treatment of pension schemes include: *i)* the argument that there is a need to encourage people to save enough to maintain post retirement living standards; *ii)* this in turn would mean that when people save enough it would reduce the cost to the state to provide means-tested social security benefits; and *iii)* it is also hoped that the general level of saving would be raised. The tax treatment of pension schemes differ widely across OECD countries (Tables B1-B2).

Regulatory aspects of pension fund activities

Quantitative regulation of portfolio holdings are in place in a number of OECD countries. Reasons include the protection of pension fund beneficiaries or benefit insurers and, in some countries, the creation of a steady demand for government securities. Limits are often imposed on holdings with relatively volatile returns, such as equities, real estate and foreign assets, although their mean return might be higher (*e.g.* on equity) than on assets with so-called stable returns (*e.g.* government bonds with a fixed coupon). There are often also limits on self investment, to protect against the associated concentration of risk regarding insolvency of the plan sponsor.

A number of countries do not impose quantitative limits but impose guidelines such as the so-called "prudent man rule". Under the prudent man rule, fiduciaries, trustees, and bank trust departments are expected to behave as careful professionals in making investment decisions. In the United States the Employment Retirement Security Act (ERISA) stipulates that the fiduciary must be knowledgeable enough to act as a careful professional, experienced and educated in trust and financial matters. "Prudence" is a design standard, not a performance standard. This is reflected in the two most significant elements of the rule: *i)* the requirement to diversify; *ii)* the exhortation to favour "seasoned" situations that similarly-placed institutions find appropriate. In the United States, the application of this design standard to investment decisions has led to the overwhelming preponderance of pension equity money being invested in the limited number of listed securities of American corporations with large capitalisation. It may also account for the increase in the "index mode" of investments.

Prudential concerns are also often mentioned as the rationale for regulatory constraints on portfolio holdings of foreign securities (Table B3). Other motives (for example, the "benchmark" orientation of fund managers) are, however, also mentioned in the literature.

Funding rules are a key aspect of the regulation of defined benefit pension funds. A defined contribution is by definition always funded. However, with defined benefit schemes one needs to make a distinction between the pension plan (*i.e.* the contractual rights of the parties) and the pension fund (*i.e.* the pool of assets to provide cover for the promised benefits). Under/over funding is the situation when the fund is worth less/more than the present discounted value of the promised benefits. Minimum funding rules seek to protect the beneficiaries against default risk by the company. Since unfunded benefits are liabilities for the company, pensioners or pension insurers (see below) may have no better claim than other creditors. Other regulatory issues concern ownership of surpluses, portability, internal transfers, fraud, disclosure, and the structure and mechanics of supervision (see Tables B1-B2, for a summary).

Table A1. **Maximum percentage that can be invested in a given class of investments**

	Domestic shares (quoted)		Domestic shares (unquoted)		Foreign shares		Foreign bonds and other securities		Real estate		Loans (mortgage)		Loans (non-mortgage)	
	Non-life	Life	Non-life	Life	Non-life	Life	Non-life	Life	Non-life	Life	Non-life	Life	Non-life	Life
Australia	-	-	-	-	-	-	-	-	-	-	-	-	-	-
Austria	30a	30e	5	5	30a	30e	-	-	30a	30e	-	-	0	0
Belgium	-	-	10a	10e	10a(2)	10e(2)	10(3)	10(3)	10(4)	10(4)	-	-	5(5)	5(5)
Canada	25a	5-25e	25a	5-25e	0	5-25e	0		10	5-25e	-	-	5	5
Denmark	40a	40e	10	10	40a,d	40d,e	-	-	-	-	-	-	10	10
Finland	20	20	0	0	0	0	0	0	-	-	-	-	-	-
France	65a	65e	65a	65e	65a	65e	-	-	40	40	10b	10f	10b	10f
Germany	30	30	10	10	6	6	5	5	25	25	50a	50e	50a	50e
Greece	30a	30e	30a	30e	30a	30e	-	-	40	50	10b	10f	10b	10f
Iceland	40a	40e	10b	10f	40a	40e	10b	10f	-	-	-	-	10b	10f
Ireland	50-60a	55e	20	2.5	50-60a	55e	-	-	60	25	15-30b	10	15-30b	45
Italy	20	20	20	20	10	20	30	50	35	50	20	50	0	0
Japan	30a	30e	30a	30e	30b	30f	30b	30f	20	20	55c	-	55c	10
Luxembourg	10	10	5	5	5	5	10	10	40	40	10a	10e	0	0
Mexico	30	30	30	30	30	30	30	30	40	40	40	40	40	40
Netherlands	-	-	10	10	-	-	-	-	-	-	10	10	5j	8j
Norway	20a	20e	20a	20e	20a	20e	30b	30f	30b	30f	30b	30f	30b	30f
Portugal	25a	25e	10	10	25a	25e	60	60	35	45	10	25	10	25
Spain	-	-	-	-	-	-	-	-	-	-	-	-	-	-
Sweden	25a	25e	25a	25e	25a	25e	-	-	25b	25f	25b	25e	10	10

Table A1. **Maximum percentage that can be invested in a given class of investments** (continued)

	Domestic shares (quoted)		Domestic shares (unquoted)		Foreign shares		Foreign bonds and other securities		Real Estate		Loans (mortgage)		Loans (non-mortgage)	
	Non-life	Life	Non-life	Life	Non-life	Life	Non-life	Life	Non-life	Life	Non-life	Life	Non-life	Life
Switzerland	30a	30e	30a	30e	25b	25f	20b	20f	-	-	-	-	0	0
Turkey	-	-	10	10	-	-	-	-	20	20	20	20	20	20
UK	-	-	10a	10e	-	-	-	-	-	-	10a	10e	10a	10e
USA(New Jersey)	-	15e	-	15e	h	i	h	i	5	10	40	60	-	-
USA (Delaware)	40a	(1)	40a	(1)	5	5	5	5	25	25	50	50	-	-

a) maximum for these classes of investment combined (Non-life)
b) maximum for these classes of investment combined (Non-life)
c) maximum for these classes of investment combined (Non-life)
d) if unquoted then ten per cent
e) maximum for these classes of investment combined (Life) which would constitute one single investment
f) maximum for these classes of investment combined (Life)
g) maximum for these classes of investment combined (Life); only for unqualified non-mortgage loans
h) investment must not exceed the value of outstanding policies in the foreign country
l) five per cent in the aggregate; two per cent in foreign countries, except for "qualified foreign investment" defined in the statute
j) unsecured loans.

1. 250 per cent (at market value) of the capital and surplus
2. unquoted shares only
3. only State and enterprises bonds outside of area A (see the Directive 89/647/EEC)
4. investments in a single real estate or in several real estate close to one another
5. five per cent with a maximum of one per cent for one single loan

Note: maxima in respect of foreign investments are separate from the currency matching requirements for foreign liabilities
Source: OECD Policy Issues in Insurance, Paris 1996, OECD submissions.

Table A2. **Currency matching requirements**

	Required percentage of currency matching of technical provision		Does currency matching extend to equalisation (claim fluctuation) reserves?		Extent to which ECU denominated securities can be used for matching	
	Non-life	Life	Non-life	Life	Non-life	Life
Australia	-	-	n/a	n/a	n/a	n/a
Austria	80	80	Yes	n/a	100	100
Belgium	80	80	Yes	n/a	100	100
Canada	100	100	n/a	n/a	n/a	n/a
Denmark	80	80	Yes	Yes	50	50
Finland	100	95	n/a	n/a	n/a	n/a
France	80	80	Yes	Yes	0	0
Germany	80	80	Yes	n/a	50	50
Greece	80	80	n/a	n/a	100	100
Iceland	80	80	Yes	Yes	50	50
Ireland	80	80	Yes	n/a	50	50
Italy	80	80	Yes	n/a	100	100
Japan	No	No	No	No	n/a	No
Luxembourg	80	80	n/a	n/a	0	0
Mexico	-	-	-	-	n/a	n/a
Netherlands	80	80	Yes	-	100	100
Norway	80	80	Yes	Yes	80	80
Portugal	80	80	Yes	Yes	50	50
Spain	80	80	Yes	n/a	-	-
Sweden	80	80	n/a	n/a	0	0
Switzerland	80	80	n/a	n/a	80	80
Turkey	100	100	n/a	n/a	n/a	n/a
UK	80	80	No	n/a	0	0
USA(New Jersey)	100	100	n/a	n/a	n/a	n/a
USA (Delaware)	100	100	n/a	n/a	n/a	n/a

Source: Table A1

Table A3. **Use of financial derivatives**

	Can they be used in respect of the investment fo technical provisions?		Can they be used in respect of the investment of capital funds?		Purpose for which the can be used	
	Non-life	Life	Non-life	Life	Non-life	Life
Australia	Yes	Yes	Yes	Yes	Hedging*	Hedging*
Austria	Yes	Yes	Yes	Yes	Hedging*	Hedging*
Belgium	Yes	Yes	Yes	Yes	Hedging*	Hedging*
Canada	Yes	Yes	Yes	Yes	Hedging*	Hedging*
Denmark	Yes	Yes	Yes	Yes	Hedging*	Hedging*
Finland	Yes	Yes	Yes	Yes	Hedging*	Hedging*
France	No	No	Yes	Yes	Hedging*	Hedging*
Germany	Yes	Yes	Yes	Yes	Hedging*	Hedging*
Greece	-	-	-	-		
Iceland	Yes	Yes	Yes	Yes	Hedging	Hedging
Ireland	Yes	Yes	Yes	Yes	Hedging	Hedging*
Italy	Yes	Yes	Yes	Yes	Hedging	Hedging
Japan	Yes	Yes	Yes	Yes	Hedging*	Hedging*
Luxembourg	Yes	Yes	Yes	Yes	Hedging*	Hedging*
Mexico	No	No	Yes	Yes	Hedging	Hedging
Netherlands	Yes	Yes	Yes	Yes	Hedging*	Hedging*
Norway	Yes	Yes	Yes	Yes	Hedging*	Hedging*
Portugal	Yes	Yes	Yes	Yes	Hedging	Hedging
Spain	No	No	Yes	Yes	Hedging	Hedging
Sweden	Yes	Yes	Yes	Yes	Hedging*	Hedging*
Switzerland	No	No	Yes	Yes	Hedging*	Hedging*
Turkey	Yes	Yes	Yes	Yes	Hedging	Hedging
UK	Yes	Yes	Yes	Yes	Hedging*	Hedging*
USA(New Jersey)	Yes	Yes	Yes	Yes	Hedging*	Hedging*
USA (Delaware)	Yes	Yes	Yes	Yes	Hedging*	Hedging*

* Also allowed to write covered call options

Source: Table A1

Table B1. **Summary of pension asset regulations**

	Portfolio regulations	**Regulation of funding (1)**
United Kingdom	Prudent man concept; 5 per cent self investment limit, concentration limit for defined contribution plans.	Maximum 5 per cent overfund of PBO or IBO. Funding only obligatory for contracted out part of social security.
Germany	Guidelines: maximum 30 per cent EU equity, 25 percent EU property, 6 per cent non-EU shares, 6 per cent non-EU bonds, 20 per cent overall foreign assets, 10 per cent self investment limit.	Funding obligatory up to PBO. Option of book-reserve funding.
Netherlands	Prudent man concept; 5 per cent self investment limit, whereby free reserves can be added up to a total limit of 10 per cent.	Minimum funding requirement is present value of ABO discounted at 4 per cent; percentage of overfunding dependent on composition of investment portfolio and volatility of relevant investment returns; maximum 15 per cent overfund of ABO, minimum is ABO itself.
Sweden	Majority to be in listed bonds, debentures and retroverse loans to contributors.	For ATO, IBO is funded. Contribution rate adjusted 5-yearly to balance fund.
Denmark	Property loans, shares and investment trust holdings limited to 40 per cent, foreign assets to 20 per cent; 60 per cent to be in domestic debt. No self investment.	Irrelevant as defined contribution; benefits must be funded externally.
France	Assets of supplementary funds (ARRCO/AGIRC) to be invested 50 per cent in EU government bonds and less than 33 per cent in loans to sponsors. insured funds to be at least 34 per cent state bonds, maximum 40 per cent property and 15 per cent Treasury deposits. No foreign assets.	Funded company schemes forbidden: book reserve funding subject to tax discrimination.
Italy	No pension law for self administered schemes. Most schemes are insured investments may be in state bonds (maximum 90 per cent), bank deposits, property, mortgages, securities, investment funds.	No pension law for self administered schemes; draft law proposes payments equal to 7 per sent of salary. Insured plans must be fully funded on a 15 year projection.

Table B1. **Summary of pension asset regulations** (continued)

	Portfolio regulations	**Regulation of funding (1)**
Ireland	Schemes must diversify prudently, any self investment to be declared.	Funding of ABO required; deferred rights indexed.
Belgium	15 per cent to be invested in government bonds, no more than 15 per cent in sponsor, 40 per cent limit on real estate, 10 per cent deposits.	Funding obligatory of ABO based on current salary, interest rate 7 per cent.
Spain	90 per cent in stocks, bonds, mortgages, property, deposits.	Funding obligatory of ABO plus 4 per cent margin; maximum interest rate 6 per cent.
Portugal	30 per cent to be invested in government bonds, maxima of 50 per cent real estate, 15 per cent self investment, 40 per cent equities and bonds not listed in Portugal.	Funding obligatory of ABO.
Norway	Maximum 20 per cent in shares; maximum 30 per cent in loans that are not issued or guaranteed by: the government or municipalities; financial institutions or EU credit institutions; and investment in other real estate than negotiable property.	Funds should, at least, cover the difference between PBO and NPV of future contributions, based on an interest rate of 3 per cent.

(1) ABO refers to the accrued benefit obligation; PBO the projected benefit obligation
Source: Davis (1995), EFRP, OECD.

Table B2. **Features of funded pension systems**

	UK	**US**	**Germany**
Nature of benefits for average member	Largely defined benefit based on final salary.	Primary cover largely defined benefit based on final salary. Supplementary defined contribution plans widespread.	Largely defined benefit with flat rate benefit based on years of service.
Taxation of funded schemes	Contributions and asset returns tax free. Benefits taxed, except tax free lump sum.	Contributions and asset returns tax free. Benefits taxed.	Employers' contributions taxed as wages; employee contributions and asset returns tax free. Benefits taxed at low rate.
Social Security	Low replacement ratio. Scheme members can contract out of earnings related social security.	Low replacement ratio.	High replacement ratio.
Regulation of portfolios	Prudent man concept; 5 per cent self investment limit; concentration limit for defined contribution plans.	Prudent man concept; 10 per cent limit on self investment for defined benefit plans.	Guidelines; maximum 20 per cent equity, 5 per cent property, 4 per cent foreign; 10 per cent self investment limit.
Regulation of funding	Maximum 5 per cent overfund of IBO or PBO. Funding only obligatory for contracted out part of social security.	Maximum 50 per cent overfund of ABO. Higher insurance premia if underfunded.	Funding obligatory for pension funds. (Pensionskassen), alb eit only up to PBO. Option of booking (tax exempt- pensions taxed at normal rate).
Maturity of funds	Mature.	Mature.	Immature.
Coverage of workforce (approx.)	50 per cent (company schemes) 20 per cent (personal pensions).	46 per cent.	42 per cent.
Insurance of benefits	No (although state guarantees payment of minimum pension if fund defaults).	Yes (special guarantee corporation).	Yes (via insurance supervisors). Booked benefits insured by Pension Guarantee Association.
Portability features	Vesting in 2 years. Indexation of accrued benefits. Transfers must be made to other pension funds.	Vesting in 5 years. No indexation of accrued benefits. Lump sum distribution permitted on transfer.	Vesting in 10 years. Indexation of accrued benefits.
Indexation	Discretionary (to date) but total or partial indexation common in practice (75 per cent).	Full indexation rare (5 per cent of schemes). Discretionary cost-of-living increases common.	Mandatory.

Source: Davis (1995) and OECD.

Table B2. **Features of funded pension systems** (continued)

	Denmark	**Sweden (ATP)**	**Switzerland**
Nature of benefits for average member	Largely defined contribution.	Defined benefit based on best income years.	Majority of schemes (60 per cent) defined contribution but with targets of 60 per cent replacement rate which contributions adjusted). 40 per cent defined benefit.
Taxation of funded schemes.	Contributions tax deductible. Fund may be taxed, including 40 per cent of lump sum.	Contributions tax free. Tax on asset returns (1991) benefits taxed at low rate.	Contributions and asset returns tax free, benefits taxed.
Social security	High replacement ratio.	Low replacement ratio; only for basic needs.	Low replacement ratio; designed to be supplemented by mandatory private scheme.
Regulation of portfolios	Real estate, investment trusts, shares limited to 40 per cent. 60 per cent in domestic debt. No self investment. Only "small proportion" can be inves ted internationally.	Majority to be in listed bonds, debentures and retroverse loans to contributors.	30 per cent limit on domestic shares; 50 per cent domestic real estate; 20 per cent foreign currency assets; 25 per cent foreign shares; overlaps are possible.
Regulation of funding	Irrelevant as defined contribution.	Contribution rate adjusted 5-yearly to ensure IBO is funded.	Funding compulsory for PBO or ABO.
Maturity of funds		Mature.	Mature
Coverage of workforce (approx.)	30 per cent (company funds) 20 per cent (personal pensions).	90 per cent (compulsory).	Above a certain salary level (SFr 23 280) 100 per cent.
Insurance of benefits		State backup as national scheme.	Yes; Government Safety Fund. Small funds backed by insurance companies.
Portability features	Immediate access to own contributions, 5 years total vesting. Transfer values can be negotiated.	Vesting immediate-national scheme and transferability perfect.	Immediate access to minimum contributions. Complete vesting for employees.
Indexation	No.	Yes.	Indexing not compulsory.

Source: Davis (1993) and OECD.

Table B2. **Features of funded pension systems** (continued)

	Japan	**Canada**	**Netherlands**
Nature of benefits for average member	Largely defined benefit based on years of service and career earning or final basic salary. Often taken as a lump sum.	Largely defined benefit based either on final salary or flat rate benefit.	Almost exclusively defined benefit, based for around 75 per cent of contributors on final salary.
Taxation of funded schemes.	Contributions tax free. Benefit taxed, except tax free lump sum.	Contributions and asset returns tax free. Benefits taxed.	Contributions and asset returns tax free. Benefits taxed.
Social security	High replacement ratio. Scheme members can contract out of earnings related social security.	Low replacement ratio.	Low replacement ratio.
Regulation of portfolios	Guidelines; maximum 30 per cent equity, 20 per cent property, 30 per cent foreign, 10 per cent one company. Minimum 50 per cent bonds.	Prudent man (since 1987); tax on foreign assets above 10 per cent; 7 per cent limit on real estate.	See Table B2
Regulation of funding	Funding optional. Tax exempt up to ABO only. (Book reserves tax exempt up to 40 per cent of liabilities).	Funding obligatory. Maximum 5 per cent overfund of PBO.	See Table B2
Maturity of funds	Immature.	Mature.	Mature.
Coverage of workforce (approx.)	37 per cent (funded plans only).	41 per cent.	90 per cent.
Insurance of benefits	Yes (under wage payment law). Mutual guarantee scheme for EPFs introduced 1988.	No (but social security provides backup).	No
Portability features	Vesting graded between 5 and 30 years for voluntary leavers. Low transfer values for voluntary early leavers.	Vesting after 2 years. Little indexation of accrued benefits.	Vesting in one year. Accrued benefits indexed. Transferability within extensive pension circuits with same conditions.
Indexation	Rare except for part replacing social security.	Provisions rare (6 per cent of private scheme s); some discretionary increases.	Indexation almost universal (albeit not mandatory).

Source: Davis (1995) and OECD.

Table B2. **Features of funded pension systems** (continued)

	Norway
Nature of benefits for average member	Largely defined benefit based on final salary. Most schemes aim to provide a benefit which, together with the State scheme, corresponds to 60-66 percent of the last income earned after a contribution period of 30 years.
Taxation of funded schemes	Contributions and asset returns tax free to a certain extent for plans which comply with the regulations of the tax law. Benefits taxed as income.
Social security	High replacement ratio for low income; designed to be supplemented by mandatory private scheme.
Regulations of portfolios	See B2
Regulation of funding	See B2
Maturity of funds	
Coverage of workforce (approx.)	Compulsory occupational pension in public sector. In the private sector, 1/3 of the workforce have occupational pension scheme and about ¼ of the overall workforce have a private pension scheme.
Insurance of benefits	Yes, via insurance supervision.
Portability features	Vesting in 3 years.
Indexation	Indexation follows social security index, which is set by the government each year.

Source: OECD.

Table B3. **Regulatory constraints on foreign investment by pension funds in selected OECD countries, 1994**

Country	Ceiling	Matching requirements
Australia	None	None
Ireland		
Luxembourg		
Netherlands	None	None
Spain		
United Kingdom		
United States (a)		
Belgium	Location in Belgium	Not applicable
Canada (a)	20%	None
Japan	30%	None
Portugal	40% (only EU)	None
Switzerland (b)	30% (global)	None
	25% (equities)	
	30% (debt instruments)	
	5% (real estate)	
	20% (foreign currency)	
Denmark	"Small proportion" stipulated	80%
	60% minimum in domestic debt	
Finland	5% (foreign currency)	None
Germany	60%	100%
Sweden	5-10%	None
Norway	None	80%

(a) Applies only to private pension funds. France and Italy are not included, because private pension schemes are almost nil.
(b) Overlaps are possible.
Source: OECD.

Investment companies (Institutions for collective investment in securities)

Investment companies are financial intermediaries that sell shares to the public and invest the proceeds in a diversified portfolio of securities. Each share sold represents a proportionate interest in the portfolio of securities managed by the investment company on behalf of the companies' shareholders. The type of securities purchased depends on the company's investment strategy.

The different types of investment companies are based on a common principle: individuals contribute savings to a large pool—the mutual fund—which is managed by a team of professional money managers. This mutual fund operation is conceptually different from asset management services offered by securities brokers (*e.g.* "SIMs" in Italy), banks and trust companies to individual clients.

There are four distinct parties involved in any type of "mutual" fund operation: (1) fund participants who contribute their savings; (2) the fund management company that invests the pool of savings and executes the necessary transactions within the framework of the rules specified in the mandate of a given mutual fund and the existing regulatory and supervisory regime; (3) the depository bank that is empowered to act as custodian for the assets of the fund, and is charged with ensuring that all transactions executed by the management company conform to the fund's regulations; and (4) the sales network that acts as a conduit for contributions to the fund. The network may consist of the branches of the depository bank or other banks, a distribution unit within the fund management company, a brokerage company or a combination.

By investing in a fund, an investor can effectively achieve the benefits of diversification at lower cost even if the amount of money available is not very large. Beyond risk reduction via diversification offered by the funds, there are reduced costs of contracting and information processing. In addition, money market mutual funds generally also provide payment services by allowing investors to write checks drawn on the fund, although this payment facility is limited in various ways.

The regulation of investment companies

Extensive regulation by governmental authorities is a characteristic of mutual fund activities in many OECD countries. A distinction needs to be made between the restrictions on the "manufacture" of investment fund products and services and restrictions on their "distribution". Although in many respects (*e.g.* investor protection) investment companies are required to operate under the regulatory and supervisory framework for securities markets, there are many special provisions that regulate their activities. Regulations cover usually the following key areas: self dealings and affiliated party transactions; management fees of professional fund managers; capital structures; investment objectives and policies; protection of physical integrity of the asset pool; fair valuation of investor purchases and redemptions; and the disclosure of reliable information to investors.

In the **United States**, all investment companies are regulated at the federal level according to the Investment Company Act of 1940. This Act established a comprehensive framework of federal regulation for the protection of United States investors, including disclosure, accounting, pricing, the use of leverage, transactions with affiliates, and the custody of fund assets. The securities issued by investment companies must be registered with the SEC. The Insider Trading and Securities Fraud Enforcement Act of 1988 requires mutual funds investment advisors to institute and enforce procedures that reduce the chances of insider trading. The purchases and sales of mutual fund shares must meet the requirement of fair dealing that the SEC and the NASD, a self-regulatory organisation, have established for all securities transactions in the United States. Fees charged by mutual funds are also subject to United States regulations. In addition to federal regulations, mutual funds are subject to the "Blue Sky" laws of each state, which include, among other provisions, restrictions on certain types of investments.

Regulation of the investment companies in ***Japan*** is conducted by the Ministry of Finance (MOF) and a self-regulatory organisation, the Investment Trust Association. Securities investment trusts (an investment vehicle in many ways similar to a US mutual fund) are regulated along the lines of the 1951 Securities Investment Trust, as amended. A securities investment trust is a contractual agreement among four parties: The investor who buys beneficiary certificates; the management company that issues the certificates and decides on the investments of the trust; the securities company that sells the certificates; and the trustee, which is a trust bank that manages the assets at the direction of the management company. If an investment trust is an open type trust, investors can purchase new certificates, there is no specific maturity date, and the size of the trust is not fixed. A unit type of trust is somewhat similar to a closed-end fund: After it is issued at fixed cost per certificate, no new certificates are sold and no new money is raised. The typical unit trust matures five years after issuing its certificates. The MOF must license securities firms (or subsidiaries) before they may act as the manager of a securities investment trust.

The regulatory situation in ***Western Europe*** has undergone important changes since the adoption of the 1985 EU Directive on Undertakings for Collective Investment in Transferable Securities (UCITS). The UCITS Directive stipulates which types of investment companies are allowed and which can advertise and market their products across the EU area. Moreover, it contains the co-ordination of an agreed upon set of minimum standards for investor protection, leaving considerable scope for EU countries to compete with each other. Consequently, some EU countries have relatively liberal investment fund regulations (*e.g.* Belgium, France, Ireland, Luxembourg and The Netherlands) that are not in conflict with the minimum standards of the UCITS Directive. The draft 1993 Directive amending the 1985 UCITS Directive investment fund companies would allow (*i.e.* when adopted) investment companies to advertise and market MMMFs and funds-of-funds across the EU area.

The 1988 ***Luxembourg*** Investment Company Act provides considerable freedom to investment companies regarding legal structure (contractual form, the joint stock company with variable capital or SICAV form, the common fund or FCP form, or any other form of collective investment) and investment objectives of the investment fund. The Luxembourg law includes also regulation of funds that are not covered by the UCITS Directive, including venture capital funds, derivatives funds, index funds, foreign currency funds, family or group of funds, government securities funds, etc. These non-UCITS funds are not allowed to be advertised and marketed across the EU area. Also, ***France*** has relatively liberal investment fund rules. Money market mutual funds (MMMFs) have grown spectacularly. But other funds have also grown steadily, including risk capital funds, funds-of-funds, index funds, and financial futures, options and warrant funds.

More "conservative" European countries such as ***Germany*** and ***Switzerland*** have reacted to these new initiatives and competition from other European countries by giving more freedom to investment companies. Germany allows now the operation of MMMF. Existing investment funds have gained greater flexibility to engage in derivatives transactions for risk management purposes; they may invest up to 10 per cent of total assets in unquoted financial assets. The new Swiss Investment Fund Act of March 1994 has considerably widened the scope for new investment fund products. Both German and Swiss investment funds have been expanding their presence in Luxembourg in response to investment fund restrictions at home and, more important, to tax factors.

Restrictions on the distribution of investment fund products (including restrictions on cross-border sales of products and services) are usually motivated by investor protection concerns. Most OECD countries other than France, the United Kingdom, Italy, Switzerland and the United States, seem not to have in place special regulations dealing with the sale and marketing of investment products.

In the ***United States*** the sale of investment fund products has traditionally been subject to tight and detailed regulations. The SEC is currently undertaking a comprehensive review of current disclosure requirements. In addition, the Commission is working on the development of a "fund profile". The profile contains the fund's key features in a standardised format designed to facilitate comparison among funds. Another noteworthy development is that US legislators are currently considering a set of amendments to the Investment Company Act designed to modernise certain aspects of mutual fund regulation, including the authorisation to allow the SEC to create a new, more investor-friendly fund "advertising prospectus. A final point of regulatory attention for the authorities is the recent sharp surge in the sale of investment products via the banking system.

The new ***Swiss*** Investment Fund Act covers the sale of investment products. According to this Act, foreign investment funds will be allowed to be marketed in Switzerland, provided that the fund management companies from the home countries: *i)* have supervisory practices and investor protection rules that are judged to be "equivalent" (not necessarily "identical" or "equal") to the one in Switzerland; *ii)* have a legal presence in Switzerland; and *iii)* have sales practices in compliance with the new Investment Act.

As noted above, the ***EU*** UCITS Directive allows the free distribution of UCIT-defined investment fund products within the European Union. However, many OECD countries have very detailed and complex investor protection rules that inhibit at present the free cross-border sale of investment products.

Direct regulation of portfolio holdings of investment funds are largely in the form of constraints on outward portfolio investments. However, these constraints are usually formulated in terms of limits on illiquid securities or in the form of asset diversification rules. For example, in the United States a mutual funds may not hold more than 15 per cent of its net assets in illiquid assets.

Annex II

STOCK MARKET DEVELOPMENT IN THE TRANSITION ECONOMIES, END 1996[1]

Stock exchange	Number of shares[2]	Shares capitalisation (US$ million)[3]	Turnover per session (US$ million)[3]	Annual turnover (US$ million)[3]	Share turnover (per cent of capitalisation)	Share capitalisation (per cent of GDP)
Russia (RTS)[4]	160	19 911.50	41.00	10 800.00	54.24	3.94
Prague	1 671	19 790.15	36.84	9 172.60	46.35	40.03
Warsaw	83	8 155.99	41.73	10.432.39	127.91	6.43
Bratislava	950	5 632.66	12.80	3 200.00	56.81	30.93
Budapest	45	5 269.09	12.23	3 031.99	57.54	12.55
Zagreb	68	1 359,12	n.a.	103.86	7.64	7.52
Ljubljana	52	1 229.47	0.58	145.25	11.81	7.32
Vilnius	350	899.93	0.33	47.23	5.25	8.98
Tallinn	16	896.20	1.39	366.30	40.87	18.80
Kiev	0	600.00	n.a.	17.00	2.83	1.38
Riga	34	115.23	0.12	11.67	10.13	2.34
Bucharest	21	72.64	0.24[5]	6.24	8.60	0.28
Skopje	3	63.61	n.a.	0.40	0.63	1.83
Sofia	26	4.86	0.04[5]	0.01	0.17	0.17
NYSE	-	5 654 815.40	-	3 082 916.10	54.52	77.99
London	-	1 346 640.70	-	1 153 221.30	85.64	121.32
Germany	-	577 364.80	-	593 936.20	102.87	23.96
Paris	-	499 989.60	-	716 507.60	143.30	32.25
Kuala Lumpur	-	213 757.40	-	60 792.40	28.44	254.17
San Paulo	-	147 635.80	-	57 024.50	38.62	21.94
Thailand	-	135 774.20	-	59 303.30	43.68	81.31
Mexico	-	90 694.00	-	35 037.20	38.63	37.63
Santiago	-	72 927.70	-	11 411.60	15.66	108.36
Buenos Aires	-	37 783.80	-	31 932.60	84.51	13.45
New Zealand	-	31 949.80	-	8 718.00	27.28	54.89

1. Data for comparative stock exchanges refer to 1995;
2. Data for transition economies refer to listed and unlisted shares while data for comparative stock exchanges refer to listed shares only;
3. Exchange rate of 6 Jan. 1997; 4. 90 stocks on RTS-1 and 70 stocks on RTS-2, all other date refer to RTS-1 only. Annual turnover is a projection of Jan. 1997 total turnover; 5. US$ thousands.

Source: Individual stock exchanges.

Chapter 11

NEW INSTRUMENTS IN THE HUNGARIAN FINANCIAL MARKETS

Derivative Markets, Instruments and Market Infrastructure in Hungary
The Main Players, Regulation and Market Size[1]

by

Zoltán Szalai
Economic Analyst, National Bank of Hungary

1. Budapest Commodity Exchange (BCE)

1.1 Organisation and regulation

BCE is a self-organised, self-regulatory, non-profit institution and closely held by its members. The legal form is special for exchanges and government permission is necessary for the establishment. BCE is subject to the "Act on Commodity Exchange and Commodity Exchange Contracts" (XXXIX/1994). The law allows establishment and operation of more than one commodity exchange (although to date, there is only one commodity exchange in Hungary). BCE must have a licence from State Money and Capital Market Supervision (SMCMS), which is an integrated supervision authority (supervises banks, stock and commodity exchanges, and other financial institutions except insurance companies). The law defines the attributes of commodity exchange in a very general way as a self-governing, self-regulatory institution, which concentrates supply and demand in a publicly pre-announced way and place. But there is no definition of "concentration" in the law. The products also are described in very general terms as "standardised". An important requirement for futures products is that they have to be cleared and guaranteed by an approved clearing and settlement house (which falls under the "Securities Act CXL/1996" -- see point 3. below). Indices based on securities are not allowed to be traded in a commodity exchange but those based on foreign exchanges and interest rates or their derivatives are.

BCE was established in 1989 as a grain exchange. In 1991 a meat subsection was created. In 1993 BCE launched the financial products section. Currently, efforts are made to create an energy section as well; the plan being to have an agricultural (grain and meat), a financial and an energy products section.

1.2 Members

Members must fulfil criteria determined by BCE. Also, the applicants must have a the licence from the State Money and Capital Market Supervision (SMCMS). The members of the non-financial sections are mainly agro-industrial producers and trading companies, co-operatives, brokers, futures brokers etc., while in the financial section members are mainly specialist futures brokerage firms, sometimes owned by banks. The law does not determine the capital and other prudential requirements for the members of BCE; these being left to the BCE's own regulations. Most of the members fall under the Corporate Law, so the capital requirements are essentially the same as for non-financial Ltds and Plcs, depending on the legal form chosen by the members.

1.3 Derivative products on BCE

i) Interest rate instruments (size of a contract): 1 months (10 M HUF) and 3 months (10 M HUF). Budapest inter-bank interest rate futures contracts [1 M BUBOR and 3 M BUBOR or BR (exactly the same as on the BSE as a result of co-ordinated product design and implementation between the two markets)].

ii) Forex futures (size of a contract): DM 1 000, US$1 000, ECU 1 000, £1 000, Y 100 000, L 1 000 000, SF 1 000, CZK 100 000.

iii) Commodities: grain and meat contracts.

iv) In April, 1998 trading of standardised options on grain was initiated.

1.4 *Organisation of trade and price discovery process:*

There are two main phases on a business day, the free phase, and the closing phase. *i)* In the free phase, the price discovery is based on competitive pricing principle. This means that a more competitive order flowing to the pit automatically cancels the formerly registered, but less competitive order. Orders made in the free phase may be withdrawn. *ii)* In the closing phase, there is no automatic cancellation of less competitive orders, and they are non-withdrawable. But only the most competitive orders will be executed. All the orders can be seen on a billboard in the trading pit throughout the business day. Quantities associated with the orders and the identity of partners are not shown, but are known by the auctioneer, and he or she can be qquestioned on these aspects during the business day by any of the traders. Post-trade quantities and identity of traders are not published.

After the close of the business day, section officials calculate settlement prices for each futures contracts on the basis of the price of the last contract in the free phase, the prices of the closing phase and bids and offers made on the closing date but not executed because of lack of counter-parties at that price. The exact algorithm of computation is fixed. Settlement prices are immediately available after the business day.

Market-makers are appointed in the financial section. Approximately 75-80 per cent of turnover is traded via market-makers who are obliged to quote bids and offers for certain futures dates, thus providing *liquidity* and *price continuity* for the market. Usually, offers and bids by market-makers are quoted in both phases. Market-makers are appointed for the whole financial section, so for one product there may be more than one market maker.

BCE so far has not yet encountered block-trading (*i.e.* trading in large volumes relative to the liquidity of the market) as a problem for market organisation and price discovery. BCE plans to provide opportunity in the future for after hours trading based on an electronic system. The traditional and the electronic trading facility will co-exist, and at the moment, BCE does not want to decide which is the most suitable for its members and their clients.

1.5 *Clearing and settlement*

All transactions executed on BCE are cleared and settled by KELER Ltd. Budapest (see below).

1.1.6 Market size and its main determinants

As can be seen from the following summary tables, all sections of the BCE have grown in recent years, with the exemption of the meat section, which reached its peak size in 1995. The most dynamic development can be seen in the financial section. One reason for the rapid growth in turnover is the relatively large and well functioning underlying inter-bank foreign exchange market. Another, more recent spur came from the exchange rate regime adopted in March 1995. In this crawling peg regime, NBH publishes the rate of depreciation of the HUF central parity against the official basket six months in advance. The fluctuation band is symmetric, allowing 2.25 per cent movement in both directions (thus a total 4.5 per cent fluctuation band). This regime serves as an anchor for expectations and provides an element that makes exchange rate developments reasonably calculable. On the other hand, the existence of the fluctuation band helps to preserve some uncertainty, adding an incalculable element to the exact futures exchange rate. This regime in principle generates expectations both above and below the central parity, preventing the development of one-way expectations, and thus contributes to market liquidity. However, realisation of this beneficial feature depends on the conduct of monetary policy, the central bank sterilisation policy and the resulting fluctuation of the exchange rate within the band as well as the interest rate spread over the international interest rate (*e.g.* LIBOR and FIBOR) which are also affected by general economic policy. Expected exchange rate developments are built into the inflationary and interest rate expectations, which in turn are reflected in the foreign exchange and interest rate futures. At times, when the HUF spread over international interest rates was high, portfolio investors reaped secured profits by converting foreign exchange to HUF, buying assets denominated in Hungarian currency yielding higher HUF profit than the international rate at the spot exchange rate, and buying back their original currencies in the futures market. In this way they could eliminate the risk of depreciation of HUF exceeding the level allowed by the official fluctuation rate. The main players using this strategy were banks, who could lend in HUF to their clients or had easy access to the government paper market. As the spread over the international rate has narrowed, the strategy's popularity has declined. The need for hedging also decreased as the credibility of monetary and exchange rate policy improved, which is reflected in the decrease of "basket trades".

Table 1. **The development of turnover on BCE**
(in million HUF.)

Year	Grain	Meat	Financial	Total	Grain %	Meat %	Financial %
1989-90	574	0	0	574	100.00%	0.00%	0.00%
1991	1 746	170	0	1 916	91.13%	8.87%	0.00%
1992	5 798	339	0	6 137	94.48%	5.52%	0.00%
1993	10 693	190	1 448	12 331	86.72%	1.54%	11.74%
1994	8 099	218	26 944	35 261	22.97%	0.62%	76.41%
1995	12 686	512	162 150	175 348	7.23%	0.29%	92.47%
1996	62 026	605	855 169	917 800	6.76%	0.07%	93.18%
1997	95 947	444	1 076 357	1 172 748	8.18%	0.04%	91.78%
Total	197 569	2 478	2 122 068	2 322 115	8.51%	0.11%	91.39%

Source: Budapest Commodity Exchange, Annual Report, 1997.

Table 2. **Open interest (1994-1998, 31 March)**
(no. of contracts)

BCE	31 Dec. 94	31 Dec. 95	31 Dec. 96	31 Dec. 97	31 March 98
Forex	45 450	363 211	689 081	1 336 445	1 814 000
Grain	2 468	4 824	21 781	10 677	10 531
Meat	29	102	44	64	58

Source: Budapest Commodity Exchange, Annual Report, 1997.

Among the *financial products*[2], foreign exchange transactions are the most popular, while interest rate products are less traded. The most active currencies are those, which are included in the basket, in relation to which the external value of the HUF is determined. From January 1997, ECU has been replaced by DEM in the basket (the basket consist of 70 per cent DEM -- earlier ECU -- and 30 per cent US$). Their presence in the basket is explained by their importance in Hungary's trade and external financial relationships. The economic role of these two currencies has been re-inforced via their involvement in the official currency basket, which assures their dominance on the foreign exchange markets. The ECU's turnover on the foreign exchange fell dramatically after it was dropped from the basket. The official, twofold explanation of the ECU's exclusion is important for the development of derivatives markets. On the one hand, the German currency can serve as a proxy representing core European currencies. On the other hand, it has a liquid spot and derivative market, which the ECU does not, thus making it easier for market participants to find counter parties for derivative contracts. Finding a counter-party in the case of the ECU transactions was at times very difficult because of the relative illiquidity of this artificial currency.

There are currencies traded on the BCE which may be important not so much because of their role in our external trading or financial relations, but rather as attractive investment assets, with exchange rate and yield patterns unrelated to those of other traded currencies.

As far as *interest rate contracts* are concerned, their share in the total turnover of BCE is still modest. BCE realised the potential of interest rate contracts as complementary to foreign exchange contracts. Present regulation bars the BCE from introducing products based on securities. An alternative to a security-based interest rate product was one tied to an inter-bank interest rate. Thus, the first interest rate contract ("interest rate 90") was based on the inter-bank deposit rate for a 90-day period. However, using this instrument proved cumbersome as compared to simply buying or selling government papers, renering the contract illiquid. A second, more promising attempt aims at cross-listing 1 month and 3 months interest rate contracts (1 and 3 BUBOR or BR) with the BSE, based on inter-bank interest rates. The contracts have been introduced to both exchanges in last October, with exactly the same terms. Turnover of the 3 months contract in BCE greatly exceeded that of both the earlier interest rate contract, and the turnover on the BSE, and is now comparable to the most successful forex futures on BCE.[3] So far, 1-month interest rate contracts on both exchanges have been largely dormant, as this time segment tends to be dominated by monetary authorities and institutional factors like the reserve requirement regime, instead of market expectations.

2. Budapest Stock Exchange (BSE)

2.1 Organisation and regulation

BSE is -- like BCE -- a self-organised, self-regulatory, non-profit institution, closely held by its members. Its legal form is the special one for exchanges and establishment requires government permission, in the same way as in the case of the commodity exchanges. BSE falls under the "Act on Securities Underwriting and Trading, on Investment Services in the Securities Field and on Securities Exchange" (CXL/1996, ch. XXV.). The law defines various securities, investment services (including non-core investment services), underwriting etc. and also defines the clearing and settlement services (ch. XXXIII) and the investor protection fund (ch. XXIV). Membership in this fund (established on 28 April 1997) is obligatory. There is no definition of "concentration" and "transparency" in the law. These are words used in the preamble in very general terms, like common attributes of all exchanges, but are neutral from the point of view of market organisation and transparency.

BSE is owned by its members as closely held Ltd. licensed by the State Money and Capital Market Supervision (SMCMS). The governance of the exchange has been modified recently to reflect more accurately the turnover made by individual members in the weighting of their votes. By law, more than one security exchange can be established, although to date only one securities exchange exists in Hungary.

2.2 Members

Applicants must fulfil the criteria prescribed by BSE. They must also have a license from the SMCMS. Firms in the field of securities investment are authorised on an exclusive basis: they are not allowed to engage in other activities than those explicitly mentioned in the law. So far banks have not been allowed to engage in securities investment services, so they cannot be members of a stock exchange. This restriction will be removed as the European Commission's Capital Adequacy Directive will be translated into Hungarian law. In case an application is refused, BSE has to explain the reasons for the denial. In the standardised section non-exchange members are allowed to become members if they fulfil certain requirements. Important prerequisites are that they have a clearing and settlement contract with a section member which is also an exchange member, and the latter declares that it will provide such services for the former and fulfils the segregation requirement as well. Besides, the stock exchange member has to declare that it guarantees all liabilities of the non-member and ensure that the required margin is maintained. (Note: the National Bank of Hungary is member of the BSE in the government securities section).

2.3 Derivative products:

i) Interest rate instruments (size of a contract): 1 month (10 M HUF) and three months (10 M HUF) Budapest inter-bank interest rate futures contracts (1 M BUBOR and 3 M BUBOR or BR (both are exactly the same as in BCE, as a result of close co-operation of the two markets), three (1 M HUF) and 12 months treasury bills.

ii) Forex futures (size of a contract): DM (10 000), US$ (10 000), ECU (10 000).

iii) Index futures (size of a contract): BUX index (BUX * 100 HUF).

iv) Non-standardised options on shares: so far turnover has been insignificant.

v) Planned products: standardised options.

2.4 Organisation of trade and price discovery process

The stages of the *trade by market-makers* are the opening, the free and the closing phases. The rules of the opening phase are the same as that of the closing phase. In the opening and the closing phases, the market-maker and the traders can make orders by entering them into the electronic order-book. For traders who do not have their own work stations, BSE has provided common work stations. In the opening phase market makers are not allowed to enter orders on their own accounts. The orders are put into the order book, the content of which is known only by the auctioneer. Then the BSE determines the opening price and executes trades by matching orders according to the trading algorithm. After determining and publishing the opening price, the content of the order-book is available to the market-maker. In the closing phase, only the auctioneer knows the orders. The BSE matches the orders, again on the basis of the algorithm, and then determines and publishes the settlement price. The algorithm for order matching in the opening and closing phases aims to match the greatest possible number of quantities at a uniform price. Competitive bids and offers enjoy priority over non-competitive ones, when matching the orders. This gives the incentive for more "aggressive" bids and offers, and is supposed to reward risk taking. In the free phase, market makers are required to quote bid and offer prices as determined by the market-making contract.

BSE can operate both as an electronic market place (including remote access) and as an open outcry market. These two trading methods are regarded by BSE as complementary, rather than competing trading facilities. So far no special trading organisation has been developed for block trading.

2.5 Clearing and Settlement

All transactions executed on BSE are cleared and settled by KELER Ltd. Budapest (see below).

Table 3. **Market size and it's main determinants**

	1995 Apr.-Dec.	1996	1997	1998 Jan.-Feb.	Total
Futures turnover on market value on BSE (billion HUF. simple)	10.16	190.94	1 415.97	675.25	2 292.32
of which					
3 month T-bill	5.91	29.22	3.26	0.00	38.39
12 month T-bill	0.00	0.00	70.06	75.04	145.10
BUX	0.53	49.15	1 004.17	370.34	1 424.19
DEM	1.41	29.39	216.28	138.70	385.78
US$	1.34	32.99	115.45	91.13	240.91
ECU	0.97	49.23	5.11	0.00	55.31
1-month BUBOR*	0.00	0.87	0.02	0.00	0.89
3-month BUBOR*	0.00	0.09	1.61	0.04	1.75

Source: Budapest Stock Exchange

Table 1. Table 4. **Open interest on BSE at market price**
(in HUF million)

	3TB	12TB	BUX	DEM	US$	ECU	1BR	3BR	Total
96/12.	1 644	0	4 360	2 916	3 659	5 598	0.04	0.15	18 178
97/12.	1 476	136	46 598	31 025	13 351	0	3.84	21.08	92 612
98/01.	1 476	34	41 229	29 494	13 120	0	2.87	17.08	85 373
98/02.	1 476	123	46 748	53 280	23 011	0	0.95	17.04	124 656

Source: Budapest Stock Exchange

The popularity of *BUX futures* started to increase in 1996. In 1997 this trend continued and resulted in a tenfold increase of BUX open interests between the end of the two years. The turnover increased by 20 times from 1996 to 1997. This dramatic development may be explained by the general optimism with regard to the stock prices and the fact that market players were quick to learn how to profit from this optimism. Some would say that there was an over-optimism present in the BUX futures market before the crash in October, 1997, as until that date investors did not experience large-scale losses resulting from the sudden reversal of the generally optimistic expectations.

Until the global decline in stock exchanges in October, 1997, BUX futures contract tended to be considerably overpriced, compared to the "no-arbitrage" requirement (*e.g.* over the price what would be justified on the basis of spot index plus a risk-free interest rate).[4] Selling futures in a futures market with implied interest rates sometimes twice as high as the risk-free interest rate, and at the same time buying shares on the spot market in roughly the same composition as in the BUX, provides assured profits for investors. Indeed, this was and still is a widely adopted strategy in several periods from 1996 onwards. In addition to this futures arbitrage profit, profit-opportunity arises whenever the futures price of the BUX drops below the no-arbitrage level. In such situations, arbitrageurs who are already "locked in" the arbitrage position should not wait until the expiration date of their original contracts, rather they may add to their assured profits by reversing ("early unwind") their position (*e.g.* selling shares on the spot market and buying BUX futures contracts). Alternatively, investors may chose to roll over their original arbitrage positions if BUX contracts with later expiration dates are available.[5] Besides non-financial firms and individuals, institutional investors are important players in creating such "synthetic" instruments. Institutional investors are particularly well placed for such strategies, because they hold considerable amount of shares and can thus economise on transaction costs in creating arbitrage positions. As we will see below, they are permitted to trade in derivative markets on a restricted basis.

A major regulatory change came into force on 24 January 1997, in permitting foreign residents to participate in the futures BUX trading. Because their share in the spot market turnover was somewhere between two thirds and three fourths, it was natural to expect that they would dominate in the futures trade as well. Turnover has indeed increased in the BUX futures from the beginning of 1997, but until the first quarter of 1998 foreign residents were not active in the BUX futures market.

In October and November, the share prices on the BSE were seriously affected by the contagion effect of the Asian crises. For example, the spot index dropped by more than 16 per cent on 28th October. From the local peak, 8 106 points on 22nd October, the spot index fell to its lowest value during the crisis on 13th November with 5 561 points (31 per cent drop). However, by 7 January 1998 the spot index had climbed back to 8 647 points, and in the late April, it exceeded the 9 000 points level. On the BUX futures market, similar price movements were recorded, although the contracts with different maturities performed differently: December 1997 contracts dropped by 17 per cent, March 1998 contracts by nearly 13 per cent and the contracts with longer maturities by less than 10 per cent.

Is it possible that the futures BUX contributed to the large drop in the value of the spot index? It would be hard to prove that this was the case. However, there are some features of the futures index trade on the BSE which indicate that the futures market played some role in the crash. But we do not know how important it may have been nor whether the BUX futures started the process or simply followed the downward movement with some positive feedback effect.

The first mechanism by which the futures BUX may have contributed to the crisis is the unwinding of futures arbitrage positions as we explained above. In a situation, where an initial over-valuation of BUX futures switches to an under-valuation position, for arbitrageurs it becomes profitable to sell on the spot market and buy on the futures market, thus closing their position. This means sellling in a falling market, reinforcing the drop of the underlying share prices. However, by simultaneously buying on the futures market, they contributed to the reversal of the falling trend.

The other feature of the BSE trading organisation which could have played a role is that trading in Hungarian shares starts earlier in the morning in London than in Budapest. Thus, at the opening stage of the BUX futures section on the BSE, traders and investors already know the London prices. On the morning of 28 October 1997 London prices incorporated a huge los and traders were sure that a serious price drop would occur that day on the BSE. So everyone wanted to sell that day, but nobody was sure that he or she could. Those risk averse investors and traders who wanted to sell at any price and wanted to be sure of it, offered their contracts at a low price. At this point the matching algorithm for the opening stage might have contributed to lowering selling prices: as the algorithm pairs the most aggressive bids and offers, risk averse players had to sell at very low prices to avoid future, potentially larger losses by failing to have their offers matched. Thus, the very trading organisation which, at normal times, helps to generate some movements in prices, may make things worse in extreme situations.

As a consequence of the crises, the limit for the daily price movement has been raised in several steps (by 250-300, then by 500-600 points and finally, by 550-700 points, depending on the maturity). In addition, the initial margins have been doubled. Some smaller investors may have been hit hard by the drop, and the broker/dealers also increased their margins *vis-à-vis* this category of investors in order to decrease their own risk exposure. With hindsight, the financial markets proved robust, although selling pressure could be felt on the spot foreign exchange market as well in this period, and the market exchange rate weakened within the official band for a couple of days.

After the crash, players on the BUX market became much more cautious. Speculators became less enthusiastic about the likely future development of the BUX. This is reflected both in the narrower futures spreads over the spot index and the lower futures premia over the three month treasury bill. Also, the cost of trading rose through the increased margin requirements for the traders and their clients. The BUX section became more mature than before, without any serious threat to the financial system.

Interest rate futures contracts[6] trading and open interests represent the smallest segment of the futures section. This may be surprising at first sight, since there is a large government paper section on the BSE, providing a liquid underlying market for futures trading. But, as we could see on BCE and we will see below on the OTC market, interest rate contracts are not widely traded on any Hungarian market. This could be taken as typical in a less mature market, in a less mature economy with high inflation and nominal interest rates. In the present Hungarian context this argument certainly has some validity. Another, frequently offered explanation is that expectations are one-sided, so it is hard to find counter-parties. This may explain part of the relative unpopularity of interest rate contracts, but hardly a large part. This is so because for interest rate futures contracts to be traded it is not necessary to have different expectations about the *direction* of interest rate movements on the two sides of the deal. It is enough to have different expectations about the *rate or size of change* of interest rate movements. Be that as it may, the Hungarian interest rate futures market is still in its infancy.

The most successful interest rate contracts by far are the futures based on the three months Treasury-bills. However, turnover of this product declined from the peak 5.4 bn HUF in April, 1996 to levels far below 1 bn HUF in 1997 on a monthly basis. Outstanding contracts also declined from 2.7 bn HUF in April 1996 to 1.8 bn in May 1997. Trading and open interests in other interest rate contracts are far below these levels. It may be that without a further decline in the inflation rate and nominal interest rate levels, the interest rate segment can not develop in the futures market.

3. Central Clearing House and Depository (Budapest) KELER Ltd[7].

3.1 Organisation and regulation

KELER Ltd. was established in 1993 on the basis of the securities and stock exchange law then in force (VI/1990, amended by XLII/1994 and by CXL/1996) and is licensed by the SMCMS. It is established as a legal entity, with privately placed and closely held shares. National Bank of Hungary holds 50 per cent of the shares whereas the two exchanges hold 25-25 per cent. In 1995 KELER Ltd. was declared a National Depository and approved by US authorities as a recognised depository institution according to the Investment Law, point 17f-5.

3.2 Settlements and clearing of derivatives by KELER Ltd.

KELER Ltd. settles and clears all derivative trades executed on both exchanges (including the non-financial sections of the BCE). It keeps the securities and cash accounts of exchange members. KELER Ltd. specifies the financial collateral and margin requirements for clearing members and monitors compliance on a continuous basis. It also settles the deals matched each day by the exchanges and settles the open positions at the time of expiration. And, like all other futures clearing houses, it guarantees futures settlements, thus eliminating credit, payment and settlement risks.

KELER Ltd. operates a guarantee system by which: *i)* it settles only for clearing members, *ii)* requires financial collateral, *iii)* determines and requires initial margin calculated to cover the maximum possible losses caused by the greatest possible price movement on a day, *iv)* requires supplementary financial collateral above a specified number of open positions. In case of spot government paper multi-level clearing membership has been introduced. In the more critical case of derivative transactions, this is not yet the case. In general, all members of the derivative sections of the two exchanges are automatically clearing members as well. One exemption to this rule are the recently introduced "locals" on the BUX futures market, who are not themselves clearing members and may clear their transactions *via* clearing members. KELER Ltd. plans to separate clearing and derivative exchange membership to strengthen its own stability and prevent losses to the clearing house and systemic risks.

The maximum price movement allowed are strict on BCE for a day, but on BSE, after a general clearing, trade can be continued. After each business day margin requirements for new positions and variation margins arising from adverse price movements will be called for. Non-compliance with these prescription may lead to suspension of trading rights or liquidation of positions.

KELER Ltd. is working on the regulation and system implementation for an integrated futures and options settlement system for both exchanges. Recently, KELER chose to implement the SPAN margining system developed by the Chicago Mercantile Exchange.

3.3 OTC transactions settled and cleared by the KELER Ltd.

KELER Ltd. settles OTC transactions only for government securities. A vast majority of these are spot and *repo* transactions. Participants in this market are banks, specialised financial institutions, securities investment firms and NBH and KELER Ltd. itself. There is no obligatory or privately negotiated margin requirement in this market segment. Settlements are effected on a gross basis, by DVP. Recently, multiple daily settlement cycles have been introduced. Contracts are made on the basis of standardised documentation. *No OTC corporate securities or forex futures and forwards, swaps and options transactions are cleared by KELER Ltd.*

4 Non-cleared, non-public OTC derivative market

4.1 Prudential regulation

4.1.1 Credit (partner-) risks

Starting from January 1997 banks has to report to the SMCMS[8] their derivative positions which must be taken into account in calculating their regulatory capital requirements. The types of derivatives are the same as in the BCBS "expanded matrix": interest rate, foreign exchange, share, and commodity derivatives.[9] The maturity break-down is more detailed and the required capital charges for the types of instruments are higher in the Hungarian regulation than even in BCBS reflecting the greater risks involved in such instruments under less stable conditions.[10] The appropriate counter party risk weights are also applicable for OTC derivatives as in the case of the balance sheet items.

4.1.2 Market risks

As there is no regulation of market risks taken by banks and they are not allowed to trade directly on the exchanges, their derivative activities are automatically OTC transactions. To date Hungary did not implement the EU "trading book" or the capital requirement for market risks suggested by the Basle Commission for Banking Supervision (BCBS). Thus, the regulation applicable for OTC derivative activities of banks is a more traditional "open position" restriction, imposed on banks overall foreign exchange mismatch arising from both their balance sheet and off-balance sheet items. According to this regulation, the restriction is defined in terms of the banks own capital that also serves to support the risks arising in general from the banking book. This means that the same capital is exposed to multiple risks.[11] Foreign exchange open position can not exceed 30 per cent of the bank's capital. Open positions must be calculated on a "gross aggregate" basis (*i.e.* "GAP"), which is also called the "Bundesbank-method".[12] This means, that equal risk weight is given to cross exchange rate movements and the movements between the HUF and other currencies. It is to be noted, that EU and BCBS adopted the so called "Bank of England" method, which allows for cross exchange rate movements partly to cancel each other in a typical bank's open position and requires less (half of the) regulatory capital than the open position *vis-à-vis* all the foreign currency open positions.

The government has already started to develop a *trading book* regulation for banks along the lines of the BCBS proposal and the EC CAD. Investment firms in securities and brokers/dealers will also be allowed to use the capital requirement for market risks instead of the current capital requirement. The latter is essentially a translation of the Basle/Cook ratio and is similar for both banks and securities firms in Hungary. But the capital requirements relevant for banks are not very useful for institutions and activities, which involve mainly market risks. For these market risks, the alternative definition of capital in the EU CAD, Annex V. which is based on the liquid elements of an institution's capital would be more appropriate.

4.2 Legal issues

There are legal ambiguities in Hungary as well, although so far legal disputes have not emerged about derivatives. For example, there are no specific regulations to assure enforceability of derivative contracts and netting arrangements. On the basis of the civil code, one can challenge the validity of derivative contracts as falling into the forbidden category of "selling something, which has not been owned". But the securities law explicitly defines derivative contracts as future liabilities or obligations, which do not count as "things" sold by a party, who did not possess them. In the case of OTC contracts, parties should sign a contract in terms of future liabilities to avoid potential legal disputes, instead of in terms of selling "things". A more serious problem is that the "Act on Investment Funds" (LXIII/1991, para. 12(4)) explicitly prohibits selling a security which has not been owned previously by the seller, and buying one, which has not been owned by the seller. This is equivalent to an outright prohibition of "short selling", without which a well developed derivative market it is hardly imaginable.

In the case of investment funds, another legal uncertainty arises from the fact that the law does not mention investment in derivatives among the permitted assets in the portfolio of the funds. In practice however, the SMCMS authorises funds to invest in these instruments for "hedging purposes", but sometimes it is hard to make distinction between hedging and speculation.

Despite these concerns, most of the potential legal obstacles to the derivative market are not so serious, as they are not directed against their use (*e.g.* the lack of explicit legal framework for netting, and for the derivative contract themselves.). Rather, they reflect realities of an earlier stage of development of the country's legal system. Nor are these kinds of obstacles specific to transition economies: most developed countries operated with the same legal ambiguities sometime in their recent past. Moreover, in newly adopted or proposed laws, at least for hedging purposes, authorities explicitly allow investments in derivatives for institutional investors, although on a small scale (*e.g.* in the case of voluntary "mutual funds" and the act on optionally obligatory funded pension plans, max. 10 per cent of their invested assets adopted at the end of 1997).

4.3 *Market size and its main determinants*[13]

Information about the main players, instruments and the size of the OTC market is important, because this segment of the derivative market has substantial partner risks. Other traded and cleared segments are less likely to cause systemic risks if appropriate regulation and infrastructure is in place, and implemented and run adequately. Although this is not completely the case in Hungary with traded and cleared contracts, safety of the market is satisfactory. By contrast, as far as the OTC market is concerned, opacity is prevalent, producing a less satisfactory situation. There is lack of information regarding standardised documentation, voluntary margining and collateralisation by the players, the typical counter-parties of the banks and the concentration of risks by institution etc. Regular data collection for derivative activities of banks, including OTC contracts, started in January 1997, based the bank's reports to the SMCMS. Statistical data collected in this way are also available to the National Bank of Hungary (NBH).

As this type of reporting is new for both the banks and the authorities, one should be aware of the possible mistakes and errors, which may make the database subject to possible future revisions and corrections. Nonetheless, based on the new data collected, we can obtain a rough picture of the market. Because only notional amounts are available, one is left to speculate on the basis of international evidence, that in general, replacement values are only a small percentage of the notional outstanding (roughly 2-5 per cent, depending on the type of instrument, time and place). Another problem with the data is that we do not know anything about their relation to the on-balance sheet and other potentially offsetting items. An increase of the notional outstanding value may either increase or decrease the overall risk of an institution.

Putting aside all these limitations, we can turn to the data. Within the total off-balance sheet liabilities of the banks, derivative activity in 1997 grew from 926 bn HUF to 2 100 bn HUF.[14] These amounts are the sum of total derivative assets and liabilities. This is a much higher pace compared to the growth of the more traditional off-balance sheet activities of the banks (more than 100 per cent, compared to less than 30 per cent). This may be partly the result of the relatively low initial level for derivatives. Their ratio within the off-balance sheet liabilities increased by more than 50 per cent.

Within the banking system as a whole, the most popular instruments *by type* are foreign exchange derivatives. Of the total derivatives notional outstanding contracts at the end of 1997, 88 per cent were forex and only

7.7 per cent were interest rate derivatives. At the end of 1996, the share of forward forex contracts was even higher, at 90 per cent, whereas futures accounted for 5.7 per cent of all derivative contracts. This pattern is typical for an emerging derivatives market, because, as we explained above in the context of the BSE, in more matured markets trading in interest rate instruments usually exceed trading in the forex contracts. Also, as we could already see above, the pre-announced crawling peg exchange rate regime and credibility of economic policy may explain the popularity of this kind of derivatives, because risks may be seen as limited and reasonably calculable. By contrast, the high level of inflation may make interest rate instruments too risky. Anyway, these relative proportions between type of derivative instruments are in line with those seen on both official exchanges.

The most popular instruments *by maturity* were in the short segment. Of all the notional outstanding contracts, instruments with maturities of less than three months accounted for 52.8 per cent, while contracts with maturites over three months and less than one year accounted for 36 per cent at the end of 1997. At the end of 1996, the maturity of the derivatives contracts were even shorter, 65.3 per cent and 27.3 per cent respectively. Thus a slight lengthening of maturites took place in each type of instrument.

The ratio of the *notional outstanding to the balance* sheet total of the banking system was about 30 per cent (total off-balance sheet items were close to 40 per cent) at the end of 1997. This seems a significant increase, but at this stage of development of the Hungarian derivative markets one should be cautious making comparisons between time periods.

As far as the *asset and liability matching* is concerned, the banking system as a whole had 30 per cent more forex liabilities than assets (1 055 bn to 798 bn HUF, *i.e.* net liabilities of 257 bn) at the end of 1997. However, this whole amount may not be a net position taking by Hungarian banks since at least part of these contracts represents hedging of on-balance sheet items. Also, the partners in some of these derivative contracts may be and actually are, players outside the domestic banking system, *e.g.* foreign banks. Moreover, the foreign exchange open position regulation induces banks to close their forex positions via forex derivatives. This became more and more important for the banks who increasingly raise funds abroad denominated in foreign currency and re-lend these funds in the domestic market in HUF.

Banks classified a very small portion of their derivative contracts. Provisions against derivative risk are negligible in relation to the notional outstanding amounts in the first half of 1997. More than 80 per cent of average outstandings was assigned above zero risk weight, but of this the overwhelming majority was given the risk weight applicable to banks incorporated in OECD countries.

The proportion of exchange traded instruments compared to the OTC derivatives traded diminished during 1997, falling below 10 per cent, from 20 per cent one year ago. For example, among the forex contracts, the ratio of *forward* (OTC) contracts have increased to *80 per cent.* Some banks are active on the BCE forex section via their broker/dealer firms. At the end of 1997, the outstanding forex futures liabilities of banks stood at 65 bn HUF, compared to the 180 bn HUF end of the year capitalisation of the forex section of the BCE. Usually, banks are buyers of futures contracts on the BCE as we explained above when discussing the their forex arbitrage activities.

5. Institutional investments

5.1 Regulatory environment[15]

Until the end of 1997, institutional investors consisted only of insurance companies, investment funds and voluntary social security "mutual funds" (or "caisses")[16] in Hungary. With the adoption of a new act on private pension funds, from the beginning of 1998 another very important class of players has been added to the above three. Of the existing four, only the voluntary "mutual funds" and private pension funds are permitted by law to engage in derivative transactions. For investment funds and insurance companies' derivative activity is "tolerated" by their supervision authorities for hedging purposes. As we could see in some detail in the explanation of some legal considerations above, this means that although the "Act on Investment Funds" and "Act on Insurance Companies" do not mention derivatives among the eligible assets, some funds and insurance companies invest, with the consent of their supervision authorities, in exchange traded futures instruments, mainly in BUX futures.[17]

The new act on the pension funds authorises them to invest in derivatives for hedging roughly on the same basis as the voluntary "mutual funds". We expect that they will become active players in derivatives, as they will compete with each other for clients, and these instruments provide cheap and flexible yield enhancing means for them.

5.2 *Derivative transactions of institutional investors*[18]

Until the stock exchange boom, institutional investors were unenthusiastic about equities and equity-based derivatives. With the boom lasting until October 1997, an attractive arbitrage opportunity opened up to them. As futures on BUX provide a considerable premium over the spot "portfolio", which replicates the composition of BUX, selling futures and holding spot share portfolio as hedging, makes this strategy safe and profitable for investors. If authorities allow BUX futures for institutional investors only for hedging, then the value of shares in their portfolio limits their activities. This was seen above when we described the typical trading strategies on the futures BUX market. Thus far voluntary "mutual funds" did not use their rights to invest in derivatives. The most active players among the domestic institutional investors in derivative trading were investment funds.

Two main constraints prevent institutional investors to play a larger role in derivative markets. One is their small size, the other is portfolio regulation. The first obstacle will be removed over time. The government incentives to institutional forms of savings and to funded social security plans seems set to continue in the future. The removal of the second obstacle needs a change in regulatory attitude, which may prove somewhat harder to obtain in the near future. It is interesting that no public debate or communication has been initiated so far on these issues, even among professionals.

Another kind of players are "funds", established as non-financial corporations which do not fall under any existing laws and regulations regulating financial intermediaries. An example is the two "funds" recently merged, managed by *Banker Ltd.* (*e.g.* 2nd Forex Factory -- in Hungarian "2. Deviza Factory", the first of which already has been closed down -- and Risk Factory -- "Rizikó Factory"). The second Forex Factory used to invest mainly in forex contracts, whereas the Risk Factory invested mainly in spot shares and futures BUX contracts. The maximum proportion in the portfolio of these risky assets is published beforehand, and the potential investors know the risky nature of the investment. Investors are asked by the fund managers to put into these "vehicles" only their risk money. The shares of both "funds" are traded on the BSE. (Their market capitalisation at the end of August 1997 was 379 M HUF and 802 M HUF respectively). The two funds have recently been merged, with the book value of the share capital above 844 M HUF, while the market capitalisation standing at nearly 590 M HUF at the end of March 1998.

6. Foreign residents and the Hungarian derivative markets

6.1 Current general approach of Hungarian authorities

To date foreign residents are not allowed to trade derivatives in Hungary, the only exception being the futures BUX contract traded on BSE. Starting 24 January 1997 this segment was open to foreigners. The consent of the National Bank of Hungary to this liberalisation was given on several conditions. These include daily reporting to the NBH of the share of the foreigners in turnover and open positions, large position-taking by foreigners, number of closed contracts and profits realised by foreigners. There are strict rules on the maximum possible price movements. In case of reaching the defined limit, immediate clearing is executed by the clearing house. Then those players, who re-deposit the required margins, can continue the trade. There are other restrictions like segregation of sub-account on behalf of foreigners held on the main accounts of the securities firm with the clearing house. Restrictions also aim to ensure that the money to be invested in BUX can only come from abroad via foreign exchange conversion, and conversely, they can put their profits in convertible HUF accounts if they can prove that the invested amount originally came from abroad. These restrictions are not intended as discriminating against foreigners, but rather, aim to minimise potential pressures on the domestic forex market in case of large-scale profit taking and repatriation by foreign investors while still allowing them to hedge market risks arising from their spot share positions.

6.2 Prospects for further liberalisation

The National Bank of Hungary as a foreign exchange authority currently does not intend to liberalise capital movements further in a stepwise fashion. For the moment, it feels that the current degree of liberalisation is quite high, and also in accordance with our international commitments (OECD, EU). Until Hungary gains more experience with the present level of liberalisation no more steps are foreseen. But we also take into account the costs of this degree of liberalisation. By costs we mean less transparent markets, arising from the fact that it is relatively easy for market players to circumvent the remaining restrictions. This has the result that the Hungarian market is virtually totally open, but the authorities do not have access to all the information which would be available with full liberalisation. Thisdisadvantage is partially outweighed by the slightly higher transactions cost caused by the remaining restrictions. In sum, the remaining restrictions are to be maintained for some time, not as part of a long-term strategy, but as a temporary necessity or safeguard. As soon as macroeconomic conditions and the implementation of adequate prudential regulation allow, Hungarian authorities will remove the remaining controls.

6.3 *Immediate plans*

Even in these circumstances, people interested in the development of Hungarian markets and their openness are not likely to sit and wait passively. Work already started in the clearing house and the exchanges to build up the necessary infrastructure for multiple currency clearing and settlements. The intended technological development will make it possible for Hungarian markets and their financial infrastructure to offer services to foreigners on a relatively large scale, without any potential interference with the Hungarian money and foreign markets or monetary policy, because the funds to be invested and the various margins and collaterals would be denominated in foreign currencies. This development will enhance competitiveness of our markets *vis-à-vis* both Western and Central and East European financial centres. The Hungarian authorities actively support these efforts of the markets.

NOTES

1. I am indebted for the two Hungarian exchanges for providing data in preparation of this note. Szergej Keresztesi, Krisztina Kasza and Attila Lovas of Budapest Commodity Exchange corrected the draft version on BCE. Zsolt Horváth and Károly Mátrai of KELER Ltd. also provided data on the performance of the two exchanges and the OTC market and made corrections on the draft version. Éva Istvánovits of the Regulation Department of the National Bank of Hungary helped in writing the legal aspects of derivatives in Hungary. Csaba Moré of the Banking Department of the National Bank of Hungary permitted to me to use his basic analysis on the OTC derivative activities of the banks based on the bank's reports to the supervision authorities. Zsófia Árvai of Economics and Research Department of the NBH helped to translate this note into English. All remaining errors and mistakes are my responsibilities.

2. More detailed data can be found in the Appendix, 1. Table.

3. See Appendix, 1. and 2. Table.

4. See the 3., 4., 5. charts in the Appendix showing price movements and implied interest rates of different BUX futures contracts.

5. For a detailed explanation of futures arbitrage, early unwinding and roll-over of futures positions see for example Sutcliffe (1997), p. 75-93.

6. See the development of BUBOR futures prices on both exchanges on 2. chart in the Appendix.

7. Sources on KELER are its official publications, various issues and communication with KELER officials.

8. SMCMS regulation 4/1996, amending the 1/1992 SMCMS regulation on the principles and calculation of capital adequacy. The Hungarian regulation does not permit the mark-to-market approach to calculate capital adequacy for OTC derivatives, only the alternative, simpler "original exposure" method.

9. BCBS (1995). The EU Solvency Ratio Directive, (EU, 89/647/EEC, Annex II) regulates only the partner (credit-) risk of interest rate and foreign exchange OTC derivatives.

10. The capital requirement in accordance with the Basle/EU regulation is intended to cover the potential replacement costs of cash flows arising from the non-performance of the partner.

11. The EU "trading book" (CAD) and BCBS "market risk" regulations require 8 per cent additional regulatory capital set aside in case of a bank's open forex position exceeds 2 per cent of its own capital.

12. On the economics of market risk regulation, and different methods to calculate open position see Levonian (1995). For a survey of how these are applied by regulators in developed and less developed countries see Harmann (1994) and (1997).

13. Detailed data can be found on bank's derivative businesses in the Appendix, 3, 4, 5 Tables.

14. See 3., and 4. Tables in the Annex on the banks derivative assets and liabilities.

15. Appendix 6 Table shows the portfolio regulations for institutional investors.

16. The law differentiates them from funds in that these "mutual funds" give formal rights to unit holders to have a say in its investment policies and other decisions. In the following, for sake of easier international comparison, but at the same time indicating the legal difference, I will use the expression "mutual funds" in between quotation marks.

17. It is to be noted that the at the beginning of 1997, nearly 80 per cent of insurance industry was owned by foreign professional owners. Thus, most of the users of derivatives in insurance industry are owned by professional investors, for whom using derivatives as hedging instruments may be legitimate or even encouraged investments in their home countries. However, even if this is the case, the legal uncertainty should be eliminated in Hungary about the usage of derivatives by insurance companies.

18. Summary tables of investment portfolio composition of institutional investors can be found in the Appendix, 7, 8, Tables.

REFERENCES

Basle Committee on Banking Supervision (1995): Basle Capital Accord. Treatment of Potential Exposure for off-Balance Sheet Items, Basle, April

DALE, R. (1994), "Regulating investment business in the Single Market", Bank of England Quarterly Bulletin, November

European Commission (1989), Council Directive on a Solvency Ratio for Credit Institutions (SRD, 89/647/EEC), Official Journal of the European Commission, No. L. 386/14, Brussels, particularly Annex II

LEVONIAN, M. E. (1994), "Bank Capital Standards for Foreign Exchange and Other Market Risks", Federal Reserve Bank of San Francisco Economic Review, pp. 3-18.

HARMAN, Ph. (1994), Foreign Exchange Risk Regulation. Issues for Industrial and Developing Countries, IMF Working Paper WP/94/141

HARMAN, Ph (1997), "Capital Adequacy and Foreign Exchange Risk Regulation. Theoretical Considerations and Recent Developments in Industrial Countries", Kredit und Kapital, 2/1997, p. 186-218.

State Money and Capital Market Supervision (1996): "SMCMS regulation 4/1996, amending the 1/1992 SMCMS regulation on the principles and calculation of capital adequacy", Budapest

SUTCLIFFE, (1997), Stock Index Futures. Theories and International Evidence, International Thomson Business Press, London.

APPENDIX

Table 1. **Turnover on the Budapest Commodity Exchange**

Product		1993	1994	1995	1996	1997	Total
DM	Turnover (M HUF)	430 360	11 165 552	67 470 984	80 193 382	317 600 517	476 860 796
	Turnover (contr.)	3 731	153 779	697 200	751 130	2 731 592	4 337 432
	Transaction (No.)	243	426	1 330	1 125	2 223	5 347
US$	Turnover (M HUF)	1 017 609	15 156 809	48 635 902	140 033 187	218 036 719	422 880 226
	Turnover (contr.)	10 228	136 163	357 610	871 174	1 097 502	2 472 677
	Transaction (No.)	401	641	1 292	1 834	4 173	8 341
ECU	Turnover (M HUF)	0	0	5 822 479	262 962 349	28 455 167	297 239 995
	Turnover (contr.)	0	0	31 435	1 303 920	134 048	1 469 403
	Transaction (No.)	0	0	33	1 404	143	1 580
Y	Turnover (M HUF)	0	609 200	40 072 626	142 309 943	140 211 150	323 202 919
	Turnover (contr.)	0	106	269 826	916 857	852 629	2 039 418
	Transaction (No.)	0	13	642	2 649	3 022	6 326
L	Turnover (M HUF)	0	0	0	76 800 590	9 690 649	86 491 239
	Turnover (contr.)	0	0	0	710 455	83 692	794 147
	Transaction (No.)	0	0	0	370	73	443
£	Turnover (M HUF)	0	0	0	85 614 665	61 758 642	147 373 307
	Turnover (contr.)	0	0	0	304 872	201 974	506 846
	Transaction (No.)	0	0	0	398	1 145	1 543
SF	Turnover (M HUF)	0	0	0	56 349 082	116 598 671	172 947 753
	Turnover (contr.)	0	0	0	419 885	849 185	1 269 070
	Transaction (No.)	0	0	0	505	1 871	2 376
CZK	Turnover (M HUF)	0	0	0	0	11	11
	Turnover (contr.)	0	0	0	0	2	2
	Transaction (No.)	0	0	0	0	2	2
Interest rate 90	Turnover (M HUF)	0	12 291	147 524	102 586	0	262 401
	Turnover (contr.)	0	160	2 016	1 661	0	3 837
	Transaction (No.)	0	4	25	44	0	73
3 months BUBOR	Turnover (M HUF)	0	0	0	10 777 823	184 005 633	194 783 456
	Turnover (contr.)	0	0	0	22 333	405 726	428 059
	Transaction (No.)	0	0	0	201	993	1 194
1 months BUBOR	Turnover (M HUF)	0	0	0	25 017 750	0	25 018
	Turnover (contr.)	0	0	0	135	0	135
	Transaction (No.)	0	0	0	6	0	6
Financial section	Turnover (M HUF)	1 447 970	26 943 852	162 149 515	855 168 623	1 076 357 160	2 122 067 121
	Turnover (contr.)	13 959	290 208	1 358 087	5 302 422	6 356 350	13 321 026
	Transaction (No.)	644	1 084	3 322	8 536	13 645	27 231

Source: Budapest Commodity Exchange, Annual Report, 1997.

Table 2. **Turnover in the derivative section of the Budapest Stock Exchange**

Product		1995. Apr-Dec	1996	1997	Total
3TB	Turnover (M HUF)	5 905	29 222	3 264	38 392
	Turnover (No.)	6 333	30 933	3 409	40 666
12TB	Turnover (M HUF)	0	0	70 060	70 060
	Turnover (No.)	0	0	8 126	8 126
BUX	Turnover (M HUF)	530	49 148	1 004 173	1 053 851
	Turnover (No.)	3 207	136 990	1 208 388	1 348 585
DM	Turnover (M HUF)	1 407	29 392	216 279	247 077
	Turnover (No.)	1 407	25 429	183 470	210 306
US$	Turnover (M HUF)	1 345	32 992	115 451	149 788
	Turnover (No.)	940	20 439	55 116	76 495
ECU	Turnover (M HUF)	969	49 228	5 110	553 069
	Turnover (No.)	494	24 299	2 339	27 132
1BR	Turnover (M HUF)	0	867	22	889
	Turnover (No.)	0	4 585	131	4 716
3BR	Turnover (M HUF)	0	872	1 614	1 701
	Turnover (No.)	0	161	3 679	3 840
Futures section	Turnover (M HUF)	10 155	190 936	1 415 974	1 617 065
	Turnover (No.)	12 381	242 836	1 464 658	1 719 875

Source: Budapest Securities Exchange, Monthly Report, March 1998.

Table 3.1 **Bank's total outstanding notional derivative contracts (1996)**
(Assets plus liabilities, end of the year, M HUF)

Type of contract Assets plus Liabilities	< 3 months	%	> 3 m.< 1 y.	%	> 1 y. < 2 y.	%	> 2 y.	%	Total	%
Interest rate derivatives	4 409	0.5%	19 976	2.2%	2 410	0.3%	25 958	2.8%	52 753	5.7%
of which:										
Single currency int. rate swaps	0		2 834		2 310		25 946			
Froward rate agreements	3 509		1 651		0		0			
Interest rate futures	98		9 066		100		0			
Interest rate options	601		6 425		0		12			
Other interest rate contracts	201		0		0		0			
Forex derivatives	588 948	63.6%	209 873	22.7%	4 309	0.5%	35 773	3.9%	838 903	90.6%
of which:										
Cross currency int. rate cont.	110 625		3 854		0		12 029			
Forward currency contracts	358 531		114 285		1 392		23 744			
Currency futures	97 433		84 452		2 917		0			
Currency options	0		0		0		0			
Other currency cotracts	22 359		7 282		0		0			
Securities and index derivatives	11 483	1.2%	22 504	2.4%	29	0.0%	0	0.0%	34 016	3.7%
of which:										
Securities derivatives	11 483		22 504		29		0			
Index derivatives	0		0		0		0			
Total	604 840	65.3%	252 353	27.3%	6 748	0.7%	61 731	6.7%	925 672	100.0%

Source: State Money and Capital Market Supervision, as reported by the banks.

Table 3.2 **Bank's total outstanding notional derivative contracts 1997**
(Assets plus liabilities, end of the year, M HUF)

Type of contract Assets plus Liabilities	< 3 months	%	> 3 m.< 1 y.	%	> 1 y. < 2 y.	%	> 2 y.	%	Total	%
Interest rate derivatives	26 880	1.3%	28 077	1.3%	6 051	0.3%	100 818	4.8%	161 826	7.7%
of which:										
Single currency int. rate swaps	2 620		14 903		6 051		98 986			
Froward rate agreements	9 204		13 174		0		0			
Interest rate futures	13 000		0		0		0			
Interest rate options	0		0		0		1 832			
Other interest rate contracts	2 056		0		0		0			
Forex derivatives	1 006 509	47.9%	720 024	34.3%	88 561	4.2%	38 653	1.8%	1 853 747	88.2%
of which:										
Cross currency int. rate cont.	58 601		37 280		0		11 785			
Forward currency contracts	828 740		475 011		61 431		26 868			
Currency futures	72 678		77 262		722		0			
Currency options	6 989		72 912		12 210		0			
Other currency cotracts	39 501		57 559		14 198		0			
Securities and index derivatives	76 085	3.6%	9 415	0.4%	1 303	0.1%	0	0.1%	86 803	4.1%
of which:										
Securities derivatives	76 055		9 310		1 303		0			
Index derivatives	30		105		0		0			
Total	1 108 474	47.9%	757 516	36.0%	95 915	4.6%	139 471	4.6%	2 101 376	100.0%

Source: State Money and Capital Market Supervision, as reported by the banks.

Table 4.1 **Bank's total outstanding notional derivative contracts, 1996**
(Assets, end of the year, M HUF)

Type of contract Assets				%	> 1 y. < 2 y.	%	> 2 y.	%	Total	%
Interest rate derivatives	2 511	0.6%	9 273	2.2%	1 255	0.3%	12 946	3.0%	25 985	6.1%
of which:										
Single currency int. rate swaps	0		1 417		1 155		24 646			
Froward rate agreements	1 759		951		0		0			
Interest rate futures	50		480		100		0			
Interest rate options	601		6 425		0		0			
Other interest rate contracts	101		0		0		0			
Forex derivatives	273 849	64.3%	86 859	20.4%	3 596	0.8%	17 564	4.1%	381 868	89.6%
of which:										
Cross currency int. rate cont.	55 486		1 922		0		6 120			
Forward currency contracts	162 651		42 329		680		11 444			
Currency futures	44 428		39 057		2 916		0			
Currency options	0		0		0		0			
Other currency cotracts	11 284		3 551		0		0			
Securities and index derivatives	4 512	1.1%	13 704	3.2%	0	0.0%	0	0.0%	18 216	4.3%
of which:										
Securities derivatives	4 512		13 704		0		0			
Index derivatives	0		0		0		0			
Total	280 872	65.9%	109 836	25.8%	4 851	1.1%	30 510	7.2%	426 069	100.0%

Source: State Money and Capital Market Supervision, as reported by the banks.

Table 4.2 **Bank's total outstanding notional derivative contracts, 1997**
(Assets, end of the year, M HUF)

Type of contract Assets				%	> 1 y. < 2 y.	%	> 2 y.	%	Total	%
Interest rate derivatives	6 604	0.7%	13 479	1.5%	2 971	0.3%	49 624	5.6%	72 678	8.2%
of which:										
Single currency int. rate swaps	1 296		7 362		2 971		48 708			
Froward rate agreements	4 100		6 117		0		0			
Interest rate futures	0		0		0		0			
Interest rate options	0		0		0		916			
Other interest rate contracts	1 208		0		0		0			
Forex derivatives	460 242	51.7%	299 705	33.7%	20 700	2.3%	17 656	2.0%	798 303	89.6%
of which:										
Cross currency int. rate cont.	29 333		18 563		0		5 553			
Forward currency contracts	392 346		179 399		6 755		12 194			
Currency futures	15 463		40 524		722		0			
Currency options	3 460		33 115		6 105		0			
Other currency cotracts	19 640		28 149		7 118		0			
Securities and index derivatives	16 185	1.8%	4 039	0.5%	0	0.0%	0	0.0%	20 224	2.3%
of which:										
Securities derivatives	16 155		3 934		0		0			
Index derivatives	30		105		0		0			
Total	482 031	47.9%	317 223	35.6%	23 671	2.7%	67 280	2.7%	890 205	100.0%

Source: State Money and Capital Market Supervision, as reported by the banks.

Table 5.1 **Bank's total outstanding notional derivative contracts 1996 (Liabilities, end of the year, M HUF)**

Type of contract Assets	< 3 months	%	> 3 m.< 1 y.	%	> 1 y. < 2 y.	%	> 2 y.	%	Total	%
Interest rate derivatives	1 898	0.4%	10 703	2.1%	1 155	0.2%	13 012	2.6%	26 768	5.4%
of which:										
Single currency int. rate swaps	0		1 417		1 155		1 300			
Froward rate agreements	1 750		700		0		0			
Interest rate futures	48		8 586		0		0			
Interest rate options	0		0		0		12			
Other interest rate contracts	100		0		0		0			
Forex derivatives	315 099	63.1%	123 014	24.6%	713	0.1%	18 209	3.6%	457 035	91.5%
of which:										
Cross currency int. rate cont.	55 139		1 932		0		5 909			
Forward currency contracts	195 880		71 956		712		12 300			
Currency futures	53 005		45 395		1		0			
Currency options	0		0		0		0			
Other currency cotracts	11 075		3 731		0		0			
Securities and index derivatives	6 971	1.4%	8 800	1.8%	29	0.0%	0	0.0%	15 800	3.2%
of which:										
Securities derivatives	6 971		8 800		29		0			
Index derivatives	0		0		0		0			
Total	323 968	64.8%	142 517	28.5%	1 897	0.4%	31 221	6.2%	499 603	100.0%

Source: State Money and Capital Market Supervision, as reported by the banks.

Table 5.2 **Bank's total outstanding notional derivative contracts 1997 (Liabilities, end of the year, M HUF)**

Type of contract Liabilities	< 3 months	%	> 3 m.< 1 y.	%	> 1 y. < 2 y.	%	> 2 y.	%	Total	%
Interest rate derivatives	20 276	1.7%	14 598	1.2%	3 080	0.3%	51 194	4.2%	89 148	7.4%
of which:										
Single currency int. rate swaps	1 324		7 541		3 080		50 278			
Froward rate agreements	5 104		7 057		0		0			
Interest rate futures	13 000		0		0		0			
Interest rate options	0		0		0		916			
Other interest rate contracts	848		0		0		0			
Forex derivatives	546 267	45.1%	420 319	34.7%	67 861	5.6%	20 997	1.7%	1 055 444	87.1%
of which:										
Cross currency int. rate cont.	29 268		18 717		0		6 232			
Forward currency contracts	436 394		295 612		54 676		14 674			
Currency futures	57 215		36 738		0		0			
Currency options	3 529		39 797		6 105		0			
Other currency cotracts	19 861		29 410		7 080		0			
Securities and index derivatives	59 900	4.9%	5 376	0.4%	1 303	0.1%	0	0.0%	66 579	5.5%
of which:										
Securities derivatives	59 900		5 376		1 303		0			
Index derivatives	0		0		0		0			
Total	626 443	51.7%	440 293	36.4%	72 244	6.0%	72 191	6.0%	1 211 171	100.0%

Source: State Money and Capital Market Supervision, as reported by the banks.

Table 6. **Restrictions on institutional investors' portfolio in Hungary**

Item	Type of asset	Voluntary social security "funds"	Insurance companies	Investment funds (excluded real estate funds)	Private pension funds.
1	Cash, cash accounts	Minimum 10 %, together with items 2 and 3 if their maturity is less than 1 year. Minimum 40 % together with items 2 and 3 with more than 1 year maturity.	Of insurance reserves, no less than 40 % minus items 2 and 3 if their maturity is less than 1 year.		
2	Government papers (including central bank paper)	Minimum 10 %, together with items 1 and 3 if their maturity is less than 1 year. Minimum 40 % together with items 1 and 3 with more than 1 year maturity.	Of insurance reserves, no less than 40 % minus items 1 and 3 if their maturity is less than 1 year		
3	Deposits with banks or deposit-like papers banks issued	Minimum 10 %, together with items 1 and 2 if their maturity is less than 1 year. Minimum 40 % together with items 1 and 2 with more than 1 year maturity. Max. 60 %, if maturity exceeds 1 year.	No more than 25 % minus item 11 of the mathematical reserves and solvency capital; of insurance reserves, no less than 40 % minus items 1 and 2 if their maturity is less than 1 year.		Deposits with institutions belonging to the same banking group may not exceed 20 % of the assets of the pension fund. Together with items 2,4,11, max. 60 %.
4	Exchange traded securities	Max. 60 %. If so classified, see item 5.	In shares, less than 10 % of the mathematical reserve and solvency capital		Max. 30 % BSE shares (20 % in foreign recognised markets). Max. 30 % OECD gov. and corp. guarantied or traded bonds.

5	Off-exchange securities	Max. 30 %	In shares, less than 5 % of the mathematical reserve and solvency capital	Max. 10 %, but max. 2 % of the same issuer.	Max. 20 % bank or bank guaranteed corporate bonds. Otherwise 10-10 % corp. and loc. gov. bonds.
6	Securities issued by pension and health care self-governing bodies (non- funded, parts of the state household)	If guaranteed by the government, max. 60 %.	Less than 10 % of the mathematical reserve and solvency capital		
7	Securities issued by non-financial companies	Max. 60 %. If non-traded on an exchange or so classified, see item 5.	Less than 10 % of the mathematical reserve and solvency capital		Max. 60 %. If non-traded, see item 5.
8	Units issued by investment funds.	Max. 60 %, depending on classification. If so classified, see item 5.	Less than 5 % of the mathematical reserve and solvency capital	Max. 10 %	Depending on the portfolio of the fund. The same as for individual papers.
9	Real estate or securities issued by real estate funds	Max. 60 % depending on classification	No more than 20 % of the mathematical reserve and solvency capital		Max. 10 %.
10	Loans to owners, investors, insured.	Max. 30 % "for members"	-		
11	Mortgage papers falling under mortgage law	Max. 60 % if guaranteed by a bank or real estate	No more than 25 % minus item 11 of the mathematical reserve and solvency capital	Max. 25 % even if issued by the same issuer, and not traded on exchange.	Max. 10 %.
12	Securities issued by public utilities	Max. 60 %, depending on classification. May be max. 30 %.	Less than 10 % of the mathematical reserve and solvency capital		-
13	Securities issued by local government	Max. 60 %, depending on classification. May be max. 30 %.	Less than 5 % of the mathematical reserve and solvency capital		Max. 10 %.

Table 6. **Restrictions on institutional investors' portfolio in Hungary** (continued)

Item	Type of asset	Voluntary social security "funds"	Insurance companies	Investment funds (excluded real estate funds)	Private pension funds.
14	Compensation note			Max. 15 %. In case of compensation note fund indicated in its name, max. 25 %.	
15	Derivative instruments	Max. 10 % of their Net Asset Value	By law: zero, in practice supervision authorities may allow for hedging positions.	By law: zero, in practice supervision authorities may allow for hedging positions. "Short selling" may be challenged on the	Only for hedging purposes. Max. 10 % of total invested assets.
16	Foreign assets	Max. 5 % of total invested assets.	Zero	Zero	Max. 30 % of the portfolio. Max. 10 % bonds if traded in Hungary
17	Note	Securities issued by the same issuer and deposits with the same bank may not exceed 20 % of portfolio.	Supervision authority may allow non-compliance with the above types of assets and ratios	Of the of the portfolio, max. 5 % in the same type of securities of the same issuer. Exemptions are: mortgage papers: max. 25 %, and government papers; no more than 10 % of the same issuer except mortgage papers: max. 25 % and government papers.	Except for government papers, securities holding may not exceed 10 % of all papers issued by the same issuer, or the portfolio of the fund. Only securities traded on recognised (by the Act on foreign exchange) exchanges are eligible to pension funds.

Source: Various laws and regulations for institutional investors.

Table 7. **Investment portfolio of institutional investors in Hungary (excluding banks)**

	1996 Q4		1997 Q1		1997 Q2	
Total institutional investments	value of invested assets (M HUF)	share in the portfolio (%)	value of invested assets (M HUF)	share in the portfolio (%)	value of invested assets (M HUF)	share in the portfolio (%)
Claims on the banking system	35 167	10.29%	36 381	9.36%	47 515	10.40%
Claims on the consolidated government (with maturity less than one year)	165 506	48.43%	190 165	48.91%	217 342	47.58%
Claims on the consolidated government (with maturity over one year)	104 096	30.46%	117 041	30.10%	139 276	30.49%
Bonds issued by non-financial firms	9 218	2.70%	13 121	3.38%	13 362	2.93%
Shares	10 635	3.11%	13 654	3.51%	20 167	4.41%
Units of investment funds	359	0.10%	601	0.15%	316	0.07%
Other items	16 758	4.90%	17 812	4.58%	18 836	4.12%
Total stock of assets at the end of the quarter	341 739	100.00%	388 776	100.00%	456 814	100.00%

Source: National Bank of Hungary, based on the reports by the institutions to respective supervision authorities.

Table 8. **Portfolio of institutional investors by type institution**

million HUF

	1996 Q4		1997 Q1		1997 Q2	
Voluntary savings in specialised social security "funds" (mainly supplementary pension funds)	value of invested assets (M HUF)	share in the portfolio (%)	value of invested assets (M HUF)	share in the portfolio (%)	value of invested assets (M HUF)	share in the portfolio (%)
Claims on the banking system	3 279	13.79%	1 916	6.87%	1 830	5.11%
Claims on the consolidated government (with maturity less than one year)	11 721	49.28%	14 968	53.71%	16 846	46.99%
Claims on the consolidated government (with maturity over one year)	6 901	29.02%	9 098	32.65%	11 649	32.49%
Bonds issued by non-financial firms	812	3.41%	274	0.98%	832	2.32%
Shares	982	4.13%	1 469	5.27%	3 550	9.90%
Units of investment funds	43	0.18%	115	0.41%	133	0.37%
Other (including: loans to members and non classified assets)	43	0.18%	30	0.11%	1 009	2.81%
Total stock of assets at the end of the quarter	23 781	100.00%	27 870	100.00%	35 848	100.00%

Table 8. **Portfolio of institutional investors by type institution** (continued)
million HUF

	1996 Q4		1997 Q1		1997 Q2	
Insurance companies	value of invested assets (M HUF)	share in the portfolio (%)	value of invested assets (M HUF)	share in the portfolio (%)	value of invested assets (M HUF)	share in the portfolio (%)
Claims on the banking system	16 418	8.16%	12 330	5.81%	19 111	8.42%
Claims on the consolidated government (with maturity less than one year)	94 069	46.73%	90 862	42.81%	95 657	42.15%
Claims on the consolidated government (with maturity over one year)	58 653	29.14%	72 342	34.09%	79 131	34.87%
Bonds issued by non-financial firms	6 956	3.46%	8 995	4.24%	7 916	3.49%
Shares	8 393	4.17%	9 871	4.65%	7 368	3.25%
Units of investment funds	0	0.00%	45	0.02%	45	0.02%
Other (including: real estates and loans for life-insurance policy holders)	16 815	8.35%	17 781	8.38%	17 710	7.80%
Total stock of assets at the end of the quarter	201 304	100.00%	212 226	100.00%	226 938	100.00%

Table 8. **Portfolio of institutional investors by type institution** (continued)
million HUF

	1996 Q4		1997 Q1		1997 Q2	
Investment funds	value of invested assets (M HUF)	share in the portfolio (%)	value of invested assets (M HUF)	share in the portfolio (%)	value of invested assets (M HUF)	share in the portfolio (%)
Claims on the banking system	15 470	13.26%	22 136	14.89%	26 574	13.70%
Claims on the consolidated government (with maturity less than one year)	59 717	51.19%	84 336	56.72%	104 840	54.03%
Claims on the consolidated government (with maturity over one year)	38 542	33.04%	35 600	23.94%	48 496	24.99%
Bonds issued by non-financial firms	1 450	1.24%	3 852	2.59%	4 614	2.38%
Shares	1 260	1.08%	2 314	1.56%	9 248	4.77%
Units of investment funds	316	0.27%	441	0.30%	138	0.07%
Other (including: futures contracts as hedging instruments, maybe negative)	- 100	-0.09%	1	0.00%	117	0.06%
Total stock of assets at the end of the quarter	116 654	100.00%	148 680	100.00%	194 028	100.00%

Source: National Bank of Hungary, based on the reports by the institutions to respective supervision authorities.

Chart 1. **The official exchange rate band, the market exchange rate and the evolution of the futures basket on BCE**

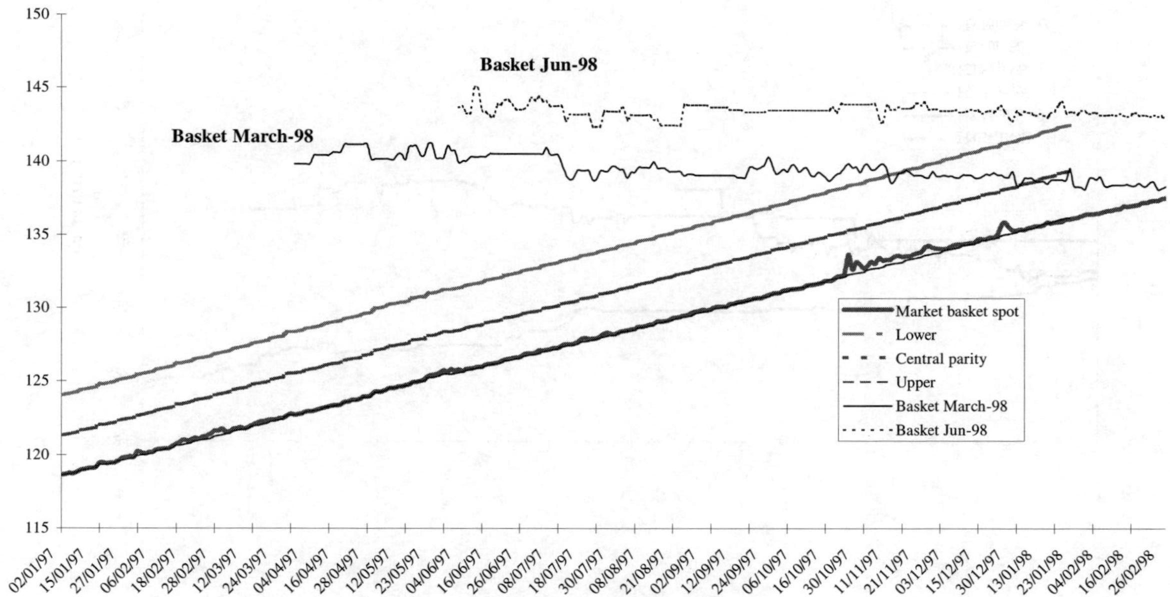

Source: National Bank of Hungary and Budapest Commodity Exchange.

Chart 2. **The 3 months interbank spot interest rates and 3 months interest rate futures on the BSE and the BCE**

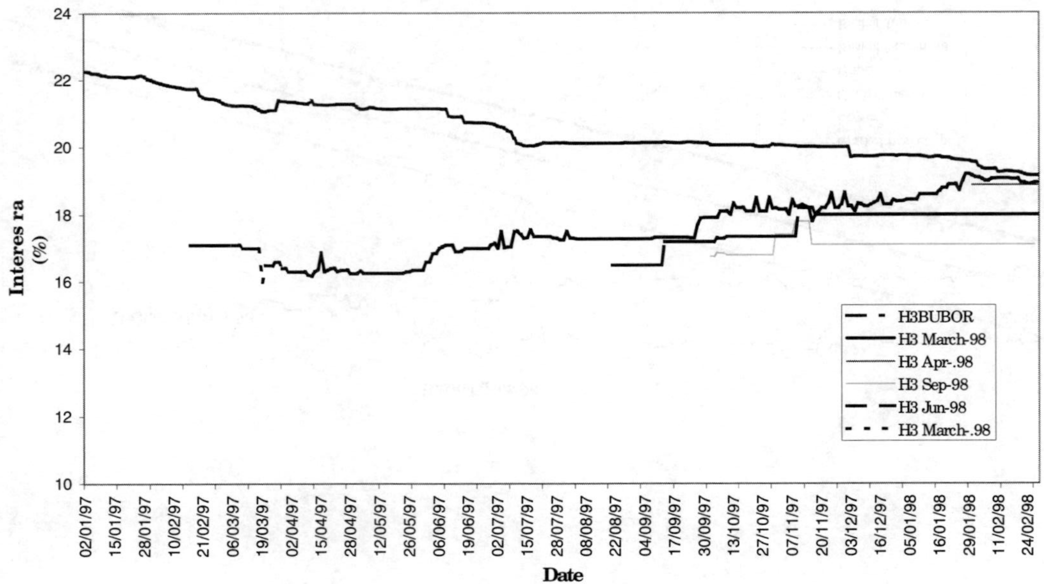

Source: National Bank of Hungary, Budapest Commodity Exchange and Budapest Stock Exchange.

Chart 3. **BUX spot and futures prices**

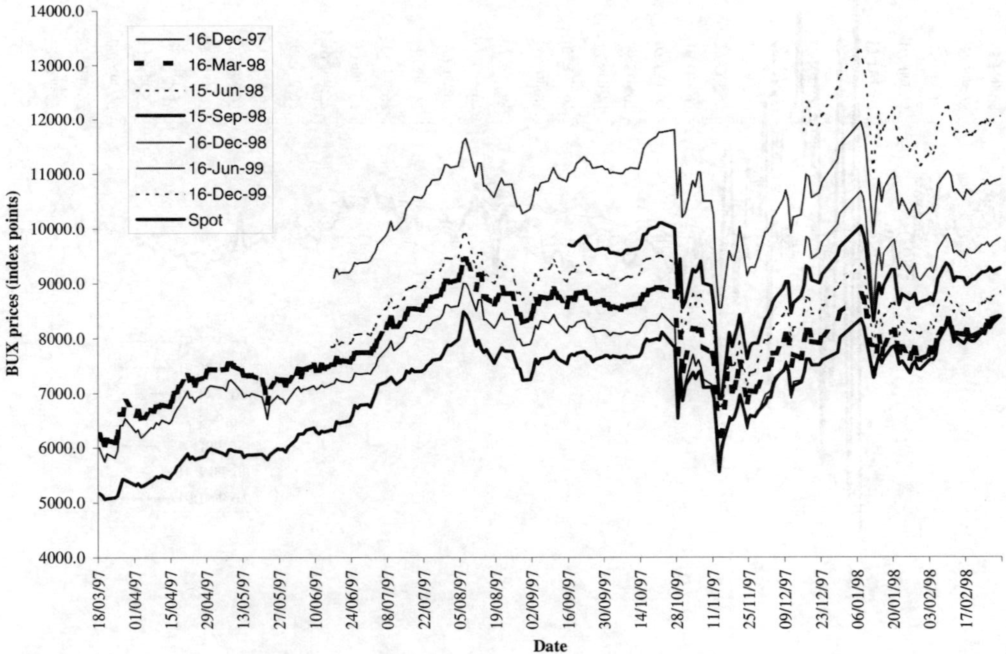

Source: Budapest Stock Exchange.

Chart 4. **Futures spreads in BUX futures prices for various maturities over the spot BUX index**

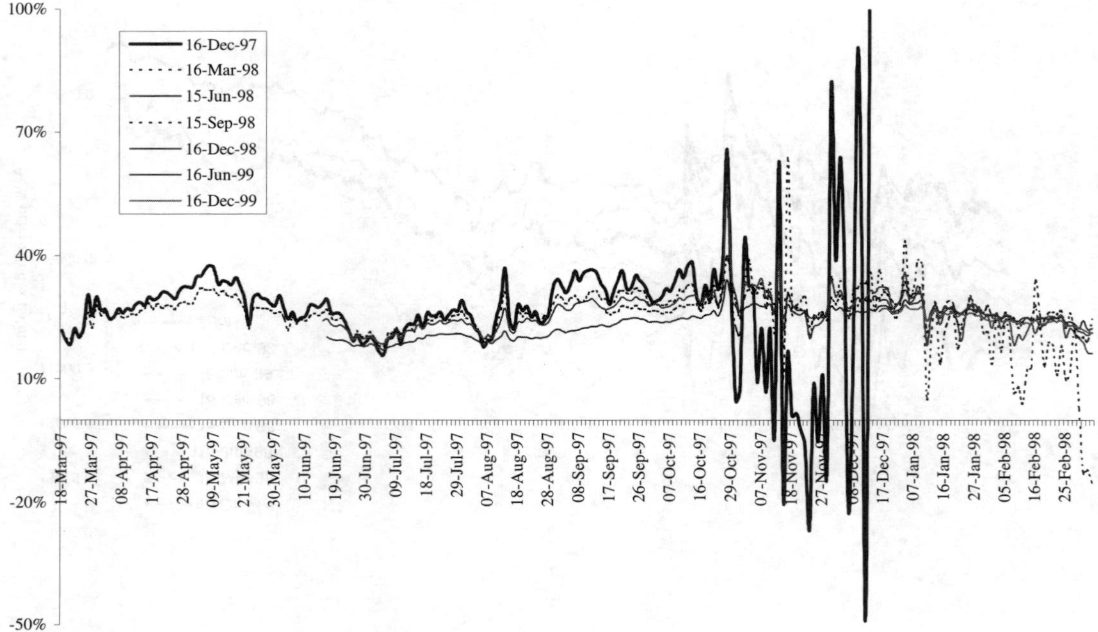

Source: Budapest Stock Exchange.

Chart 5. **Futures premia over riskless interest rate (3TB) implicit in BUX futures prices**

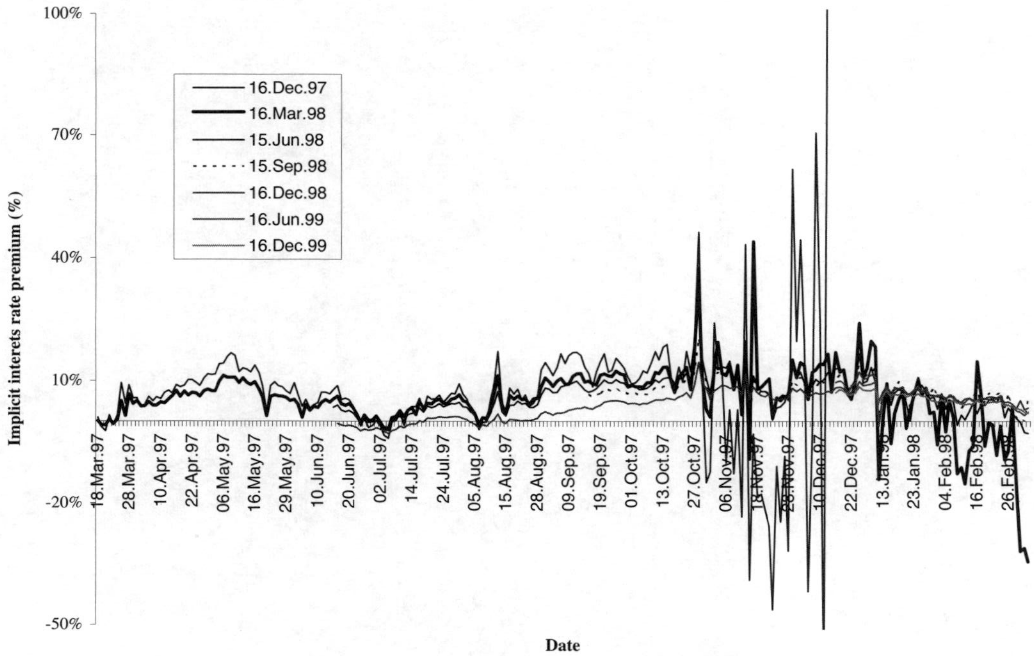

Source: National Bank of Hungary and Budapest Stock Exchange.

Chapter 12

THE PROVISION OF CLEARING AND SETTLEMENT SERVICES FOR THE RUSSIAN FUTURES MARKET

Submission by
The Central Bank of The Russian Federation

The history of the Russian futures market dates back to October 1992 when US dollar futures were traded for the first time on the Moscow Stock Exchange. At present futures are regularly traded on 15 commodity, stock and currency exchanges in Moscow, Voronezh, Omsk, Samara and St. Petersburg. In 1993 futures trade turnover totalled 131.5 billion roubles in current prices and it rose to 6.127 trillion roubles in 1994, 64.954 trillion roubles in 1995 and nearly 20 trillion roubles in the first half of 1996. In 1993-1995 and the first half of 1996 the US dollar futures contracts accounted for nearly 98 per cent of the entire market futures trade turnover; the remainder being accounted for by operations with commodity futures.

At present the average daily futures trade turnover is around 275 billion roubles ($50 million). It should be noted that last September the Moscow Interbank Currency Exchange (MICEX) began trading futures on the US dollar and the average weighted GKO price in the secondary market. The overall futures trade at MICEX rose from 23.5 billion roubles in September 1996 to 96.7 billion roubles in October and 275 billion roubles in November and nearly 70 per cent-80 per cent of the futures trade turnover in the Russian Federation has ever since been ensured by banking capital. At the same time, the structure of futures trade has changed significantly. The share of the US dollar futures has dropped to 15 per cent, while that of the government securities futures, mainly the government short-term bonds (GKOs) and federal loan bonds (OFZs) rose to more than 80 per cent.

One of the reasons for this structural change is that during the first half of 1996 the Moscow Commodities Exchange, one of the major organisers of futures trade with an average daily US dollar futures trade turnover of

240 billion roubles ($60 million), began to withdraw gradually from the market. When its clearing and settlement system collapsed, all trade on the exchange ended.

Futures and options exchange trade attracts traders because it allows them to achieve two objectives, depending on what their interests are: hedge price risks on available assets and engage in speculative operations. Unlike other forms of public trade, the organised market has the main advantage of ensuring market players practically 100 per cent contract guarantees.

The provision of clearing services is an indispensable condition for the exchanges organising futures and options trade and creating an organised financial market.

Clearing and settlement services are provided to the organised market participants by special institutions, such as clearing houses, which enable the parties to a deal (seller/buyer) to manage independently their positions opening up after the deal is closed.

The futures trade in the Russian Federation has so far relied both on the provision of clearing services by the exchanges and the provision of clearing services by contract. The clearing houses of the Russian Exchange, Moscow Exchange and Moscow Central Stock Exchange, for instance, operate as the structural units of these exchanges, while the Moscow Non-Ferrous Metals Exchange and the Central Russian Universal Exchange obtain clearing services under contract with the Clearing Centre -- Moskovskaya Raschetnaya Palata.

In accordance with the Russian Federation legislation, the provision of clearing and settlement services for trade in the futures markets, organised by the exchanges on their own or by contract, is subject to state regulation in the form of licensing. Paragraph 1 of Article 28 of the Russian Federation Law on Commodity Exchanges and Exchange Trade reads: "To ensure the execution of the forward, futures and options transactions on the exchange, the exchange shall organise the provision of settlement services by setting up settlement institutions (clearing centres), which shall be created in accordance with the established procedure, or by contracting a bank or other credit institution to organise the provision of settlement (clearing) services".

Section 1 of Article 80 of the Federal Law of the Russian Federation on the Central Bank of the Russian Federation (Bank of Russia) stipulates that "the Bank of Russia is a body co-ordinating, regulating and licensing the organisation of settlement systems, including clearing systems, in the Russian Federation".

The Bank of Russia so far has issued only one banking licence to the Moscow-based Clearing Centre -- Moskovskaya Raschetnaya Palata -- to provide clearing services as an independent kind of activity. The parameters of the Bank of Russia licences do not meet the requirements established for this kind of activity, because the clearing centres (houses) providing clearing services for exchange trade in the futures markets must be either subject to restrictions or prohibited from extending credit to legal entities and natural persons.

The Russian Government is currently considering a draft of a federal law "On Exchanges and Exchange Activities", which requires the exchange clearing and settlement houses to provide guarantees for exchange trade. This should include a ban on crediting in any form.

The situation in the Russian Federation today is unique in the sense that other traders in the futures markets provide clearing services on their own without having Bank of Russia permission to do so.

The absence of regulation in this sphere of business in the form of licensing provoked a series of crippling crises in the clearing service sector, especially as concerns futures trade on the commodity and stock exchanges. The worst crises broke out in 1994 on the Moscow Central Stock Exchange (MCSE) and in 1995 on the Moscow Commodities Exchange (MCE). The MCSE crisis occured after two companies had lost nearly 20 billion roubles to other market players and the exchange's further existence was put in jeopardy because the pledged collaterals of these market players were not secured by real monetary assets. The exchange survived the crisis but its traders incurred heavy losses. That crisis had a direct impact on the Moscow Commodities Exchange because the MCSE traders opened opposite positions on it to obtain additional hedging against their risks.

The systemic crisis resulting from the collapse of the MCE's clearing and settlement house had grave consequences for the development of trade in the futures markets. It affected 200 commercial banks which traded on the MCE. The crisis originated from receivables which the MCE clearing house had contracted from the the Mytishchinsky Commercial Bank and the Natsionalny Kredit Bank of 24 billion roubles and 8 billion roubles respectively, by depositing its free mortgage funds in these banks. Late in December 1995 the negative effect of these receivables in the currency futures market sharply increased and settlement companies (clearing members) began to rapidly withdraw funds from the clearing house, causing a shortage of working capital and disrupting payment schedules. Eventually, a run on all free funds took place and positions were closed.

The MCE managed to repay only 4 billion roubles, and in early 1996 trade on the exchange stopped. The hardest hit were the Moscow Branch of the Savings Bank (Sberbank) of Russia, to which the MCE's clearing house owed 4 billion roubles, Mosbiznesbank (owed 3.6 billion roubles by MCE, of which 3 billion roubles were client funds) and Rossiisky Kredit (the MCE clearing house owed it 1 billion roubles).

It should be recalled that the crisis in the futures market also affected the interbank market. Conducting operations with foreign currency, banks concluded long-term forward deals in the interbank market and hedged them by opening short counter positions in the futures market. Among the parties to such deals were many small banks, such as Gloria-bank, Tandem, etc., which used both markets to conduct purely speculative and rather risky operations.

The Bank of Russia takes into account the growing role of the futures market as a segment of the financial market and the importance of the organisations providing services in this market (exchange clearing houses and clearing centres). As it has already been said, this segment of the market is not regulated yet and the Bank of Russia has no adequate and uniform information about the derivatives transactions conducted by credit organisations.

At present the best organised system of reporting and accounting exists in the sphere of conversion futures operations conducted by authorised banks. According to Bank of Russia Instruction No. 42 of 22 May 1996, "On the Procedure for Reporting Conversion Operations by Russian Federation Authorised Banks -- Major Operators in the Interbank Currency Market", the authorised banks compile daily reports in established form on the forward currency operations they conduct within the limits of the open currency position and these reports are submitted to the Bank of Russia International Operations Department. Provisions No. 290 (Bank of Russia Order No. 02-198 of 10 June 1996) on the Procedure for Keeping Accounts of the Currency Operations in Credit Organisations set the rules for recording in the balance sheets of authorised banks their futures transactions which give rise to claims and obligations in foreign exchange (forward and futures deals, swap transactions, etc.). A procedure has been established for keeping accounts on the operations conducted on the organised securities market with government paper derivatives. These procedures are described in Bank of Russia Provisions No. 307 "On the Procedure for Effecting Settlements on Operations with New Financial Instruments on the Organised Securities Market" which was approved by Bank of Russia Order No. 02-242 of 6 June 1996.

Taking into consideration all the factors described above, the Bank of Russia has begun within its powers and in accordance with applicable legislation to create a system of regulation of clearing services in the financial markets, including licensing non-bank credit institutions conducting operations in this sector. Specifically, the Bank of Russia intends:

- to work out provisions for licensing the exchange clearing houses and clearing members of the exchange clearing houses;

- to regulate the types of banking operations conducted by the exchange clearing houses and clearing members of the exchange clearing houses;

- to work out special economic standards regulating the activities of the exchange clearing houses and their members;

- to work out accounting rules for clearing services;

- to work out settlement instructions and rules for the exchange clearing houses and establish the procedure for and conditions of opening rouble and foreign-currency accounts by the exchange clearing houses in the Bank of Russia institutions; and

- to establish the procedure and working rules for the exchange clearing houses in the liquid assets market (licensing the exchange clearing houses as professional securities market participants).

In addition, taking into account commercial banks' activity in the futures markets and the increased risks involved in the operations conducted in these markets, the Bank of Russia is beginning to regulate credit organisations' participation in these operations. This action has also been prompted by the desire to stabilise financial markets as a whole and protect the interests of commercial banks' customers. The immediate plans of the Bank of Russia in this sphere are:

- to set requirements for the risks taken by credit organisations making transactions in the futures markets;
- to establish the procedure and conditions for the accounting of the futures deals by credit organisations;
- to set requirements for the compulsory internal structuring of credit organisations conducting operations in the futures markets as brokers, dealers or customers giving instructions on their own behalf and the corresponding qualification requirements to the personnel of commercial banks; and
- to set compliance requirements for the credit organisations operating in the futures markets.

OECD PUBLICATIONS, 2, rue André-Pascal, 75775 PARIS CEDEX 16
PRINTED IN FRANCE
(14 98 10 1 P) ISBN 92-64-16119-8 – No. 50379 1998